Pierre Boulez

A World of Harmony

## Contemporary Music Studies

A series of books edited by Nigel Osborne, University of Edinburgh, UK

# Pierre Boulez

# A World of Harmony

Lev Koblyakov

harwood academic publishers
Switzerland • USA • Japan • UK • France • Germany
Netherlands • Russia • Singapore • Malaysia • Australia

First published 1990
Second printing 1992
Third printing 1993

**Harwood Academic Publishers**

Post Office Box 90
Reading, Berkshire RGI 8JL

Private Bag 8
Camberwell, Victoria 3124
Australia

820 Town Centre Drive
Langhorne
PA 19047
United States of America

Glinkastrasse 13-15
0-1086 Berlin
Germany

3-14-9, Okubo
Shinjuku-ku, Tokyo 169
Japan

Emmaplein 5
1075 AN Amsterdam
Netherlands

The cover photo of Pierre Boulez and all musical examples, including pages from the orchestral score of *Le marteau sans maître*, have been reprinted by kind permission of Universal Edition (London) Ltd.

**Library of Congress Cataloging-in-Publication Data**

Koblyakov, Lev, 1948–
    Pierre Boulez : a world of harmony / Lev Koblyakov.
        p.  cm. — (Contemporary music studies, ISSN 0891–5415 ; v. 2)
    Bibliography:  p.
    Includes index.
    ISBN 3-7186-0422-1 (hard cover)
    ISBN 3-7186-0553-8 (soft cover)
    1. Boulez, Pierre, 1925–  Marteau sans maître  I.-Title.
    II. Series.
    MT115.B7K6  1990
    782.4'8125—dc20                                    89–7460
                                                        CIP-
                                                        MN

# Contents

# Introduction to the Series

The rapid expansion and diversification of contemporary music is explored in this international series of books for contemporary musicians. Leading experts and practitioners present composition today in all its aspects—its techniques, aesthetics, technology and its relationship with other disciplines and currents of thought—as well as use the series to communicate actual musical materials.

The series also features monographs on significant twentieth century composers not extensively documented in the existing literature.

# Preface

This book, which was my PhD thesis, was completed at the Hebrew University of Jerusalem. I carried out the analysis of *Le marteau sans maître* between 1975 and the end of 1977. The concluding chapter was written subsequently. Since then my knowledge of *Le marteau* and Pierre Boulez' musical thought has broadened. Nevertheless I have decided to publish the work without changing it, otherwise another book would have emerged. This analysis of *Le marteau* can also serve to show that it was possible to analyse a totally serial composition without seeing any sketches for the work.

I am indebted to Nigel Osborne and Peter Nelson, who both generously took the time to read the typescript and to check and edit the English. The publication of this book was assisted by a generous grant from Siemens AG.

*Lev Koblyakov*
*Spring 1989*
*Jerusalem*

*To my Mother, Judith Koblyakov*

# Introduction

The purpose of the present study is the investigation of harmony in the music of Pierre Boulez based on his composition *Le marteau sans maître* (1952–55). By harmony we mean two phenomena. On the one hand, in the narrow meaning of the word, we shall understand by this term the whole pitch structure of the composition. On the other hand, in its wider meaning, we understand proportionality, balance of the parts of a musical form, their harmoniousness. Both of the above phenomena will be demonstrated in this analysis of *Le marteau sans maître*, which will make it clear that they form an inseparable unity in the music of this composition.

*Marteau* by Boulez includes three cycles of movements; therefore the structure of the present study consists of three chapters where in turn each of the three cycles is investigated, with the results being summed up in the fourth chapter, the conclusion. Each cycle is analysed in a different way. In the first cycle attention is paid mainly to the analysis of pitch structure and formal proportions. The second cycle is analysed the most comprehensively, as the relationship of all the parameters is the principal subject here. In the third cycle attention is paid mainly to movement 9, the conclusion of the composition. Throughout this study references are made to most of the other compositions of Boulez composed both before and after *marteau*.

In *Le marteau sans maître* Boulez turned for the third and last time to the poetry of René Char. Boulez had used other texts of this poet in his earlier cantatas *Le visage nuptial* (1946) and *Le soleil des eaux* (1948). The name *Le marteau sans maître* itself is taken from Char, who at the end of the 1920s and the beginning of the 30s wrote several sets of poems which he united in one cycle with this title. For the three cycles of his own composition Boulez chose three separate poems. From this collection *marteau* is probably one of the first instances of music written to a surrealist text.

Several significant trends in music first appeared in the 1950s. Among them is serialism, which developed the ideas of the Schoenberg school borrowed via their considerable development by Webern. The serialization of all parameters was probably first achieved by Boulez in *Structures Ia for Two Pianos* (1951). After that followed *Polyphonie X* (for orchestra), *Structures* Ic, Ib, *Oubli, Signal, Lapidé* (for mixed chorus) (1952), two *Etudes concrètes* (1951–52), and finally *Le marteau sans maître* (for contralto and six instruments).

But the serialization of all parameters alone is not sufficient for the creation of a good composition with a unique new form. Something more is needed. A special direction must be produced: special types of serial organization have to be created. It is also necessary to master and control the serial organization on the basis of a *musical* concept, without subjecting the latter to the full automatism of the serial organization. All this was accomplished in *marteau* and together with the high musical quality of the composition, has resulted in success.

*Le marteau sans maître* is one of the most important works of Boulez and of the mid 20<sup>th</sup> century. It reflects some of the most characteristic features of the thinking of the time, while putting them into a new and beautiful form. *marteau* is a kind of focal point in the creative output of Boulez, as, on the one hand, it embodies the basic ideas of his previous works of the 40s and 50s and, on the other hand, it has turned out to be a source of essentially new ideas, which were later developed in many other of his works. *marteau* was a turning–point for Boulez, and probably one of no less importance than that which happened in composing *Structure Ia*. This turning–point was the transition from a simple or little developed serial organization to one complex in conception and specially directed.

What can musical analysis be? What is the working method of a musical investigator? Boulez himself gives the following definition:

> 'I have often pointed out that analysis is only of real interest when it is *active*, and it can only be fruitful in terms of its deductions and consequences for the future.'[†]

> 'Let us define what may be considered the indispensable constituents of an "active" analytical method: it must begin with the most minute and exact observation possible of the musical facts confronting us; it is then a question of finding a plan, a law of internal organization which takes account of these facts with the maximum coherence; finally comes the interpretation of the compositional laws deduced from this special application. All these stages are necessary; one's studies are of merely technical interest if they are not followed through to the highest point—the *interpretation* of the structure; only at this stage can one be sure that the work has been assimilated and understood.'[‡]

The special nature and the difficulty of analysing serial music are a result of its complex organization. The problem is that, besides the serialization of all parameters, numeric codes are used, which help in the hierarchic development of the serial system. Besides, with Boulez the general series of a composition is mostly only the organism generating a network of derivative series, and usually takes no direct part in the music. Thus the investigator ought to have at least some sketches by the composer himself, otherwise he will have to perform a task of incredible complexity.[§] Of course *musical intuition* is of enormous importance for analysis. In particular, the author of the present study could only complete the following analysis to a great extent through its help. Musical intuition assists analysis if there is an intimate knowledge and aural familiarity with the composition. In such a case the investigator tries to imagine the main direction of the composer's thinking and practically, so to speak, to compose the music anew.

The structural analysis of the works of the recent past, serial music in particular, is rather important today. The young generation of composers born after the war is in many cases unaware of the compositional technique of the composers of the preceding generation owing to the almost complete absence of precise analyses. This analysis of *Le marteau sans maître* is a modest attempt to fill the gap.

---

†   *Boulez on Music Today*, pp.16–17. See also the discussion of the problem continued on p.17.
‡   Op.cit., p.18. In our work we have tried to follow the advice of Boulez, therefore possibly our following analysis of *marteau* can be assessed as active.
§   Hence the almost complete absence of structural analyses of works of serial music (Boulez, Stockhausen, Nono, etc.). We could never see any sketches to *marteau*, the whereabouts of which are unknown.

# Chapter I

# Analysis of the First Cycle

The first cycle of *Le marteau sans maître* comprises the 1st, 3rd and 7th movements:

1. Avant L'artisanat furieux,

3. L'artisanat furieux,

7. Après L'artisanat furieux.

The 9th movement of *marteau* consists of three sections, the last of which is the coda (see bars 88–95, 100–102, 128–143, 154–158, 164–188). In organization this section is related to the first cycle of *marteau* and will therefore be discussed with it.

The whole of the first cycle and the coda of the 9th movement use the technique of frequency[†] multiplication, the frequencies making up a twelve–note series. This type of organization was used for the first time in the works of Boulez and it was created and developed by him. All the musical parameters: pitch, system of durations, dynamics, number of attacks, etc., are subjected to the common impact of this organization.

The pitch organization is based on one general series, which by different divisions creates an ensemble of series of frequency groups.[‡] The general series as such is not included in the first cycle. The division of the general series into groups of frequencies is connected with the application of the proportion row 24213, which is consistently rotated, thus producing the following five derived series (each figure denotes the number of sounds in each group).

Each derived series has a one–sound group and the positions of these sounds (within the original series) divide the series by the same proportions but in reversed order (compare the proportion of Ex. 2 with row IV in Ex. 1a).

Each of the five marked sounds could become the basis of a transposition for its derived series. Boulez however starts by an additional pitch transposition of the derived series, with the exception of derived series IV, which keeps the E flat transposition. Series I and III go down by a major second, so they are based on the sounds F sharp and C natural instead of G sharp and D natural respectively. Series II and V go up by a minor second, so instead of the A natural and F sharp transpositions they

---

† Boulez uses word frequency instead of sound (see *Boulez on Music Today*).
‡ Or sound groups, or blocks. Boulez also calls them sonorities (see *Notes of an Apprenticeship*, p.167). For the sake of brevity we will also call them just groups.

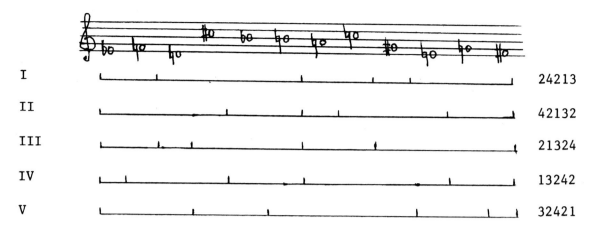

I      24213

II      42132

III      21324

IV      13242

V      32421

Ex. 1a

Ex. 1b

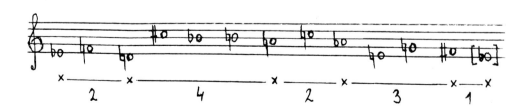

Ex. 2

will have B flat and G natural respectively.

Now each of the abovementioned series, by multiplication of frequency groups, creates five *harmonic fields*. Moreover, each frequency group in the derived series is multiplied by another frequency group, thus producing new groups. Since a series has five groups, multiplication results in twenty–five groups, ten of which appear twice. This can be denoted by letters.[†]

|    |    |    |    |    |
|----|----|----|----|----|
| aa | ab | ac | ad | ae |
| ba | bb | bc | bd | be |
| ca | cb | cc | cd | ce |
| da | db | dc | dd | de |
| ea | eb | ec | ed | **ee** |

Ex. 3

E.g., to obtain block aa, group a is multiplied by itself, any repeated sounds appearing only once (see Ex. 4).

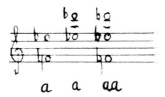

Ex. 4

The elimination of repeated sounds leads to the number of sounds in a group never being more than 12. When dividing the general series into five groups, as in the first cycle of *marteau*, the number of sounds in a group cannot in fact be more than 10.

With multiplication each of the five derived series is to produce five harmonic fields. Each system of five harmonic fields will be called a *harmonic domain*. Thus we have five domains (see Diagram I, where they are denoted by Roman numerals). This diagram shows that Boulez replaces in each domain the horizontal field a by a field consisting of a derived series.

Each domain has its system of blocks of different structure. Sometimes however identical blocks can be found, coinciding even in transposition, though belonging to different domains. Such a coincidence results from the existence of a single division system of the general series, as shown above. Each domain is based on the transposition of its derived series, which creates, so to speak, a higher system of pitch interrelation of domains: I, F sharp; II, B flat; III, C natural; IV, E flat; V, G natural.

Those domains can be found in the 1st, 3rd, and 7th movements of *marteau*, while for the coda of the 9th movement the composer uses the inversion of the general series and a row of proportions in retrograde order 31242 (see Ex. 5a and 5b).

---

† See also a short description of the multiplication process in Boulez, *Notes of an Apprenticeship* (pp. 167–168) and *Boulez on Music Today* (pp. 79–80).

I          31242

II        23124

III       42312

IV       24231

V         12423

**Ex. 5a**

**Ex. 5b**

One–sound groups create within this series the same interrelation of proportions, though in retrograde order (compare the proportion in Ex. 6 with the proportion from row V in Ex. 5a).

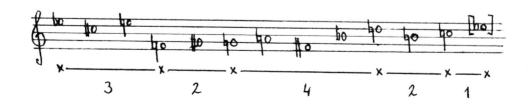

**Ex 6**

These five sounds become transposition bases for their derived series, and then produce domains. In the coda of the 9th movement of *marteau* for each of the five domains only the harmonic fields b and d are used; that is why they are the only ones given in Diagram II.

Now we can begin the analysis of the general form and the description of the harmonic domains in the first cycle of *marteau*. The 1st movement of the composition includes five sections or nine subsections in which all the five domains are presented (see Ex. 7, and also the score appended).

| bars | 1-10 | 11-20 | 21-32 | 33-41 | 42-52 | 53-60 | 60-68 | 69-80 | 81-95 |
|------|------|-------|-------|-------|-------|-------|-------|-------|-------|
| domains | I | V | III | IV | II | V | II | IV | III |
| number of domains per one section | 1 | | 3 | | 1 | | 3 | | 1 |

Ex. 7

As seen in Ex. 7, all five sections create a symmetry by the number of fields included in them (13131). On the other hand, each domain is found to be used twice, the exception being domain I which reappears only in the 7th movement of *marteau*, which is built completely on this domain. Fermatas separate the five sections of the 1st movement and at the end of each domain (or subsection) there is a compression of tempo (*presser*) or its retardation (*poco rit.*), while each domain begins *a tempo*.[†] It is also noteworthy that by switching domains V and II a consecutive movement of domains from I to V appears; then a reverse movement of the domains begins (with bar 53), where domain II is between domains V and IV. Thus a concealed mirror symmetry is expressed, which exists also with the position of the domains (see also bars 21–52, domains III–IV–II, and bars 60–95, domains II–IV–III).

The 7th movement of *marteau* is something like a widened conclusion of the 1st; it also includes five sections (Ex. 8).

| bars | 1-7 | 8-17 | 18-29 | 30-37 | 38-47 |
|------|-----|------|-------|-------|-------|

Ex. 8

The 3rd movement is built on a strictly consecutive alternation of domains, using only fields b in prime form and d in retrograde (see our score appended and Ex. 9). Thus the 3rd movement is divided into two parts, and they in their turn into two sections.[‡]

In the 3rd movement the composer uses twice field b in domain III and field d in domain I, the fields in both cases being first given in retrograde, and then in prime form (see bars 10–15 and 42–48 in our score appended). Boulez possibly chose those fields for repetition because they consist of 12 sounds only and in fact are transposed derived series. Due to the repetition of two fields their total number in the 3rd movement amounts to twelve.

---

† This expresses some extent of homage on the part of Boulez to Webern, who also made use of a change of tempo with the change of structural sections.

‡ This corresponds to four stanzas of a poetic text. From the traditional viewpoint bars 1–5 (domain I) can be considered an instrumental introduction. Then the following sections contain about the same number of bars: 10+11+11+11 (see Ex. 9). Other features of symmetry will be shown later.

| bars | 1–5 | 6–9 | 10–15 | 16–21 | 22–26 | 27–30 | 30–33 | 34–37 | 38–42 | 42–48 |
|---|---|---|---|---|---|---|---|---|---|---|
| domains | I | II | III | IV | V | V | IV | III | II | I |
| number of fields per section | | 3 | | | 2 | | | 3 | | 2 |

**Ex. 9**

The progression of domains in the 3rd movement from I to V and then back from V to I displays clearly the general idea of the structure of the first cycle of *marteau*. The 3rd movement is a kind of compressed variant of the same form. This is probably also why Boulez decided to change the precise order of domains in the 1st movement of *marteau* in order to avoid a literal repetition of the same scheme. Thus there are two subcycles within the first cycle:  1) the 1st and 7th movements;  2) the 3rd movement.[†]

In the coda of the 9th movement percussion instruments take part too. It consists of five sections symmetrically divided into nine subsections (see Ex. 10, where the horizontal fields b and d are shown in brackets). Such a structure connects the coda of the 9th movement with the 1st movement of *marteau*. In contrast to the 3rd movement where groups from the fields b and d move in prime order, in the coda of the 9th movement groups from the fields b move in retrograde order (i.e., from be to ba), and groups from the fields d in prime order. An exception is domain I where the groups of both fields move in prime order (see our score appended). In the coda the alternation of fields b and d is more varied than in the 3rd movement (see Ex. 10). The coda of the 9th movement is a peculiar variant of the 3rd movement.[‡]

| bars | 88–91 | 92–95 | 100–102 | 128–133 | 134–137 | 138–148 | 154–158 | 164–173 | 174–188 |
|---|---|---|---|---|---|---|---|---|---|
| domains and fields | V(b) | (d) | ——— | IV(b) | III(b) | IV(d) | III(d) | II(b,d) | I(b,d) |
| number of subsections per one section | | 2 | 1 | | 3 | | 1 | | 2 |

**Ex. 10**

Let us now return to the 1st movement of *marteau* for more detailed analysis and note the number of groups in the domains. The structure of each domain is based on the use of about 15 groups, i.e., three fifths of the total group number, which we will agree to call a semi–domain. Thus, the 1st, 4th, 8th and 9th subsections include two semi–domains (see Ex. 11).[§]

The 1st and 5th, as well as the 2nd and 4th sections have almost the same number of groups (shown by arrows). The number of groups in the domains is the following: I—30, II—30 = 15+15, III—45 =

---

† It is interesting that the 3rd and 7th movements equal the 1st movement in the number of bars: 48+47 = 95.
‡ The 9th movement is really a double not only of *Bel édifice et les pressentiments*, but also of *L'artisanat furieux*, although the text is not used again in the coda of the 9th movement.
§ In bar 88 there is an additional repetition of group ba, that is why one group is added in Ex. 11 where bars 81–95 are marked.

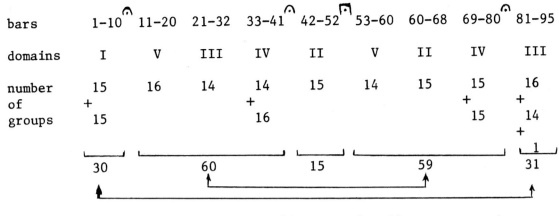

Ex. 11

14+31, IV—60 = 30+30, V—30 = 16+14. The 7th movement of *marteau* has the following number of groups in five sections, where the fifth section complements the first, and the fourth complements the second (see Ex. 12).

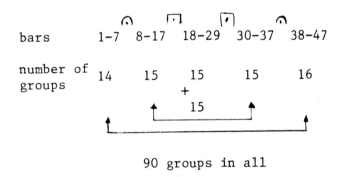

Ex. 12

Domain I is of great importance due to its widened repetition in the 7th movement. Its total number of groups is 120 (30 in the 1st movement and 90 in the 7th), the number of groups of all the other domains being 165 (30+45+60+30). The distinction of domain IV (60 groups) is due to the fact that it is based on the transposition of E flat, which is the initial sound of the general series. The 1st and 7th movements of *marteau* include 19 semi–domains (13+6) with 285 groups (195+90), which equals 15×19. The total number of groups in the first cycle, the coda of the 9th movement included, is 285+60 (3rd movement) + 50 (coda), which is 395 (36×11-1).[†]

The sequence of harmonic fields and groups within each domain is also subjected to a special organization. In domain I (bars 1–10) there is a double movement of groups, where one row creates a group sequence with the flute and vibraphone (Ex. 13a), and another, a group sequence with the

---

[†]  The division of the total group number of the first cycle by 11 appears to be coincidental. We mention it nevertheless, as it plays an important part in temporal and other proportions both of the first and of the second cycle (to be demonstrated further).

guitar and viola (Ex. 13b). In the following examples the harmonic field taken horizontally (given in square brackets) is identical everywhere with the derived series and replaces field a (see the following examples and our score appended).

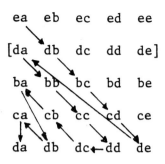

Ex. 13a   (Bars 1–10, upper row) Domain 1

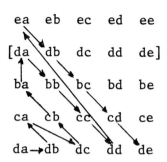

Ex. 13b   (bars 1–10, lower row) Domain I

Examples 13a and 13b show both group rows to have the same place in the scheme, the upper row beginning with group ea and ending with da, and the lower one, vice versa, going from da to de.[†] The movement from group to group is diagonal. Each of the five diagonal fields consists of one, two, three, four, and five groups respectively.

Independently of the exposition of the fields and the number of groups in them, the transition from one field to another one is denoted in the score by the symbol "|" if the borderline is within a bar, and by a full bar line if the borderline passes between bars.[‡]

In two sections where domain II is used (see bars 42–52 and Ex. 14a, bars 60–68 and Ex. 14b), a diagonal movement can be found too, the slope of the diagonal being in opposite directions in the two domains.

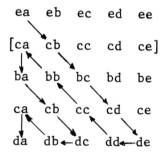

Ex. 14a   (bars 42–52) Domain II

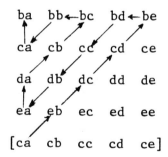

Ex. 14b   (bars 60–68) Domain II

In the first section of domain III (bars 21–32) the movement of the groups is consecutive along the vertical (Ex. 15a).

With the repetition of domain III in bars 81–95 two semi–domains can be found (bars 81–93 and 87–95); in bars 87–93 they are simultaneous. The composer has given prominence to the latter domain in the 1st movement of *marteau* by adding the remark *presser* or *poco rit.* to the end of each field, and *a tempo* to the beginning (with the exception of bars 87–91). See Ex. 15b and 15c. Ex. 15d shows that with the combination of both rows in bars 81–95 a domain is obtained in which all the

---

† In this and the following examples the composer can change the places of the horizontal fields within a domain in different ways. E.g., in bars 1–10 the upper horizontal field is e with [d], b, c and d following. More details are given below.

‡ There are cases where this rule is not observed (misprints or deviations by the composer himself).

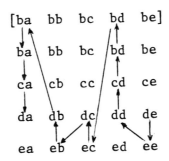

**Ex. 15a**  (bars 21–32) Domain III (14 groups)

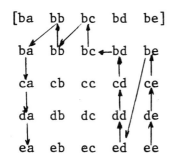

**Ex. 15b**  (bars 81–93)(16 groups) Domain III

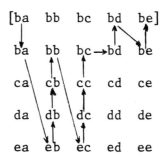

**Ex. 15c**  (bars 87–95)(14 groups) Domain III

[ba  bb  bc  bd  be]

2ba 2bb 2bc 2bd 2be

ca  cb  cc  cd  ce

da  db  dc  dd  de

ea  eb  ec  ed  ee

**Ex. 15d**  (bars 81–95)

groups are performed, and the groups of the horizontal field b are taken twice.

In examples 16a,b,c, square brackets show the connection of horizontal harmonic fields. In bars 69–80 the upper row of groups (Ex. 16a) is symmetrical with the bottom row (Ex. 16b). In the former case the movement begins with group ba and ends with be; in the latter, vice versa, it begins with be and ends with ba. The dotted arrow in brackets can be said to note the transition from one semi–domain to another. Similarly in bars 33–41 the transition appears to take place from the last group (da) of the bottom row (Ex. 16d) to the first group (de) of the upper row (Ex. 16c), which is shown by the dotted arrow. It should be noted that in Ex. 16d the first group is ae, and in Ex. 16c the last group is ea.

Ex. 16e shows that the connection of groups of the upper and lower rows in bars 33–41 creates a domain where all groups are used, while the groups of the horizontal field d are taken twice.

Finally, the two presentations of domain V (bars 11–20 and 53–60) are shown in Ex. 17a and 17b.

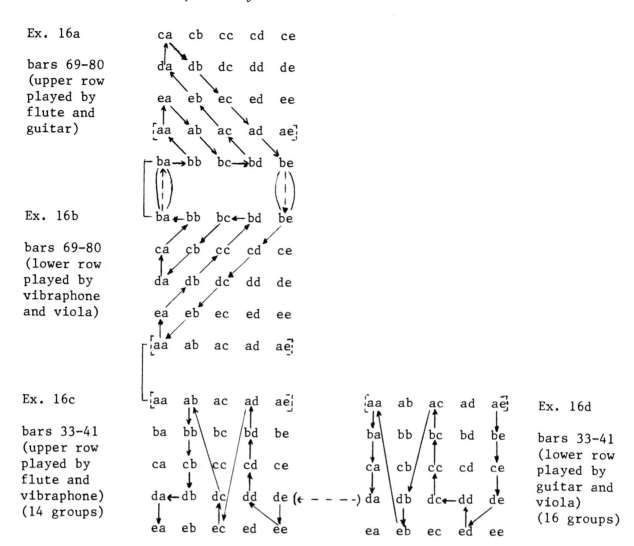

Ex. 16a

bars 69–80
(upper row
played by
flute and
guitar)

Ex. 16b

bars 69–80
(lower row
played by
vibraphone
and viola)

Ex. 16c

bars 33–41
(upper row
played by
flute and
vibraphone)
(14 groups)

Ex. 16d

bars 33–41
(lower row
played by
guitar and
viola)
(16 groups)

Ex. 16a–d  Domain IV

Ex. 16e  Domain IV

As mentioned above, only domain I is used in the 7th movement of *marteau*. In bars 1–7 (Ex. 18a) the vertical field e sounds simultaneously with other fields. In the scheme of Ex. 18a the use of this field after the vertical field d is shown in brackets. In bars 38–47 (Ex. 18b) the vertical field d sounds

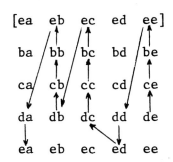

**Ex. 17a** (bars 11–20) (16 groups) Domain V

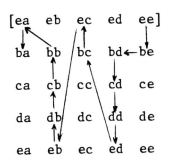

**Ex. 17b** (bars 53–60)(14 groups) Domain V

simultaneously with the vertical fields c and b. The vertical field e sounds after that, then follows the vertical field a (the group movement begins with both encircled groups [dc] and bd). Thus Boulez changes the sequence of vertical fields (see our score with analysis). In Ex. 18c arrows in brackets show the theoretically required sequence of fields.

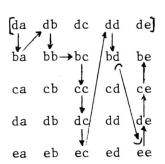

**Ex. 18a** (bars 1–7)(14 groups)

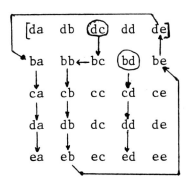

**Ex. 18b** (bars 38–47)(16 groups)

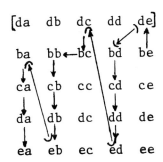

**Ex. 18c** (bars38–47)(16 groups)

In bars 8–17 and 30–37 Boulez changes the usual alternation of diagonal fields from a field containing one group to a field of five groups or vice versa. In bars 8–17 (Ex. 19a) Boulez begins with group da, i.e. with a diagonal field including four groups, then goes on to fields of five, two, one, and three groups, finishing the movement with group ea. Similarly in bars 30–37 (Ex. 19b) the alternation of diagonal fields is the following: fields of five, one, four, two, and three groups, the movement beginning with group ce and finishing with bc.

In bars 18–29 the movement of the diagonal fields belonging to two semi–domains takes place by turns. In Ex. 20a the above arrows show the alternation of the fields of the first semi–domain,

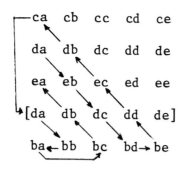

Ex. 19a  (bars 8–17)

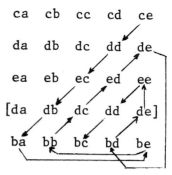

Ex. 19b  (bars 30–37)

and the arrows below, of the second one; the figures denote the number of groups in the fields. In Ex. 20b group da sounds with the additional C natural as a grace note which turns this group into ca (therefore in Ex. 20a group da noted in round brackets).

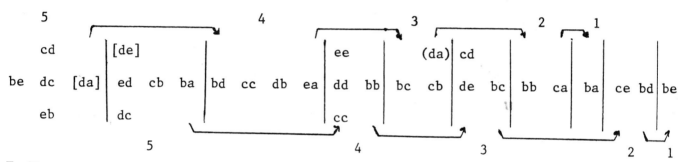

Ex. 20a

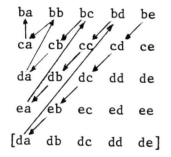

Ex. 20b  (bars 18–29)(first row)

Ex. 20c  (bars 18–29)(second row)

With the alternation of the variants of domain I within the 1st and 7th movements of *marteau* there is a gradual movement from the upper horizontal field e back to field b, and then in the retrograde direction. That means that in the 1st movement of *marteau* (bars 1–10) the upper horizontal field is field e; then in bars 1–7 of the 7th movement it is the upper horizontal field d, further in bars 8–17 it is field c, etc. (see Ex. 21, also 13, 18, 19, 20).

In Ex. 22 all the eight variants of the presentation of domain I are noted in special order. Square brackets show the connection of variants of the domain in which the last horizontal field of one variant of the domain is the same as the first horizontal field of the following variant. I.e., when looking at Ex. 22 from the top downward, we find that the first variant begins with the horizontal field c and ends with b, the second variant begins with field b and ends with [d], then one beginning

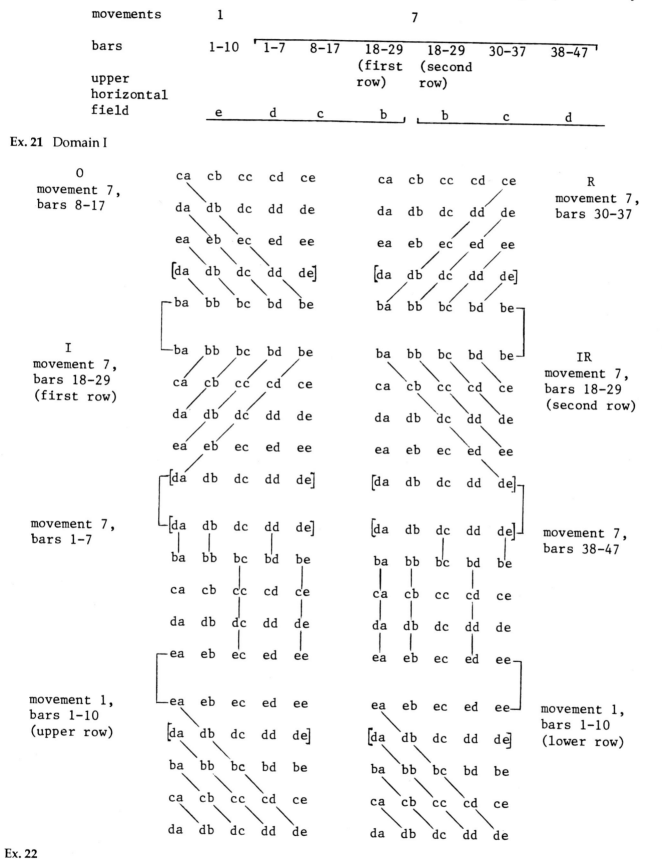

Ex. 21 Domain I

Ex. 22

with [d] and ending with e, and finally beginning with e and ending with d. Only one more variant beginning with field d and ending with field c is lacking to complete this circle (see Ex. 23).

```
                                             it is absent
          c - b   b - [d]  [d]-e   e-d     (d - c)
              L___J    L___J  L___J L_____J
```

Ex. 23

Ex. 22 also shows that another part of the scheme is used in each of the four variants of domain I (bars 8–17; 30–37, 18–29—first and second rows). Hence, if bars 8–17 can be noted as 0, then bars 18–29 (first row) can be noted as I, bars 30–37 as R, and bars 18–29 (second row) as IR.

As seen from many of the above examples, Boulez often changes the places of horizontal fields within different domains. This was mentioned when discussing Ex. 13a and 13b. The composer always switches the fields consistently according to the same principle as he did in dividing the general series into parts (see Ex. 1a). Therefore he can shift the horizontal fields within a domain, if read downwards, in an invariable form: abcde (i.e., 12345, or 23451, 34512, etc.). In Ex. 24a and 24b the shift of horizontal fields is shown, which is usually gradual (i.e., 51234, 12345, etc.). All the domains, with the exception of II, include the row 12345 as the initial and most important one; it is used 9 times.

| bars | 1–10 | 11–20 | 21–32 | 33–41 | 42–52 | 53–60 | 60–68 | 69–80 | 81–95 |
|---|---|---|---|---|---|---|---|---|---|
| domains | I | V | III | IV | II | V | II | IV | III |
| sequence of horizontal fields | 51234 | 12345 | 12345 | 12345 | 51234 | 12345 | 23451 | 34512 | 12345 |
| | 51234 | | | | 12345 | | | 23451 | 12345 |

Ex. 24a  (movement 1)

| bars | 1–7 | 8–17 | 18–29 | 30–37 | 38–47 |
|---|---|---|---|---|---|
| sequence of horizontal fields | 12345 | 34512 | 23451 | 34512 | 12345 |
| | | | 23451 | | |

Ex. 24b  (movement 7)

Ex. 25 shows the movement of groups along the diagonal and the vertical in all the semi–domains. Thus in 10 cases there is a movement along the diagonal and in 9 along the vertical. Both these directions are of equal importance. As mentioned above, for the 3rd movement of *marteau*, as well as for the coda of the 9th movement the composer chose the movement along the horizontal.

Let us discuss in greater detail the semi–domains where movement takes place along the vertical fields. In Ex. 26a,b,c,d the movement is noted for the groups used only; for greater clarity this can be compared to the respective examples mentioned above.

| Along the diagonal | | | | Along the vertical | | |
|---|---|---|---|---|---|---|
| domain | movement | bars | | domain | movement | bars |
| I | 1 | 1–10 (two rows) | | I | 7 | 1–7 and 38–47 |
| | 7 | 8–17 and 30–37 | | | | |
| | 7 | 18–29 (two rows) | | | | |
| II | 1 | 42–52 and 60–68 | | | | |
| | | | | III | 1 | 21–32 |
| | | | | | | 81–93 and 87–95 |
| IV | 1 | 69–80 (two rows) | | IV | 1 | 33–41 (two rows) |
| | | | | V | 1 | 11–20 and 53–60 |

Ex. 25

It is noteworthy that in Ex. 26a,b,c,d the vertical fields of four groups are always in another part of the semi–domain with reference to the fields of two groups. E.g., if a field of four groups is above, the field of two groups is below, and vice versa. Such a use of vertical fields always creates one complete horizontal field including five groups. This field is always field b or d (marked in brackets). The arrows in Ex. 26a,b,c,d show the direction of the movement within any vertical field. We see that there are several pairs of semi–domains where the same direction of movement within a vertical field can be observed. See domain III (bars 81–93 and 87–95; Ex. 26a), domain IV (bars 33–41, both group rows; Ex. 26b), 7th movement (bars 1–7 and 38–47; Ex. 26d). The group with which the movement begins is encircled in every case. In Ex. 26d the group with which the movement is to begin is given in brackets. The following regularity can also be observed within these pairs of semi–domains: where a vertical field of 4 groups is used in one semi–domain, a vertical field of 2 groups is used in the other semi–domain, and vice versa (e.g., see bars 81–93 and 87–95 in Ex. 26a). It is noteworthy that in bars 21–32, 33–41, 11–20 the vertical field of 4 groups is always in the upper part of the domain, and one of 2 groups in the lower part, while in bars 81–83, 87–95, 53–60 and in the 7th movement (bars 1–7 and 38–47), on the contrary, a field of 4 groups has a lower position and a field of two groups has an upper one (see Ex. 26a,b,c,d).

It should be mentioned finally that examples 13–20 and 26a,b,c,d show that when using diagonal and vertical fields, Boulez always chooses a group movement such that in each semi–domain of the first half of the 1st movement of *marteau* groups of the horizontal field d (bars 1–52) prevail, and in the second half of the 1st movement (bars 53–95) and in the 7th movement, groups of the horizontal field b prevail. Thus there is always one complete horizontal field d or b. This unites the 1st and 7th movements with the 3rd movement of *marteau* (and with the coda of the 9th movement). However, as already mentioned, in the 3rd movement, conversely, only horizontal fields b are used in the first half, and fields d in the second half. As seen from the above analysis, the development of all the movements of the first cycle, the coda of the 9th movement included, is based on the exploration of the horizontal fields b and d. This is concealed in the 1st and 7th movements and obvious in the 3rd movement and the coda of the 9th. The composer confined himself to these fields in the 3rd movement and the coda because of the small size of the movements.

It is important to bear in mind that the use of groups in domains is linked with the idea of restricted aleatorics. In effect, the use of groups in domains follows two principles only: 1) a definite number of groups is to be used (in this case 15 or 14/16); 2) the movement from group to group is to have a certain meaningful direction, i.e., it is not to be directed chaotically, as is shown above. Boulez' technique of multiplication leads to the aleatoric structure of form, which was incorporated by the

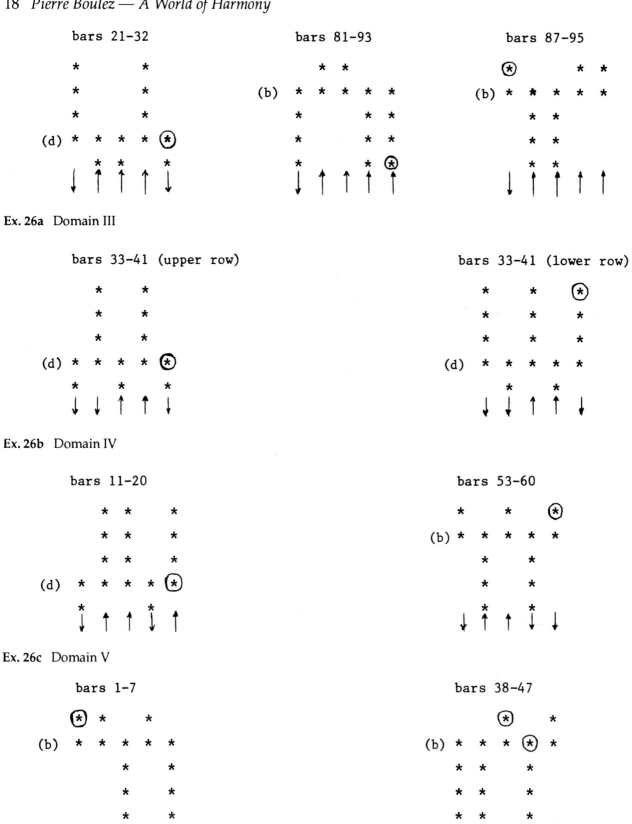

**Ex. 26a**  Domain III

**Ex. 26b**  Domain IV

**Ex. 26c**  Domain V

**Ex. 26d**  Domain I (movement 7)

composer some years after finishing *marteau* in works combining both principles (e.g., in his Third Sonata, in *Structures II*, and in *Domaines* especially).

Let us return now to the 3rd movement of *marteau*, which holds a central position in this cycle. Its first half also has features of mirror–symmetrical structure from the viewpoint of the performance of fields and groups by flute and voice (see our score appended, bars 1–26 and Ex. 27). The field in domain I performed by the flute can be seen to correlate with the field of domain V performed by the voice without text (!).[†] In the field of domain II the extreme groups ba and be are performed by flute and voice, the middle groups bb, bc, bd being performed by voice only. In the field of domain IV, conversely, the extreme groups ba and be are performed by flute only, then by voice respectively, the middle groups being performed by flute and voice. Thus the fields of domains II and IV are compared, having also their own inner symmetrical structure. The groups of two fields of domain III are also situated symmetrically (vertical dotted lines show the simultaneous beginning of the groups). It should be added that the distribution of the text in domains II, III, IV also has features of symmetry, as in the fields of domains II and IV eight syllables or five words are used in each, while in the field of domain III there are two syllables only which correspond to the first and the last sound of the field.[‡]

In the second half of the 3rd movement only the field of the central domain III has features of symmetry from the viewpoint of the performance of the groups by flute and voice (see Ex. 28). Besides, the disposition of two fields in domain I also has features of mirror symmetry (see bars 42–48 in our score appended). Here group de in bar 42 and the same group in bar 48 are performed differently. In bar 42 all three sounds are performed by voice with the flute only doubling the first sound; in bar 48, conversely, all the sounds are performed by the flute with the voice doubling the first one only. In both cases the doubling sound is performed *staccato–portamento* and lasts one quaver. The group dd in bar 43 has the sound b natural performed by the flute and doubled briefly by the voice; in bar 47, conversely, the longer sound is performed by the voice and its shorter doubling by the flute. Group dc in bar 44 has a longer duration with the voice and a shorter doubling with the flute; in bar 46, conversely, the longer duration of the group is with the flute and a shorter doubling with the voice.[§] And finally, group da is performed first by voice, then by flute (also with short doubling). The presence of doublings (unisons) in both fields of domain I assists in creating a feeling of a peculiar cadence in the conclusion of the 3rd movement.[¶] A comparison of Ex. 27 and 28 displays the fact that each of the 12 fields has its own instrumentation;[*] it changes with the transition to another field.

As to the exposition of the text in the second half of the 3rd movement, attention should be paid to the appearance of symmetry in the use of the last two groups of the field of domain V, then of the whole field of domain IV, and, finally, of the first two groups of the field of domain III (Ex. 28).

It is also noteworthy that the number of changes of performer within the 3rd movement is 23 (in Ex. 27 and 28 this is marked by figures in brackets). There are 10 changes in the first half (bars 1–26) and 13 in the second one.

Here we take up the analysis of the harmonic unity in the domain of the first cycle. Owing to the special structure of the domains mentioned above, the following characteristics can be found. First of all, any two horizontal fields of one domain[**] have only one group in common consisting of the same sounds. This group introduces an element of recapitulation when repeated in another field

---

†   One of the reasons for removing the text here is obviously the desire to emphasize the symmetry of the positions of flute and voice.

‡   It is interesting that even the number of syllables in the whole text of the 3rd movement is 47(4×12-1).

§   There is an alternation of long and short variants of groups from voice to flute and back (see groups de, dd, dc in bars 42–44 and 46–48).

¶   Thus something new is used in the conclusion of the music (since doubling can be found only twice before, the sound B natural in bar 13 and the sound C natural in bar 34).

*   In bars 10–15 both fields are partly superimposed, therefore a new result appears, although the fields themselves are performed by separate instruments.

**   An exception is a special horizontal field replacing field a.

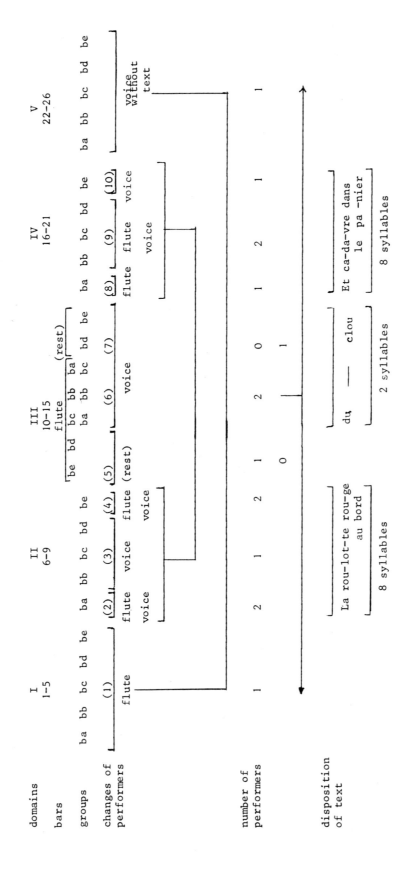

Ex. 27 (movement 3, bars 1–26)

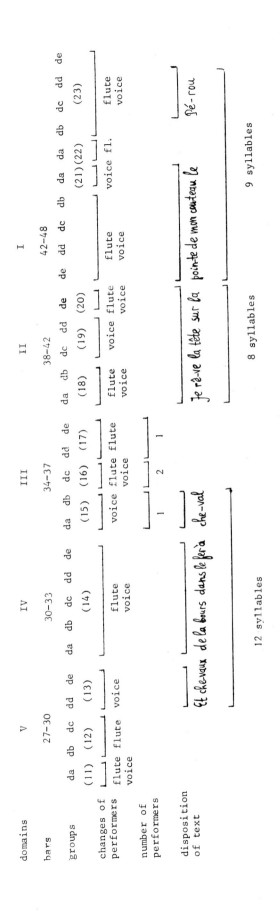

Ex. 28 (movement 3, bars 27–48)

(see Diagram I). E.g., in the 3rd movement of *marteau* the sounds of five groups bd (see the first half of the movement) are later repeated in the second half of the movement in groups db. E.g., compare bar 4 (group bd) and the first half of bar 46 (group db) in domain I, etc. This introduces an additional element of mirror symmetry into the structure of the 3rd movement of *marteau*, since, if in the horizontal harmonic field b group bd is the fourth, in the harmonic field d group db is the second (see Ex. 29).

Secondly, the groups of any one horizontal or vertical field are usually even more similar in structure than groups of different fields of the same domain. E.g., groups of the horizontal field d of domain II have the following similarity (see Diagram I): dc and dd are augmented triads; db and de consist of two augmented triads at a semitone distance (these groups have the same sounds); the groups dc and dd taken together create the groups db and de; finally, da consists of three augmented triads, as if being the sum of groups db and dc (a literal coincidence, since the same sounds are used), or dd and de, or db and dd, or dc and de. Therefore a musical fragment based on this field has a high degree of harmonic unity (see bars 38–42 in the 3rd movement of *marteau*).[†]

Thirdly, there are similar and identical groups belonging to different domains. This is seen especially when comparing domains I and III. Therefore it is not by chance that in the absence of domain I at the end of the 1st movement of *marteau* domain III seems to replace it. See the end of the 1st movement where the last five sounds of bar 95 coincide with the first five sounds of bar 1 (without taking into account the grace note). Furthermore, the group ea of six sounds with the vibraphone in bar 93 coincides with the groups ea and da (also six sounds) in bar 1.

Finally, there is a similarity between fragments in different movements of the first cycle, and also between groups in Diagrams I and II. E.g., two neighbouring groups in the 3rd movement (bars 16–19, ba and bb, domain IV) and a group in the coda of the 9th movement (bar 164, be, domain II) do not only have the same structure, but also fully coincide in their compositional usage.

Many other examples of sound–pitch unity can be given. Multiplication of frequency groups allows the creation of harmonic unity, since complex groups resulting from it break easily into simpler ones. As we know, every domain except the fourth, includes two horizontal fields of simple (unmultiplied) groups. Ten groups from these two fields are based on the structure of the general series (Ex. 1a, 1b).

An important means of relating groups both of the same field and of different ones is the rather frequent use of a common sound, which is usually played once only. Such a sound is found usually at the end of one group and at the beginning of the next one, connecting both groups by means of a ligature (e.g., see bars 1–2, 3–4, 4–5, 5–6 in the 3rd movement of *marteau* and many others).[‡] This method, together with the liquidation of repeated sounds within one group appearing with group multiplication, allows the material to be presented in a more concentrated way and, especially with a one–voiced or two–voiced texture, also allows versatile melodic lines (see 3rd movement and the coda of the 9th movement) to be created.

With multiplication each harmonic field acquires its own density. Five horizontal fields in one domain alternate in the order of the proportion characteristic of the given domain but with the replacement of field a by a field consisting of a derived series. E.g., domain I is characterized by the row 24213. Hence the first horizontal field [d] will have the density of 1, the second field b, 4, the third c, 2, etc. The interrelation of groups within all the fields of a given domain will normally be about the same. E.g., in domain I group ba will have a density of 4, group ca, 2, group da, 1, etc. A

---

[†] Furthermore all this field d is repeated with texture changes in the first section of the 9th movement (see bars 35–39). It is not by pure chance that Boulez places this fragment of the 3rd movement at the end of the first section of the 9th movement, as the word *la tête* ("the head") is repeated here and it unifies the text of the first and third cycles. That is the reason why Boulez also changed the texture of the fragment, as the voice in the 9th movement could not use the rest of the text of the 3rd movement. Hence in the 9th movement the voice partly performs the former flute part, and other instruments the part of the voice (see bars 35–36, 38–39 of the 9th movement).

[‡] Hence a new, non–traditional kind of syncopation.

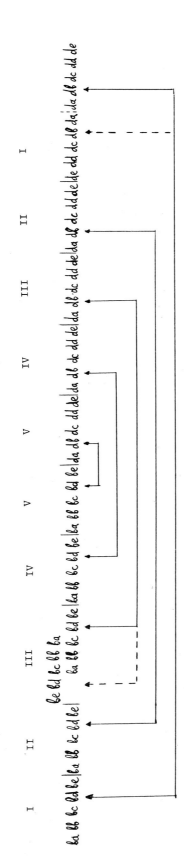

Ex. 29 (complete structure of movement 3)

horizontal field with a density of 1 will always consist of 12 sounds, while fields with a density of 2, 3, and 4 will respectively have about 20, 28, 34 sounds instead of 24, 36, and 48 sounds. This results from the fact that with group multiplication repeated sounds are not included in the created complex group. Hence the actual number of sounds is smaller in these fields. Therefore the real density of the horizontal fields will be approximately 1, 1.7, 2.4, 2.8, corresponding to the conditional density 1, 2, 3, 4. With consecutive alternation of any one horizontal field, e.g., b, of all the domains, the density of this field changes, as can be seen from the proportion scheme of Ex. 1a. E.g., fields b of all five domains will have the density 42132, i.e. for domain I the density of field b is 4, for domain II the density of field b is 2, etc. For field d the proportion of the 4th row 13242 will be used; hence domain I will have field d with density 1, domain II will have density 3, etc. The alternation of fields of different density is clearly displayed in movements 3 and 9 (coda) of *marteau*. The horizontal fields in the coda of the 9th movement are based on the inverse of this row of proportions, therefore in the scheme of Ex. 5a the second row (23124) conversely reflects the proportions of fields d, and the fourth (24231), the proportions of fields b (see Ex. 30 and 31).

| domains | I | II | III | IV | V | V | IV | III | II | I |
|---|---|---|---|---|---|---|---|---|---|---|
| fields | b | b | b | b | b | d | d | d | d | d |
| density | 4 | 2 | 1(+1) | 3 | 2 | 2 | 4 | 2 | 3 | 1(+1) |

**Ex. 30**  Movement 3

| domains | V | IV | III | IV | III | II | I | |
|---|---|---|---|---|---|---|---|---|
| fields | b | d | b | b | d | d | b,d | b,d |
| density | 2 | 2 | 4 | 2 | 3 | 1 | 3,2 | 1,4 |

**Ex. 31**  Coda of movement 9

Although the sounds in a harmonic multiplication system are absolute pitches, i.e. they can be in different registers, in some cases the composer distributes the pitches creating twelve–sound rows with a specific structure. In these cases the point is the vertical structure of a row resulting from the disposition of all its sounds in an ascending order. E.g., by connecting the sounds of groups dc, dd, and de of field d in domain II (see bars 40–42 in the 3rd movement) a row is produced with a mirror–symmetric structure (if the place of sound d natural is changed, which is shown by an arrow). See Ex. 32, where numbers indicate the value of the interval in semitones, and two vertical arrows point to two centres of symmetry.

**Ex. 32**

This structure is identical with the vertical structure of the main series of the 5th movement of *marteau* (see bars 1—beginning of 3 in the viola part). It is also an almost complete transposition of the vertical row from *Le soleil des eaux* (bar 2 after the number 3).† See Ex. 33, where the missing sounds are given in square brackets.

Ex. 33

Another example is field b of domain III with the flute in bars 10–14 in the 3rd movement of *marteau*. With the position of the sound D sharp changed, a vertically symmetrical row appears with a diminished seventh (see Ex. 34).

Ex. 34

Other examples can be found. Furthermore, in the third cycle of *marteau* (in the 5th, and especially in the 9th movement) vertical rows acquire a primary importance in pitch organization.

A characteristic feature of the harmony of the first cycle (as well as of other compositions of Boulez) is the absence of the interval of a minor second (i.e., a semitone) both along the vertical and along the horizontal. Avoiding this interval is one of the bases of the register distribution of absolute pitches. This enhances the transparent and light character of the music. Only one trill consisting of the interval of a minor second can be pointed out in the 3rd movement of *marteau* (bars 41–42). This trill hints at the material of the 5th movement. It is not by chance that it is included in a vertical row almost identical with a row in the 5th movement (see Ex. 32). In the coda of the 9th movement of *marteau* there are two other trills: one in bar 132, another at the conclusion of the composition (bar 187), which by their nature are also linked with the material of the 5th movement. One of the rare examples of the use of a minor second is bar 8 in the 1st movement of *marteau*, where the viola plays the notes B flat and B natural in sequence. The sound B natural here from the viewpoint of avoiding a semitone should have been an octave higher.

The register position of sounds is sometimes also connected with their specific musical execution. E.g., in the last section of the coda of the 9th movement (bars 164–188) G natural (as sounding) is used by the flute mainly in the extreme registers as the highest and lowest sounds (bars 164–169, 175, etc.). On the other hand, in the preceding section (bars 154–158) the repeated second octave C

---

† Thus Boulez uses here a quasi–quotation from his earlier cantata (1948).

sharp (sounding) is in the centre of the flute range.

Since the frequencies within groups can be presented in any order, the role of intervals is considerably lessened. This is also affected by the fact that certain groups, by virtue of their sound composition, fully occupy some section of the chromatic scale. E.g., group ba of domain I (see Diagram I) has the notes of the chromatic scale from A flat to D natural (see also groups bb and be from the same horizontal field). One of the aims of creating the technique of frequency multiplication was the elimination of the leading role of intervals, which played an important role in dodecaphonic music, with Webern especially. On the other hand, the composer has the possibility of making some intervals especially prominent, creating an intervalic unity to some extent, and also a greater individualization of certain fragments. This intervalic unity is of secondary importance in pitch organization, though it can be perceived by listeners and even by analysts as something of primary significance. As an example we can take the 3rd movement of *marteau* where the interval of a major second is somewhat prominent. The flute part in bar 1 begins with it and ends with it in bar 5. It also begins with it in bar 9. This interval is emphasized also in the vocal part in bar 9 and then in bars 12–13. We also note that it ends the 3rd movement of *marteau*.[†] This interval is a reminder of the beginning of the general series. The emphasis on the intervals of the general series is aided by the intervals being multiplied by themselves. E.g., self–multiplication of a minor third or major third results in groups consisting of a diminished or augmented triad only. E.g., see group cc from domain I, group cd from domain II, group dd from domain III, etc.

In the second cycle of *marteau* Boulez uses the opposite method of presenting intervals with multiplication, where one or several intervals acquire primary importance. Sometimes these intervals are easily recognizable by ear (e.g., see bars 54–102 in the 2nd movement of *marteau*, and sometimes they are purposefully veiled when each sound of the interval is performed by two different instruments (see bars 1–4 in the 4th movement of *marteau*).[‡]

The multiplication technique also decreases the role of separate sounds while increasing the role of sound groups.

In the coda of the 9th movement of *marteau* the frequencies on the flute, which have a definite pitch, are often performed together with the frequencies of percussion instruments without definite pitch, thus creating a double row of groups. The percussion part has the same serial organization as the flute part.

*Tam–Tam aigu* has 13 attacks, *Gong grave* and *Tam–Tam très profond* have 12 each. There are 13 attacks consisting of two sounds.[§] (5 attacks of high and middle instruments, 5 of middle and low instruments, 3 of extreme instruments). The total number of simple and double attacks is 24 (11+13). At the very end of the coda *Grande Cymbale suspendue* sounds once, thus the total number of attacks reaches 25 (see Ex. 35).

Five attacks from the percussion instruments (two simple and three double) in bars 100–103 correlate with 10 groups (or two fields) from the flute in bars 88–95. Ten attacks of the percussion instruments (five simple and five double) in bars 128–143, 155–157 correspond to the 20 groups from the flute in the same bars. And finally, ten attacks of the percussion instruments (five simple and five double) in the last section correspond to 20 groups performed by the flute. Thus 25 attacks of the percussion instruments, which in number seem to form a special domain consisting of five almost identical fields, correspond to 50 groups of the flute. Hence one field with the percussion instruments corresponds to two fields with the flute.

---

†   In the conclusion of the movement, as in its beginning, the major second is presented as a major ninth.
‡   This will be discussed in greater detail in the analysis of the second cycle of *marteau*.
§   The duration of both sounds is the same in these attacks.

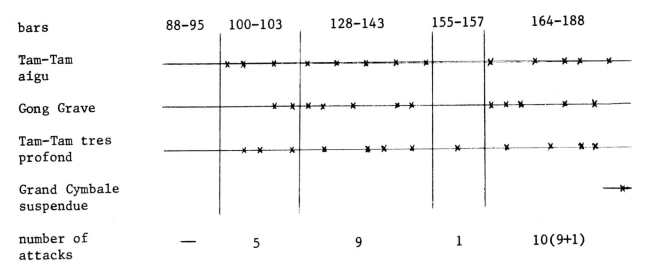

| bars | 88-95 | 100-103 | 128-143 | 155-157 | 164-188 |
|---|---|---|---|---|---|
| Tam-Tam aigu | | | | | |
| Gong Grave | | | | | |
| Tam-Tam tres profond | | | | | |
| Grand Cymbale suspendue | | | | | |
| number of attacks | — | 5 | 9 | 1 | 10(9+1) |

Ex. 35

Let us note the form proportions of the 1st and 7th movements of *marteau* from the viewpoint of the duration of each section. One semiquaver, which is the duration base of the whole of *marteau* is taken as the durational unit (see Ex. 36 and 37).

| domains | I | V | III | IV | II | V | II | IV | III |
|---|---|---|---|---|---|---|---|---|---|
| duration in semiquavers | 100 | 90 | 102 | 104 | 90 | 72 | 74 | 98 | 152 |

296

244

9X11+1    27X11-1    8X11+2    22X11+2    14X11-2

396                              396

36X11                            36X11

882
80X11+2

Ex. 36  Movement 1

| sections | I | II | III | IV | V |
|---|---|---|---|---|---|
| duration in semiquavers | 76 | 86 | 130 | 76 | 70 |

438
40X11-2

Ex. 37  Movement 7 (Domain I)

As seen from both examples, the duration of the 1st movement relates to that of the 7th approximately as 2 to 1 [882:438 = (80×11+2) : (40×11-2)]. The total duration of both movements equals

$$882+438 = 1320 = 120 \times 11 = 5 \times 24 \times 11.$$

Let us note the duration of each domain within the 1st and 7th movements (Ex. 38). The 3rd movement has the following proportions (Ex. 39).

domains

| | | |
|---|---|---|
| I | $100 + 438 = 538 =$ | $49 \times 11 - 1$ |
| II | $90 + 74 = 164 =$ | $15 \times 11 - 1$ |
| III | $102 + 152 = 254 =$ | $23 \times 11 + 1$ |
| IV | $104 + 98 = 202 =$ | $18 \times 11 + 4$ |
| V | $90 + 72 = 162 =$ | $15 \times 11 - 3$ |

Ex. 38

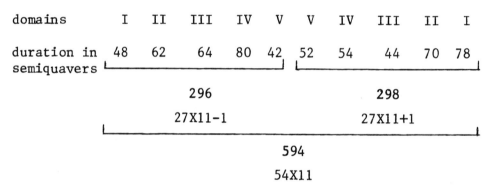

| domains | I | II | III | IV | V | V | IV | III | II | I |
|---|---|---|---|---|---|---|---|---|---|---|
| duration in semiquavers | 48 | 62 | 64 | 80 | 42 | 52 | 54 | 44 | 70 | 78 |

296
27X11-1

298
27X11+1

594
54X11

Ex. 39   Movement 3

The duration of the 1st, 3rd, and 7th movements is $1320+594 = 1914 = 174 \times 11$. The duration of the 1st and 7th movements relates to that of the 3rd as $1320:594 = (120 \times 11):(54 \times 11) = 20:9$. It should be noted that both the whole form of the three movements and its different sections have durations almost precisely divisible by 11. This is not a coincidence. In the second cycle of *marteau* the duration of many sections, of all the 8th movement and of the whole cycle is also divisible by 11.

We shall mention briefly the dynamic organization of the first cycle. In the 1st and 7th movements Boulez uses five dynamic gradations (Ex. 40), and in the 3rd movement and the coda of the 9th he uses ten (Ex. 41).[†] This corresponds to the division of the general series into five parts. The twofold widening of the dynamic scale in the 3rd movement and the coda of the 9th seems to correspond to the twofold compression of the tempo rate found in these movements as compared to the 1st and 7th. In Ex. 40 and 41 each dynamic step is denoted by a respective number.

$$\textit{ff} \quad \textit{f} \quad \textit{mf} \quad \textit{p} \quad \textit{pp}$$
$$1 \qquad 2 \qquad 3 \qquad 4 \qquad 5$$

Ex. 40

---

† *Quasi piano* is not used at all and is therefore given in brackets; *quasi forte* is found in the 3rd movement only.

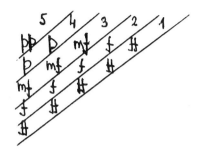

Ex. 41

Four types of dynamic usage can be identified in the 1st and 7th movements.

1. The presence of one dynamic gradation within each diagonal field and of non–repeating dynamic steps along the horizontal and the vertical. This can be found in the first semi–domain in bars 18–29 in the 7th movement (Ex. 42) and in the semi–domain in bars 30–37 of the 7th movement (Ex. 43).

Ex. 42   (bars 18–29, first row, movement 7)

Ex. 43   (bars 30–37, movement 7)

In bars 1–10 of the 1st movement non–repetition of dynamics within diagonal fields is also used (see Ex. 44a and 44b). If the examples are combined, we find an even distribution of dynamics where all the five dynamic gradations are taken six times each.

Ex. 44a   (bars 1–10, upper row);

Ex. 44b   (bars 1–10, lower row);

A similar phenomenon is observed in bars 42–52 of domain II in the 1st movement (see Ex. 45). In this case there is just a small rearrangement of dynamic steps (13524) as compared to Ex. 44b.

2. The presence of unrepeated dynamic steps within diagonal fields. This can be found in bars 8–17 and in the second semi–domain which is situated in bars 18–29 of the 7th movement (see Ex. 46 and 47). There is a certain deviation from this rule here. In these examples there is a tendency towards the non–repetition of the dynamics along the horizontal and the vertical too, which is denoted by numbers in brackets for the horizontal field consisting of five groups.

The non–repetition of dynamic steps within diagonal fields is also observed in bars 60–68 (domain II, 1st movement of *marteau*, see Ex. 48), as well as in bars 69–80 (domain IV, 1st movement, upper and lower group rows, see Ex. 49a and 49b).

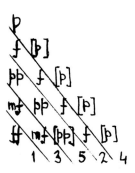

**Ex. 45**  (bars 42–52)

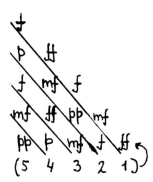

**Ex. 46**  (bars 8–17)

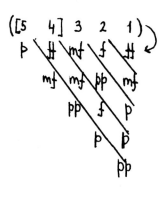

**Ex. 47**  (bars 18–29, second row of groups)

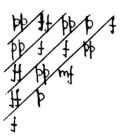

**Ex. 48**  (bars 60–68)

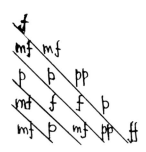

**Ex49a**  (bars 69–80) (upper row)

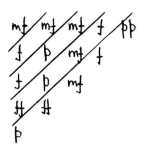

**Ex. 49b**  (bars 69–80) (lower row)

3. The group movement takes place along the vertical fields. In this case it is rather difficult to find the organizing principle of the dynamics. It can be surmised that the composer decided not to repeat the dynamics within the vertical fields. As an example the semi–domain in bars 38–47 of the 7th movement is taken (see Ex. 50 where *diminuendo* from *fortissimo* to *piano* is shown in brackets). Here the complete horizontal field consisting of five groups also includes non–repeating dynamic steps. The dynamics are presented similarly in bars 81–95 (domain III, 1st movement of *marteau*, see

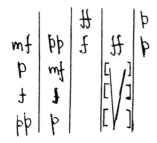

Ex. 50   (bars 38–47) movement 7

Ex. 51   (bars 81–95) movement 1

Ex. 51). Here also the only complete horizontal field consists of non–repeating dynamic gradations.

4. Last of all, the dynamics can be used in a restricted or defective way. In bars 21–32 (domain III, 1st movement of *marteau*) two dynamic gradations are used, each vertical field having one gradation (see Ex. 52).

Ex. 52   (bars 21–32, movement 1)

In bars 33–44 (domain IV, 1st movement) both group rows have one dynamic gradation only (*mezzo forte*).

It should be mentioned again that the durations and the number of attacks are also organized by means of the multiplication technique.

The multiplication technique, which creates harmonic fields consisting of frequency groups, eliminates the priority of the horizontal and vertical, establishing a new diagonal dimension. That is the difference between this serial technique and dodecaphony. Furthermore, the content of the "voice" notion changes; it is created by the alternation of groups consisting of a varying number of sounds. That is why the density of such a voice varies constantly (e.g., see bars 11–32 in the 1st movement or the coda of the 9th movement etc.) The presence of two voices can be spoken of only with two different groups sounding simultaneously (e.g., see bars 1–10 in the 1st movement).

As can be seen from this analysis, the form of all the movements of the first cycle of *marteau* develops from the initial division of the general series into five parts. Thus the freely chosen number five plays a primary role in creating the immediate form of the composition, while the number twelve lies at the top level of the composition and does not take any direct part in its organization.[†]

Another important new device is the use of derived series of frequencies when the general twelve–sound series does not have a direct role in the structuring of the music. This is the start of

---

† We should mention as an exception the form of the 3rd movement of *marteau* where Boulez adds two fields, thus bringing their total number to twelve (see Ex. 29). Another exception is the use of horizontal fields consisting of 12 frequencies (which happens rarely). As already mentioned, each domain (the fourth excepted) includes two such fields (see Diagram I).

a new stage in the development of serialism, where compositions acquire a complex multi–stepped hierarchy.

From all the above it becomes clear that the development of serial thinking required the creation of a special organization, leading music away from a structure completely built on the repetition of the twelve–sound series, whilst retaining a horizontal structure. At the same time this new organization did not have to break with the fundamentals of serial organization. This task was fulfilled by Boulez through the invention of the multiplication technique.[†] This technique can be contrasted with the organization in which sound groups have no direct common kinship based on serial organization and are used quite freely, as can be observed in the music of Cage and some other composers.

The multiplication technique after being first applied in *marteau* was used by Boulez in many compositions. Boulez uses it every time in a different way according to the intention of the composition. The works in question are the Third Sonata, *Structures II, Don, Tombeau, Eclat, Eclat–Multiple, Figures–Doubles–Prismes, Domaines, Cummings ist der Dichter*. In these compositions the multiplication technique often goes hand in hand with other serial techniques.

The general series of *marteau* is used as the basis for Boulez' orchestral composition, *Tombeau* (1959–62), which concludes the five–movement cycle *Pli selon pli*.[‡] E.g., see bars 1–8 of the principal instrument, the piano, where the same first derived series of frequencies sounds with the same initial division proportions, 24213, and the transposition E flat, as in Ex. 1b. Here the idea of multiplication is widened and includes orchestra groups organized by timbre similarity. Each orchestral group except for the brass instruments becomes the principal in turn; at this point it carries the main harmonic fields (i.e. derivative series, see Ex. 1b). In the first half of *Tombeau* the principal groups of instruments present the main fields as *cantus firmus*, i.e. 24213, 42132, 21324, etc., 25 fields altogether. Other groups of instruments either double the groups of main fields or present other frequency groups. See, e.g., the piano part from bar 43 together with Diagram I, where the full horizontal field b of domain II can be observed, then field b of domain III, field b of domain IV, field c of domain III, etc. This composition displays the possibilities of using the multiplication technique in creating music for a large orchestra. One of the possibilities is the use of heterophony which will be discussed in greater detail later.

In the orchestral composition *Don* frequency groups identical with those in *marteau* and *Tombeau* are partly used. This is not coincidental, as *Don* which begins the cycle *Pli selon pli*, really includes the material of all the later parts of the cycle. E.g., at figure 16 wood–winds use a block consisting of the frequencies of group db. Then at figure 17 for five bars the flutes perform frequencies of group dc. At the same time the trumpet (in D) plays the group dd for five bars. Furthermore the violins repeat group db for six bars. And finally, the trumpet (in D) performs group da for four bars. All these groups creating an almost complete horizontal field d belong to domain IV.

In *Cummings ist der Dichter* Boulez uses the same general series which is presented at the very beginning of the composition as a derived series of three blocks, which is furthermore given in retrograde form (see Ex. 53).

It is interesting that already in the finale (bar 210) of his Second Sonata (1948) Boulez uses three blocks which together form a twelve–sound series almost identical with the general series of *marteau* (only the sound C natural has to change its place) taken in retrograde form. In Ex. 54 numbers denote the sound order in the series (compare Ex. 53 and 54).

Multiplication technique can be combined with a heterophonic texture. E.g., two identical frequency groups sound simultaneously, while being different in duration, rhythm, dynamics,

---

†  It should also be mentioned that the so–called group technique used by Stockhausen was for him a principle of serial organization more or less as new and important as the multiplication technique was for Boulez.

‡  This general series of *marteau* was first used by Boulez even before *marteau* in his choral composition *Oubli, Signal, Lapidé* (1952), which has remained unpublished.

**Ex. 53** (*Cummings ist der Dichter*)

**Ex. 54** (Second Sonata)

number of attacks, frequency order, etc. To a very small degree, and rather veiled, this can be observed already in the 1st cycle of *marteau*. Such a method has been in part used in *Structures II for Two Pianos* (1956, 1961). E.g., in Chapter I in the second bar after number 60 piano II performs the same frequency group as Piano I (left hand), which is different in all other characteristics (see also other places). In orchestral music such a combination of multiplication technique with heterophonic texture can play an enormous part in the organization of the musical texture (see *Tombeau*).

Last of all, it should be mentioned again that the multiplication technique leads to the creation of the restricted aleatoric form. *Domaines* (1968–69) for the clarinet and 21 instruments, where the general series from the Third Sonata is used, is a characteristic example.

Thus, this kind of serial organization has proved important for the mature period of Boulez' creation.

# Chapter II

# Analysis of the Second Cycle

The second cycle of *marteau* includes four movements which occupy the even–numbered places in the composition:

II      Commentaire I de *Bourreaux de solitude*

IV     Commentaire II de *Bourreaux de solitude*

VI     *Bourreaux de solitude*

VIII   Commentaire III de *Bourreaux de solitude*

The organization of the second cycle is based on the same general series which was used for the organization of the first cycle. This series is used in *marteau* only once in its main four forms in movement 6.[†] In Ex. 55 it is given with the indices of all the parameters within the organizational system of the second cycle.

**Ex. 55**

From this series Boulez deduces 11 derived series, the variation of which forms the whole second cycle (Ex. 56).

These 11 series consist of 12 attacks, which are divided into positive (regular sounds) and negative (sounds made by a percussion instrument without definite pitch). As seen in Ex. 56, each series has

---

†   This will be discussed in greater detail further.

Ex. 56

its individual structure consisting of the position and number of positive and negative attacks and of the structure of the former.

These 11 series are united into five groups as shown in Ex. 56, thus producing a series sequence 2 2 1 3 3. Such a sequence of groups of series is usually observed throughout the cycle with the exception of the second half of the 6th movement (for the first time in bars 1–11 of the 2nd movement), while the series within each group can alternate more freely. The "names" of series given in Ex. 56 are chosen by the shortest duration in a series.

Within the 2nd, 4th and 8th movements all the series are presented as defective only. This means that the various parameters of a series, such as duration, dynamics and pitch organization, are used only partially, i.e. they do not have all the 12 gradations. A complete or non–defective series must be based on a scale with all the 12 gradations.

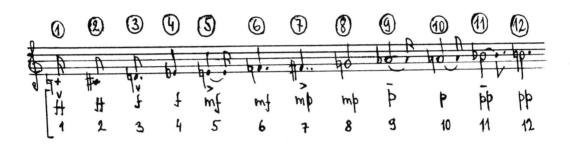

Ex. 57

Boulez combines the dynamics and the modes of attack in the second cycle in one scale which is shown in Ex. 57. Therefore everything said further on dynamics will also refer to the sphere of attacks.[†] For the sake of convenience durations and dynamics can be expressed by figures, the encircled figures referring to durations only. A note which equals a semi–quaver will be noted ①, etc.; similarly the loudest dynamics will be noted 1, etc. (Ex. 57).

In order to obtain defective series a composer can divide a 12–step scale into 2, 3, 4, 6, or 12 parts, i.e. he has five possibilities of dividing the whole scale into equal parts. E.g. with the division of the dynamic scale into two halves it becomes possible to use twice either scale 1–6 or 7–12.

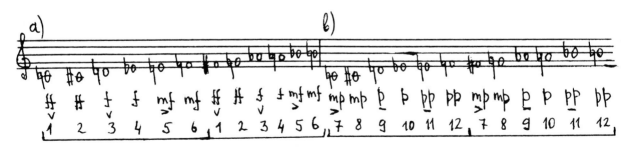

Ex. 58

With the scale divided into 3 parts three variants appear, 1–4, 5–8, 9–12. In the same way the scale is divided into 4, 6, and 12 parts, the number of variants growing and the dynamic amplitude of

---

[†] The symbol *sfz* is to be found in movements 4 and 6; in the other movements of the cycle the symbol v can only be found.

each series decreasing (the whole series can have one dynamic index only, e.g. 5, etc.). The scale of durations and pitches is divided similarly. E.g. in Ex. 59 the division of duration scale into 3 parts is shown, and in Ex. 60 the division of the pitch scale into 2 parts.

Ex. 59

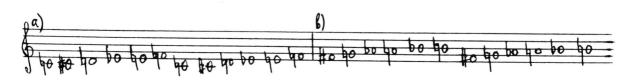

Ex. 60

Ex. 61 presents the general principle of division of a 12–step scale by all the parameters. Hence, e.g., when dividing the scale into two halves the indices 1–6 or 7–12 only can be used, while 2–7, 3–8, etc. will be considered as deviations from the scheme and therefore not used. The same refers to the division into 3, 4, 6, and 12 parts, which is shown by brackets.

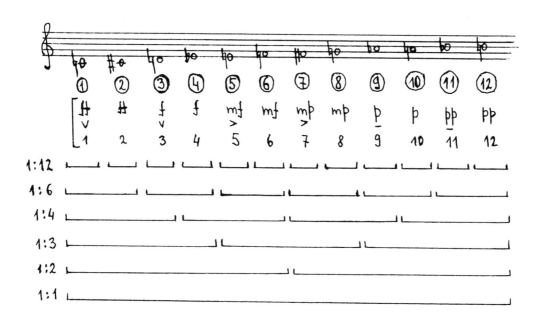

Ex. 61

In the second cycle Boulez used the defective dynamics scale completely, and the duration scale within the range 1–8, while the division of the pitch scale is found in one section of movement 8 only (division into two halves). Thus 27 defective variants of the dynamic scale and 17 of the duration scale are obtained.

In the second cycle Boulez uses several ways of determining durations.

1.  All the real sound durations are denoted.

2.  By means of one or less often two (very rarely three) grace notes. The grace note can be at the beginning or at the end of the note, or at both ends:

Ex. 62

This form of notation is mainly found in movement 8, beginning with bar 21. Such notation is especially typical of the flute part trying to render a polyphonic texture (see also bars 81–93 where this notation is used for all instruments).

3.  There is a notation for the beginning or end of the note (rarely elsewhere) i.e., a smaller part of the required duration. This can be observed in the whole of the second cycle especially in movements 2, 4, and the beginning of movement 8. The missing part of the duration seems to be implied (in the supplied score with the analysis the dotted line and the figure in brackets denote the implied duration of the note).

Ex. 63

As a variant of this mode Boulez sometimes denotes several sounds connected in one figure, which have the same duration equal to the time of all the sound (but only in the case of the same dynamics).

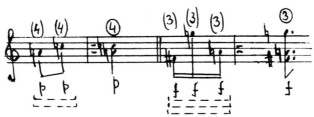

Ex. 64

The form of the whole second cycle is built on 11 sections of different size consisting of the consecutive exposition of five groups of series within each section. We shall mention briefly the main characteristics of these sections.

It is clear from Ex. 65 that the series are gradually freed from defectivization. That is the main feature of development.

We shall now discuss each section in greater detail. The sections I–V are the shortest in the whole cycle, each of them consisting of 11 series only. These series are represented in Scheme I with their duration taken into account (see Comments to Schemes). The scheme shows that five groups of series in each of the five sections are presented differently. E.g. in section II the first and second groups end simultaneously, after which without any interval the fourth and fifth groups begin; this spot (the beginning of bar 19) is almost in the centre of series development in the third group. Sections II–IV overlap partially, hence the maximum density here amounts to seven series. In Diagram I the series of sections I–V given in sequence are denoted. It is clear from this diagram that Boulez uses the division of the 12–step scale of durations and dynamics equally for each series. This means that if the duration scale is divided into 3 parts, the dynamics scale is divided in the same way, the dynamics always having the scale section at the opposite end to the scale section for durations. E.g., in a series for the flute and xylorimba (bars 1–3) the scale of durations and dynamics is divided into 3 parts, the durations occupying the section 1–4, and dynamics the other end, i.e. 9–12. If the durations have the section 4–6, dynamics have 7–9, etc.[†] All the five sections have durations within the range of 1–8 and dynamics of 5–12 respectively. Furthermore Boulez often gives the same indices of durations and dynamics of a series, which enter one group. E.g., the series F natural and G natural in bars 1–3 have the durations 1–4 and dynamics 9–12. At the same time each of the five groups of series, due to the different division of the 12–step scale, has a special section of the durations and dynamics scale. Section I has the row 3 4 12 6 2; this means that the first group of series uses the division of the scale into 3 parts, the second into 4, the third into 12, etc. If we observe the scale division with one group of series during 5 sections, we see that the composer alternates the division index without repetition. E.g., the first group of series (F natural and G natural) in section I has the division index 3, in section II it has 4, in III–2, in IV–12, in V–6. The rows of figures under Diagram I represent along the horizontal the division principle of the scale by sections, and along the vertical, for groups of series. This quadrangle shows that no figure along the vertical or the horizontal has the same position twice.

In section VI the defective series undergo multiplication. Due to that each of the main 11 series can be said to be multiplied by all the two–, three–, and four–sound structures of attacks which it has. E.g., the F natural series has three attacks consisting of more than one sound and producing intervals: minor third, perfect fourth, and major second. Therefore Boulez multiplies successively frequencies of each attack of the F natural series by these intervals. Three different multiplied series result from that. One of them has the index of multiplication to a minor third; the other to a perfect fourth, the third to a major second. With the mutual multiplication of frequencies of polyphonous attacks the resulting sonority often acquires repeated sounds, which are eliminated[‡] (similar to the mode of multiplication in the first cycle of *marteau*). E.g., in bars 54–56 of movement 2 the F natural series is presented by the viola in a multiplication by the attack structure of a minor third. Another series, e.g., E flat, has one triphonous attack (minor second and major second), one quatriphonous (two minor seconds and a major second), and one diphonous (minor third). Therefore Boulez creates three different multiplied series which differ in their density. Thus the whole multiplied series becomes similar to the harmonic field in the first cycle of *marteau*.

---

† The pointers in two places of Diagram I denote a small discrepancy between durations and dynamics.
‡ As an exception Boulez keeps these sounds at the very beginning of section VI in bars 54–59 of movement 2. E.g., the F natural sound in bar 55 is produced twice within one multiplied sonority.

| sections | I | II | III | IV | V | VI | | VII | VIII | IX | X | XI | coda |
|---|---|---|---|---|---|---|---|---|---|---|---|---|---|
| movements | 2 | 2 | 2 | 2 | 2 | 2 | 4 | 8 | 8 | 8 | 6 | 6 | 6 |
| bars | 1-11 | 11-25 | 21-32 | 29-40 | 40-53 | 54-114 | 1-105 | 1-20 | 20-50 | 46-138 | 1-33 | 33-92 | 91-94 |
| characteristics | defective duration and dynamics | | | | | † | | | defective pitch dynamics | defective dynamics | no defectivization | | |

multiplication    transposition

retrograde movement of groups of series

series are deduced from the general series IR

dispersion of series and their general attacks (and frequences)

the general series (IR,O)

Ex. 65

---

† In one short fragment of section VI dynamics is not defective

Section VI can easily be divided into four parts from the viewpoint of attack presentation in multiplied series:

| movements | 2 ("trio") | | 2 | 4 | 4 |
|---|---|---|---|---|---|
| bars | 54–102 | | 103–114 | 1–47 | 47–105 |

Ex. 66

In the "trio"[†] of movement 2 and in the first half of movement 4 the sounds of the multiplied sonorities are presented simultaneously, while in bars 103–114 of movement 2 and in the second half of movement 4 the sounds of an attack are usually presented in turn (see the appended score and Comments) e.g., the attack of two sounds in G natural and B flat in the former case will be:

Ex. 67a

In the latter case it is usually:

Ex. 67b

This is most important from the artistic standpoint, as the music sounds much more diversified. Primarily·for this reason, in the former case, the viola plays *pizzicato* only and the flute is absent.[‡] Furthermore, the "trio" in movement 2 and the first half of movement 4 are presented in a similarly quick tempo ($\downarrow$ = 120; $\downarrow$ = 132). Also the concluding section of movement 2 (bars 103–114) and the second half of movement 4 have similar slow and moderate tempos ($\downarrow$ = 63; $\downarrow$ = 76).[§]

Although section VI is clearly divided into four parts, the structure here is also based on the division into five parts, which is determined by the alternation of five groups of series. Therefore the "trio" in movement 2 is divided into two sections (bars 54–74 and 74–102). Thus the form of section VI is:

---

†   For the sake of brevity we call this part "trio", as three instruments are played here.
‡   Boulez does not introduce it in the second half of movement 4 either.
§   Tempo $\downarrow$ = 92 is also found in movement 4.

| series | g natural<br>f natural | a natural<br>f sharp | c sharp | b natural<br>g sharp<br>e flat | b flat<br>e natural<br>d natural | |
|---|---|---|---|---|---|---|
| movements | 2 | 2 | 2 | 4 | 4 | |
| bars | 54–74 | 74–102 | 103–114 | 1–47 | 47–105 | |
| number of mul-<br>tiplied series | 16(14) | 19(22) | 12 | 39 | 45 | = 131 |
| number of<br>simple series | 32 | 46 | 28 | 96 | 98 | = 300 |

Ex. 68

The numbers in brackets (Ex. 68) denote the number of series which should have been in the section. The number of polyphonous attacks, whose frequencies were used for multiplication within each series must be the same, which is on the whole observed by Boulez (see Ex. 69, where the figures denoting structure of polyphonous attacks render the intervals with the number of semi-tones. The figures in brackets say how many series there should have been). The composer seems to take two series from F sharp and give them to F natural. Then the series F natural and G natural have the same number of presentations. The series F sharp and A natural are presented roughly the same number of times, which also serves the purpose of symmetry (see Scheme II). The A natural series should be presented one time more, which does not happen because of its special presentation in bars 85–91. Boulez has increased the number of presentations of the several E flat series with a triphonous attack at the expense of presenting that series with a diphonous attack, mainly, it seems, to increase sound density. Ex. 69 shows that the total number of polyphonous attacks in all the 11 series is 36, which makes 27 two–sound attacks, 8 three–sound and 1 four–sound. Thus, 36 = 27+8+1 = 27+9. 27:9 = 3:1. If the number of diphonous multiplied series is calculated and related to the number of tri– and quatriphonous series, approximately the same relation will result (with the initial data given in brackets in Ex. 69): 132 = 98+34; 98:34≈3:1.

The system of series transpositions used in section VI has features of symmetry. The transpositions can be grouped around the central sound which is the "leading" sound of the series which bears its name (Ex. 70). The attacks grouped around this sound and showing the transpositions of these series, are usually placed symmetrically. Most symmetrical groups of sounds have a sound in common, which in one group is the upper and in another the lower one. E.g., the G natural series the group–transpositions C natural–E flat and A natural–C natural have the C natural in common. In less frequent cases the group–transpositions are symmetrical with relation to the central sound without having a sound in common. E.g., in the B natural series the group–transpositions D natural–E flat and G natural–A flat are at the same distance from the central B natural sound. Ex. 70 also shows that the F natural and G natural series have the same transpositions where possible.[†]

In section VI, as in sections I–V, each of the five groups of series has its own durational organization. The series which are included in one group acquire the same indices of the 12–step scale division. E.g., for the G natural and F natural series, 2 3 4 (see Diagram II). Besides, all the 11 series use three different division indices. An exception is presented by the series A natural and F sharp which have two indices each, but together produce three different indices 3 4 6. Thus, each

---

† The G natural series has one deviation marked by a cross.

| series | f natural | g natural | f sharp | a natural | c sharp | g sharp | e flat | b natural | d natural | e natural | b flat |
|---|---|---|---|---|---|---|---|---|---|---|---|
| structure of polyphonous attacks | 3 2 5 | 3 2 2 1 | 1 1<br>2 2 3 3 | 1<br>3 2<br>1 | 1<br>4 4<br>3 | 2<br>2<br>2 | 2<br>3 2 1<br>1 1 | 3 2 2 1 | 2<br>1 1 3<br>3 | 1<br>3 3<br>2 | 2 1 3 |
| number of presentations | 2 4 2 | 2 2 2 2 | 3 3 2 2 | 4 2 3 | 4 4 4 | 7 7 | 1 5 3 | 4 4 4 4 | 3 3 3 3 | 5 5 5 | 6 6 6=131 |
| | (2) | | (3 3) | (3) | | | (3 3) | | | | |
| | 2 | 2 | 3 | 4/3 | 4 | 7 | 3 | 4 | 3 | 5 | 6 |

Ex. 69

Ex. 70

| sub-sections | I | II | III | IV | V | VI | VII | VIII | IX |
|---|---|---|---|---|---|---|---|---|---|
| bars | 54–59 | 59–64 | 65–68 | 68–74 | 74–79 | 79–85 | 85–91 | 92–97 | 97–102 |
| tempos ( ♪ =) | 120 | 132 | 120 | 132 | 132 | 132 | 120 | 120 | 132 |
| series | g♮ f♮ | f♮ | g♮ | g♮ f♮ | f# | a♮ | a♮ | f# | f# |
| intervals of multiplication | 3  3 | 2 | 2 | 1  5 | 1 2 | 3 | 2 $^1_1$ | 3 | 1 2 |
| number of multiplied series | 2  2 | 4 | 4 | 2  2 | 3 | 4 | 5 | 4 | 3  =  35 |
| number of simple series | 4  4 | 8 | 8 | 4  4 | 9 | 8 | 12 | 8 | 9  =  78 |
| direction | $1_0 1R$ $1_1 1R$ | $2_0 2R$ | $2_0 2R$ | $1_0 1R$ $1_1 1R$ | $2_0 1R$ | $2_0 2_0$ | $2_0 1R;1_1 1R$ | $2_0 2R$ | $2_0 1R$ |

Ex. 71

division index is used in three groups of series (see Diagram II, a separate row of figures). Dynamics have a similar organization, with the exception mainly of the first half of movement 4, where dynamics often cease to be defective[†] (see Diagram V).

The instruments present the various series differently. In bars 54–74 and 105–114 of movement 2 each series is presented by one instrument only (see Scheme II), while in bars 74–102 of movement 2 and in all of movement 4 not only each series, but also many frequencies within their polyphonous attacks seem to be divided among different instruments producing in movement 4 especially a complex system of *Klangfarbenmelodie*, where series lines are absolutely indistinguishable to the ear (which obviously is the author's intention).[‡]

In the addendum to the work we give a fragment of movement 4 (bars 1–4), where, for better understanding of organization, three multiplied series are denoted in different colours: the E flat series is red, G sharp is blue, and B natural is black (see page 149).

The whole "trio" in movement 2 is divided by Boulez into nine subsections having nine serial ensembles, or into six subsections according to tempo alternations (120 and 132). (Ex. 71).

Each of the two parts of the "trio" (bars 54–74 and 74–102) has characteristics of mirror symmetry in the number of multiplied and simple series, in their position and direction, and also in multiplication intervals (see Ex. 71 and Scheme II). In bars 92–97 of the "trio" the series F sharp is presented, although in bars 79–85 the A natural series sounds, which disturbs the symmetry, nevertheless symmetry is preserved in almost all the numerical indices, e.g., in the number of multiplied series (3 4 5 4 3) and simple series (9 8 12 8 9). See also Diagram III, where the data are given for each series.

The last section of movement 2 of *marteau* (bars 103–114), presenting only the C sharp series consists of three fragments different in tempo (63, 76, 63). Boulez slows down on purpose. On the one hand, this returns to the tempo of sections I–V, on the other, this makes it possible to present multiplied series on two levels. This makes the musical texture much more dense, bringing it in bars 111–114 to the simultaneous sounding of 14 series voices ("mutation"), and complicates the playing of the music, (e.g., the flute presents 4–5 series voices simultaneously). See Scheme II and also Diagram IV, where the series which are presented on two levels are marked by a cross.

The first half of movement 4 (bars 1–47) consists of five subsections different in length, where tempi 132 and 120 alternate.

| tempos ( ♩ =) | 132 | 120 | 132 | 120 | 132 |
|---|---|---|---|---|---|
| bars | 1–4 | 5–8 | 9–16 | 16–35 | 35–47 |

Ex. 72

Those subsections are in their turn subdivided into very small fragments of different length. They are 37 in number and are separated by fermatas. The appearance of such a structure results from Boulez emphasizing the beginning and the end of each series by a fermata. The series are presented in such a way that the number of fragments (37) almost reaches the number of series (39). It is clear from Scheme III that in bars 1–16 Boulez alternates the series B natural without silences, and the series G sharp and E flat with silences; in bars 16–47 the silences disappear altogether. Besides, to increase sound density, Boulez adds another, a fourth "line" of multiplied series (from the end of bar 13 to bar 29 the G sharp series, then B natural, and in bars 36–47 the G sharp series), which brings

---

[†]  Some other deviations are observed too.
[‡]  Both modes of series presentation can be found in bars 103–104 of movement 2.

the texture to 11 series voices (in bars 17–18 and 42–45).

And last, the second half of movement 4 (bars 47–105) also consists of five subsections which vary in tempo and produce a symmetrical structure. Multiplied series are united into ten blocks. The beginning and the end of each block are shown by a fermata, thus producing 12 fragments of different length[†] (see Ex. 73, Diagram VI, Scheme III).

| bars | 47–63 | 63–72 | 73–85 | 85–90 | 91–105 |
|---|---|---|---|---|---|
| tempos ($\downarrow$ =) | 76 | 92 | 63 | 92 | 76 |
| series | d♮ e♮ b♭ | d♮ | b♭ e♮ | d♮ | e♮ b♭ d♮ |
| number of multiplied series | 3 5 6  ⌐14⌐ | 3 | 6 5  ⌐11⌐ | 3 | 5 6 3  ⌐14⌐ |
| number of simple series | 6 10 12 | 9 | 12 10 | 6 | 15 12 6 |
| direction | O R O | O | O R | R | R O R |
| intervals of multiplication | 3 3 2 | 2/3 | 1 3 | 1 | 1/2 3 1 |

Ex. 73

Within each block there are series of the same name and direction. They begin with the same attack, which created a greater block unity.

Boulez uses three kinds of series distribution in the blocks:   1) the series begin simultaneously,   2) the series end simultaneously,   3) the series are situated in "pyramid" fashion, i.e. symmetrically to each other (see Scheme III). Such a block structure can be schematically depicted by three triangles. This is shown in Scheme III down to the right, where the duration of each block is rendered by the length of the triangle base, which is given with a ten–time diminution (the arrow points to the direction of the block series, O or R).

If the 9th block is switched to the E natural series, and the 8th to the B flat series (which is denoted by two vertical dotted arrows), then a complete mirror symmetry will appear in their general distribution. Then block 10 will be symmetrical to block 1 in series distribution and direction, block 9 to 2, 8 to 3, etc. For Boulez, however, it was more important that each series (D natural, E natural, and B flat) should have three different kinds of blocks. That is why there is a small deviation from the mentioned full symmetry. Symmetry is also expressed in the fact of the second block beginning directly after the end of the first block series which is shortest in duration. Similarly the shortest series of block 10 begins almost directly after the ending of block 9. Block 3 begins directly after the end of block 1; similarly block 8 ends directly before the beginning of block 10. Blocks 4 and 7 are situated between the neighbouring blocks and sound as one "voice". Besides that block 9 is in the very centre between blocks 8 and 10.

---

† There should have been 13 fragments, but Boulez has no fermata in bar 103, before the very end of the movement.

Since Boulez is interested in creating symmetry within each of the three series (D natural, E natural, B flat), the durations of blocks 1 and 10 are the same, the durations of blocks 2 and 8 are the same respectively, while in the B flat series all the blocks are equal (i.e. 3, 5† and 9). In this case the symmetry is emphasized by the fact that, as mentioned, each of the three series (D natural, E natural, B flat) has the same number of multiplied series in each block, and besides, each of the three series begins with the same attack in all of its blocks. The mirror symmetry of structure is even expressed in the attacks of the percussion instrument at the beginning and end of five subsections (vertical lines in Ex. 74 separate the subsections).

Ex. 74

The presentation of the series in each block reflects in a veiled form the imitative texture but understood in a new way (this can really be seen at other points of section VI especially in subsections 2 and 3). This is most obvious in blocks 4 and 7, where the beginning of each series can even be caught by ear.

Block 8 is culminating in density, as in bars 91–93 there are 15 series voices; with the overlapping of blocks 8 and 9 the density also reaches 15 voices (bars 98–99) and even 16 (bar 97). Thus, this fragment has the highest density in the whole of section VI and even in the whole of the second cycle of *marteau*. Generally a characteristic feature is the creation of highest density in each subsection of section VI, usually shortly before its ending.

Thus, the principle of contrast lays the basis for the organization of section VI, where all the five subsections vary in presenting the series (as mentioned, the subsections 1 and 2 are more similar). Subsection 4 is probably the most freely created, and 5 the most strictly. That is also a contrast between the two halves of movement 4 of *marteau*.

Let us take up section VII and movement 8 of *marteau*. This short section resembles in structure sections I–V, where series are also presented by individual instruments though there are transpositions (see Diagram VII). In section VII, as further in IX, pitch transpositions seem to be more or less a free act of the composer. In section VII some series are presented several times, therefore their total number reaches 17.

The additional six series are somewhat of a continuation of the preceding series, as they begin without pauses (see Scheme IV). All the series sounding twice begin with the same frequency, e.g. two F sharp series (see the Tables of series). The position of two pairs of series is mirror symmetrical: two E flat series (R and O) equal in duration and two G sharp series (O and R) also equal in duration (see Scheme IV). Boulez included additional series to make the texture more dense (the vibraphone and the xylorimba play eight series each, one series is played by the flute).

Section VIII (bars 20–50) seems to include only series with a defective pitch structure.‡ Here the pitch scale can be said to be "compressed" to its half; to the dimensions of a perfect fourth. In such a case the sounds of the series which are outside the given half scale, are replaced by sounds at a

---

†   Boulez shortened the duration of block 5 by two semiquavers.
‡   This section is analysed only partially due to its great complexity. Hence the general statements refer to the investigated material only (see the Tables of series).

tritone distance. E.g., in bars 21–29 the vibraphone presents a B flat series transposed up a major second (all the series of this section are presented in transposition only). Its full structure is presented in Ex. 75a, and its defective structure in Ex. 75b (arrows denote the transposed sounds).

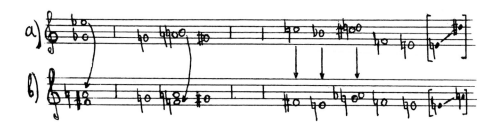

Ex. 75

The E natural–A natural range is chosen here, the scales of durations and dynamics being complete.[†]

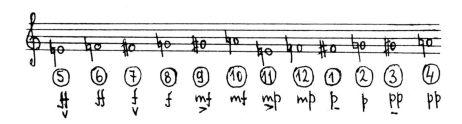

Ex. 76

In section VIII all the attacks of any one series follow at equal time intervals, therefore the duration of a series can be equal, e.g., 5×12, or 6×12, etc. (while in connection with the duration of the last attack the real duration of a series can be a little shorter or longer). The even sequence of attacks can be determined by the beginnings or ends (of their durations), however, in all the series found in this section it is determined by the attack beginnings. In Ex. 75 above the series under discussion has attacks following each other with intervals of seven semiquavers, hence its length is 7×12 = 84. In section VIII seven series only have been found, four of them in the form of halves. In this section Boulez probably decided to use also incomplete defective series.

The sequence of five groups of series is presented in section VIII in a retrograde order.[‡]

In its great duration section IX falls behind section VI only (within the range of three *commentaires*). It is presented in bars 47–138 and partially overlaps the ending of section VIII (therefore there are fermatas in bars 46 and 50). Section IX also has a much veiled five–part structure with the central fragment emphasized by fermatas.[§] (Ex. 77).

---

[†]   In bar 26 B flat of the vibraphone and F sharp of the xylorimba must be played by the opposite instruments.
[‡]   Section VIII begins eight semiquavers before, overlapping with section VII (bar 20). In this case in bar 19 there should have been a fermata. Boulez however, has it eight semiquavers later in bar 21.
[§]   The division into series is not too clear in the first fragment.

| bars | 47–61 | | 61–67 | 67–71 | 71–103 | | | 102–138 | | |
|------|-------|----|-------|-------|--------|----|----|---------|----|----|
| series | f♮ g♮ | | f♯(a♮) | c♯ | e♭ g♯ b♮ | | | d♮ e♮ b♭ | | |
| number of series | | | 2 | 3 | ⌊5 3 5⌋ | | | ⌊4 4 4⌋ | | |
| | | | | 3 | 13 | | | 12 | | |

Ex. 77

In Diagram VIII one can observe the contrasting features of the five fragments. E.g., in the central fragment three C sharp series sound with three instruments simultaneously, each series is based on two levels at a tempo ♩ = 63, which brings it close to bars 111–114 of movement 2 in *marteau*.[†]

The fourth fragment has a three–part structure with features of symmetry (bars 71–80, 81–93, 93–103), with the middle part consisting of five series presented by different instruments with the division index of dynamics by 2 (the attack sequence is determined by the beginning), and the surrounding parts consist of four series with the division index of dynamics by 4 (the sequence of attacks is determined by their endings of durations and takes place every two semiquavers).[‡]

In the fifth fragment the D natural series is always presented on three levels, each by a different instrument [§] (see the Tables of series; Ex. 78 presents the series of bars 102–106 as O, with the transposition a minor third down).

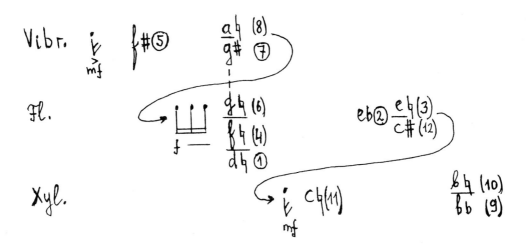

Ex. 78

In Ex. 78 arrows present the real structure of the series which is divided into 3+6+3 attacks; the vertical dotted line denotes the simultaneous beginnings of both attacks.

Another typical point should be mentioned. In the fourth fragment the duration system of all the series can be said to be "transposed" together with the transposition of their pitch structure. E.g., in bars 71–74 the G sharp series is present in transposition by a minor third down. In this case the

---

[†] It is interesting that the series of xylorimba and vibraphone (bars 67–71) are mutually retrograde. They also have the same transposition (see the Tables of series).

[‡] The symmetry is even linked to dynamics 7–9 with the series in bars 78–80 and 93–95, while all the other series have 10–12.

[§] No uniform sequence of attacks is used in presenting the series on several levels (i.e., the C sharp and D natural series).

F natural sound is selected, which is 1 in duration, instead of the former G sharp. In the fifth fragment the system of durations is preserved despite the transposition of pitch structure. E.g., in the D natural series the shortest duration will always be that of the D natural sound (see Diagram VIII). The dynamics system, on the other hand, is preserved in the fourth fragment, and in the fifth it is "transposed" together with the pitch system.[†]

The uniform sequence of attacks in section IX, as opposed to section VIII, is based, with a few exceptions, on a row of figures connected with the division of the 12–step scale into equal parts, i.e., 1 2 3 4 6. This uniform sequence of attacks is used in sections VIII and IX mainly due to the absence of duration defectivization. In section IX this is also linked to the wish to compress the time of a series duration (the number most often used is 2, less often 1, 3 and 4, while the last series of the section only has 6, which is connected with the general slowing down at the end of movement 8, see Diagram VIII). It should also be mentioned that in section IX, if the uniform sequence of attacks is determined by their beginning, then all the sounds within each polyphonous attack begin simultaneously (like in section X, but differently from VIII). And vice versa, in attacks determined by endings of their durations, the sounds within their range end simultaneously.

A characteristic feature used for the first time in section IX is the alternation of series, in which the beginning and the end of a series usually overlap a little with the neighbouring series instead of their being simultaneous as before (the exceptions are bars 67–71 and 81–93). Due to this a rather large section of the form has a relatively small number of series. Even with only three instruments, which often pause, the music begins to sound thin; e.g., compare the last 4 bars in sections IX and VII. Then the series alternation becomes the basis of section X, and also of the main section of the *marteau* finale.

All the 5 fragments of section IX contrast in the use of the percussion part. E.g., in the 4th fragment the dynamics are ppp, in the 2nd fragment only the alto and tenor bongos are sounded, and in the 4th all the four bongos play in turn. In the 1st fragment the duration of sounds of the percussion instrument reaches 12. In the 3rd fragment only the soprano and bass bongo sound, while in the 5th, the first three bongos and the alto besides. Then, at the very end of the 5th fragment and in movement 8, when the B flat series is presented, there are attacks of the alto bongo and maracas sounding simultaneously (bars 120–123 and 126–138); this last section of the form seems to create the coda of movement 8.

Finally, we will discuss movement 6 of *marteau*. The organization of the whole of movement 6 is based on one scheme connecting all the four parameters, where each sound has 12 durations and 12 dynamic grades (see Diagram IX). This becomes possible only with the complete elimination of series defectivity. Diagram IX shows, e.g., that the C natural sound, which has the duration of 1 semiquaver, will always have the dynamics of 1; if the same sound has a duration of 2 semiquavers, it will always have the dynamics of 12, etc. In this diagram the chromatic pitch row is placed horizontally, the growing row of durations is vertical, and the fading dynamic row is diagonal and falling from left to right. Hence any chromatic scale with all the parameters or any complete series is always placed diagonally (also from left to right). Diagram IX shows that only two sounds, C natural and F sharp, coincide in duration, which is one semiquaver, and in dynamics, which is also 1 (*fortissimo sforzando*). Therefore only these sounds create diagonal chromatic scales with coinciding duration and dynamics. E.g., besides the mentioned C natural and F sharp, also C sharp, equal in duration 2, coincides with dynamics 2; D natural, equal in duration 3, coincides with dynamics 3, etc. Thus the two chromatic scales falling diagonally can be called privileged, the scale from the C natural sound equal to 1 in duration and dynamics being of greater importance, since it is the basis for the general series.

---

†   On the dynamics system more will be said further in explaining Ex. 79.

The other ten diagonal rows have the following property: the position of the duration scale in each of them is symmetrical to the position of the dynamic scale, the centre of symmetry being the sound C natural (or F sharp). E.g., the diagonal scale with the sound C sharp equal to 1 in duration will have the B natural sound equal to 1 in dynamics, etc. This is shown in Ex. 25, where the sounds of the upper scale equal 1 in duration, and of the lower one, 1 in dynamics.

durations

dynamics

Ex. 79

It is very important to remember that Diagram IX is the basis not only of movement 6, but also of the whole second cycle of *marteau*. Therefore, all the defective series follow the same rules of correlation of duration and dynamics scales. Since 1 for duration and 1 for dynamics are not always used, they are replaced by the smallest index of those parameters. E.g., in sections I–V the F natural series always has the G natural sound equal to the lowest dynamic step used in that series instead of 1 (see the Tables of series, where this correlation can be checked by control scales). With pitch transpositions the systems of duration and dynamics are either transposed to the same intervals (sections VI and VII) or are not transposed (partly section IX, as mentioned in its analysis above). In section VI with multiplication the indices of durations and dynamics are determined by the upper sound of the attack (see the control scales in the Tables of series).

By Diagram IX each sound can be checked and the few deviations noted both in movement 6 and in the whole of the second cycle. This diagram is the basis of some sections of movement 9 of *marteau* as well.

Section X (bars 1–33) is built of eleven series deduced from the general series IR. It also has five parts, its main structure being produced by five groups of series, which are in the relation of IR to the five groups of the O series (with the C natural sound as the symmetry centre of both rows).

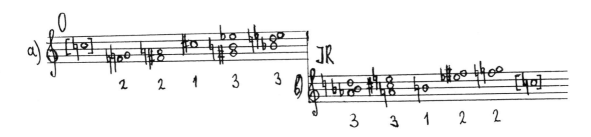

Ex. 80

It is clear from Ex. 80 that, e.g., the F natural series in the left row corresponds to the G natural series in the right one; G natural in the left row corresponds to F natural in the right one, etc., the result being the following series system (Ex. 81):

| Series deduced from the general series 0 | Series deduced from the general series IR | Series by durations (and dynamics) | Series by structures | bars |
|---|---|---|---|---|
| f ♮ | g ♮ | d ♮ | e ♭ | 1-5 |
| g ♮ | f ♮ | g ♯ | a ♮ | |
| f ♯ | f ♯ | b ♭ | c ♯ | |
| a ♮ | e ♭ | c ♯ | b ♭ | 6-14 |
| c ♯ | b ♮ | a ♮ | g ♯ | |
| g ♯ | e ♮ | e ♮ | b ♮ | |
| e ♭ | a ♮ | b ♮ | e ♮ | 13-17, 21-24 (voice) |
| b ♮ | c ♯ | e ♭ | d ♮ | 17-24 |
| d ♮ | b ♭ | f ♯ | f ♯ | |
| e ♮ | g ♯ | f ♮ | g ♮ | 25-33 |
| b ♭ | d ♮ | g ♮ | f ♮ | |

**Ex. 81**

**Ex. 82**   Series deduced from the general series IR

Every two series corresponding to each other must have the same general structure, i.e. alternation of positive and negative attacks and number of sounds in each attack, although the attack structure and their sounds differ in the two series (see Ex. 81). Ex. 81 and 80 are similar from the point of symmetry; that means that any series of the right row in Ex. 81 will have the dynamics of the left row, and vice versa. E.g., the G natural series in the right row, which has the G natural sound equal to 1 in duration, will have the F natural sound equal to 1 in dynamics, and vice versa. Hence there is an additional link between the two groups of eleven series, i.e. between the series of sections X and XI.

The series deduced from the general series IR are then linked in five pairs (in Ex. 82 this is shown). Both series in each pair exchange structures, while keeping their organization of durations and dynamics (see Ex. 82).[†] The F sharp series, as seen from Ex. 81 and 82, is never replaced by another, as it has a place of privilege in the scale in Diagram IX. Thus all the series in section X, except F sharp, have the proper organization of durations and dynamics, but not their pitch structure. This must aim at avoiding complete structural stability, which is more characteristic of the finale of *marteau*, and also at some liberation from the rigid bonds of structure.[‡] The five–part form of section X is also seen in the bars marked in Ex. 82.

---

[†]   As seen from Ex. 82, three out of five such pairs consist of series placed next to each other.

[‡]   That has something in common with the creation of additional transpositions for the four domains in the first cycle of *marteau* (i.e. for movements 1, 3 and 7); here too the domain based on the leading sound of E flat was not transposed.

Ex. 83

Ex. 84

Ex. 83 presents the 11 series of section X before structures interchange, i.e. in their purely theoretical form; their denotations coincide with Ex. 81. If the attacks including more than one sound are compared in the 11 series built from the general series O with the respective attacks of the 11 series built from the series IR, it becomes clear that the latter attacks consist almost always of greater intervals (compare Ex. 56 and 83). Due to that the series of section X are so–called widened variants of the series presented in the three *commentaires*. This reminds us of Bartók's *Music for Strings, Percussion and Celesta*, where the main theme of the first movement, which has a chromatic scale within a perfect fifth, is then repeated in the finale in widened form, in a lydian–mixolydian mode within an octave. That could be one of the reasons why Boulez decided to present once in the whole of cycle II all the 11 series deduced from the general series IR, and not O, in succession and without defectivization of parameters.

The deducing of 11 series from the general series IR is connected with its being affected by the same proportions which were taken for the general series O, but following in retrograde order.

In Ex. 84 the series are presented as they are in section X, i.e. with all the structural permutations. Their notations coincide with Ex. 82 (attack alternations by their beginnings, which are or tend to be uniform, are given in brackets). Ex. 84 shows that the last four series also have additional deviations in their structures:  1) in the E flat series sounds of many frequencies are changed, and also to a small extent its general structure;  2) in the F sharp series the structure and sounds of three attacks are changed;  3) in the F and G natural series the general structure and sounds of attacks are radically changed; the scales of durations and dynamics, 12 attacks and 12 sounds are preserved everywhere (compare Ex. 83 and 84).[†] From this viewpoint section X can be subdivided into two parts: in one the first seven series are presented (bars 1–17 and 21–22, 24 in the vocal part), in the other one the following four (bars 17–33). In this second part the composer frees the series to a great extent from rigid structure, which brings it closer to section XI (it can be called a transition to section XI, especially in bars 25–33). It is interesting that the E flat series in bars 17–20 is compressed by the composer and has only 6 different sounds producing in a concealed way two minor triads at a semitone distance (from C sharp and D natural). The third fragment resembles somewhat the beginning of the development (bars 27–28 and 41) in the first movement of Webern's Symphony op. 21.

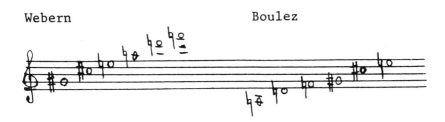

Ex. 85

In section XI (bars 33–92) the 11 series are almost always presented in a dispersed or incomplete way. The exception is the section which can be called a "reprise" (bars 75–92), in which three complete series are presented. They are: D natural (O, it is presented in compressed form, attacks follow each other at intervals of a semiquaver); E natural (R) and B flat (O) (bars 75–77, 79–85, 85–91).

---

†   The E flat series has 11 sounds only, the supposed 12th sound is added by us in brackets. The dotted arrow shows that the C sharp sound should theoretically be separate as the 8th attack (instead of an attack of the percussion instrument). All the 4 series have repeated sounds.

The series can be divided into fragments of different lengths, up to single attacks, which can also be presented in incomplete form. Simultaneous beginnings of different attacks having a complete or incomplete number of sounds are also to be found. All those series fragments are freely presented in different combinations.[†] That, as well as the structural deviations in section X, is possible due to one scheme unifying all the parameters (Diagram IX).

One feature connects section XI with I–V, i.e. the beginning and the end of the second cycle: all the series are presented here in their main transpositions.

Diagram X gives all the sounds of section XI. Figures denote the bar numbers where those sounds are; if the bar number is in brackets, this means that the sound is noted in the score partially or (seldom) that there is no proper correspondence between the duration and the dynamics of the sound. The main purpose of Diagram X is to follow the presentation of any fragments of series. The chromatic scales on which the series are based, are given here, as in Diagram IX, diagonally, from up left to right. E.g., a partial presentation can be observed of the F natural series in bars 34–37, where it has 8 sounds.

| sounds | f♮ | f♯ | g♮ | g♯ | a♮ | b♭ | b♮ | c♮ | c♯ | d♮ | e♭ | e♮ |
|---|---|---|---|---|---|---|---|---|---|---|---|---|
| bars | 34 | 34 | – | 36 | 35 | (36) | – | 37 | (36–37) | – | 34 | – |

**Ex. 86**

Ex. 87 shows the number of sounds in each series.

| series | c♯ | d♮ | e♭ | e♮ | f♮ | f♯ | g♮ | g♯ | a♮ | b♭ | b♮ | | |
|---|---|---|---|---|---|---|---|---|---|---|---|---|---|
| number of sounds | 33 | 29 | 35 | 45 | 38 | 40 | 39 | 27 | 29 | 31 | 34 | = | 380 |

**Ex. 87**

Each series has an average of $380:11 \approx 34$ sounds; that means that if all the sounds were used the same number of times, each series would be presented about three times.

In the place of series, the main role in the structure and development of section XI is played by freely created "materials" composed with the attack sounds of different series. We shall call them "materials", since they preserve their connection with thematicism only conditionally. Material here is a certain sound complex including 7–13 sounds[‡] from different series, which is then repeated several times throughout section XI, the distribution of the sounds within the material being free and variable (some sounds are sometimes skipped or added). Between the materials presented there are a few sounds not belonging to the materials, and also separate sounds from various materials. There are 10 materials in all, which in the score appended to the present study are denoted by Roman numerals in the order of their appearance.

---

† The sequence of the five groups of series characteristic of the previous sections, is not observed here.
‡ As an exception material III consists of four sounds.

bars / materials

**Table 1**

| bars | 33 | 33–34 | 34–36 | 36–37 | 36–39 | 37–39 | 39–41 | 40–43 | 42–46 | 45–50 | 44–47 |
|---|---|---|---|---|---|---|---|---|---|---|---|
| materials | | I | II | III | IV | V | VI | VII | VIII | VIII | VI |

**Table 2**

| bars | 48–50 | 48–51 | 52–53 | 52–55 | 53–56 | 57–60 | 58–61 | 61–62 | 63–66 | 63–67 | 68–74 long 𝄐 |
|---|---|---|---|---|---|---|---|---|---|---|---|
| materials | VII | IV | (IV) | V | IX | VI | V | X | VII | IV / X | |

1) 68–71–IV
2) 68–74–X
3) 69–74–VII
4) 72–74–V

**Table 3**

| | Meno lento / Moins long 𝄐 | Ancora | meno lento | | | | | | | très court 𝄐 |
|---|---|---|---|---|---|---|---|---|---|---|
| bars | 75–78 | 79–80 | 80 | 81–82 | 82–83 | 83–84 | 85 | 85–86 | 87–89 | 89–92 |
| materials | | VIII | VI | IV | II | I | (IX) | IV | VIII | IX |

1) FL.–IV
2) Xyl.–III
3) Vibr., guit.–I
4) Viola–VIII

Ex.88

Ex. 34 shows the materials presentation throughout section XI, which can be divided into three parts, bars 33–46, 45–74, 75–92. In part 1 eight different materials are exposed one after the other. Part 2 begins with the appearance of the vocal part, from this point the materials start repeating, besides two new materials are exposed. Part 3 ("reprise") can be subdivided into three fragments, which almost coincide with the presentation of the series D natural, E natural, B flat: bars 75–78 (simultaneous presentation of materials by different instruments), bars 79–84 (retrograde movement of materials), bars 85–92 (repetition of the three materials which sounded in the vocal part with the text; this is like a condensation of the vocal part, and also a special coda of section XI); in the second and third fragments the materials alternate in compressed form. The second part is a development of the materials; incomplete presentations of materials (together with complete ones) are found here reaching the stage of separate sounds, as well as free sounds not included in the materials. E.g., only half of material V is presented, bars 52–55, 58–61, 72–74. Thus, this part is more unstable. In the third part all the materials are complete, the only exception being I in bars 83–84.[†] In the first fragment of the third part all the four materials seem to be "extended" and take a longer time. In the second fragment almost all the attacks in the materials follow at one semiquaver intervals. In the third fragment the materials IV and VIII are compressed to one main attack and one (IV) or two (VIII) additional ones; thus the maximum compression of the materials takes place at the end of the reprise.

As seen in Ex. 34, different materials are presented a different number of times, from two (materials II, III, IX, X) to seven (material IV) and have different values. The first part of the section consists of 10 materials, the second of 16, the third of 12 (4+5+3) (see Ex. 88).

We shall take material IV as an example. It is first presented in bars 36–39 by the flute mainly. It is composed by the following eight sounds (only the sounds of this material are noted).

**Ex. 89a**   (bars 36–39)

The characteristic feature here is the presence of three sounds having 8 in duration, and also the position of all the sounds in a chromatic scale within a perfect fifth. In bars 48–51 this material is presented simultaneously with material VII and has six sounds only.

**Ex. 89b**   (bars 48–51)

---

† Material VI has seven sounds instead of X.

Further, in bars 52–53 only a fragment of the material is presented, while in bars 63–67 Boulez adds two sounds more at the end of the material.

**Ex. 89c** (bars 52–53)

**Ex. 89d** (bars 63–67)

In its further presentations the material acquires the following shape. (See Ex. 89e, f)

**Ex. 89e** (bars 68—71)

**Ex. 89f** (bars 75–78)

Boulez treats material IV and others as series, namely, 1) attacks in them follow each other's ending or their regular alternation is established, as in Ex. 89g†, where they come every semiquaver;‡

---

† From the viewpoint of the material the B natural sound should begin with the third semiquaver in the bar, but from the point of the E natural series this sound should begin at the bar beginning.

‡ Freer partial presentations are used too.

Ex. 89g   (bars 81–82)

Ex. 89h   (bars 85–86)

2) if the attacks consist of two (or more) sounds, those sounds are always simultaneously repeated despite the changes of the material (e.g., the sounds G natural and B flat in most examples analysed, and also additional sounds C sharp and E flat in Ex. 89d and 89h);   3) the material can be presented by a group of instruments or by one of them, and can be vocal too. In the last presentation (Ex. 89h) Boulez compresses all the material to one main attack (8 sounds) and one additional (2 sounds).

Like a series, the material can begin with any attack. With the materials repetition the sequence of attacks must mainly be preserved, which happens in Ex. 89. (Exceptions:   1) in Ex. 89a the C natural sound should be theoretically either at the very beginning of the material or at its end, which is proved by the following material presentations;   2) in Ex. 89b the B flat sound should be at the beginning or at the end of the material). A material, like a series, can be presented in its original motion (O) or in retrograde motion (R); if the former presentation of material IV in Ex. 89a is accepted as O, then Ex. 89b has O, 89d has R, 89e has O, 89f has R, 89g has R.

We shall discuss briefly material IX.† Its appearance coincides with the words *Le Balancier* in the voice part (bars 53–56).‡

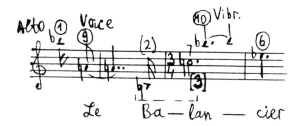

Ex. 90a   (bars 53–56)

Ex. 90b   (bar 62)

It is interesting that Boulez separates the seventh sound of this material and places it in bar 62 with a new beginning of the vocal part (Ex. 90b). When this material is repeated at the end of section XI, the composer compresses it to three attacks and separates the E flat sound placing it before.

---

†   For lack of space the development of each material cannot be discussed at length. See the Appendix where all the materials are transcribed.

‡   The C natural sound in bar 55 does not coincide in duration and dynamics; to achieve coincidence duration should be 3 and begin simultaneously with the B natural sound (see in details further).

Ex. 90c (bar 85)  Ex. 90d (bars 89–92)

Materials IV and VIII can be considered most important, they are more often repeated and sound three times in the "reprise", also being presented in the vocal part. Then materials V, VI, VII follow, presented four times each. The choice of materials and their alternation in the "reprise" (bars 75–92) depend to a great extent on the presentation of the three above–mentioned series, as the materials are chosen according to their having the sounds required by the series. If the materials do not include all the sounds needed by the series, the composer introduces the sounds lacking, even if they are never repeated later. E.g., the sounds E natural having 3 in duration, G natural with 6, C sharp with 12, D natural with 1 in bars 75–77 required by the D natural series.

A characteristic feature of all the materials is the fact that usually almost all their sounds are within some section of the chromatic scale. Materials can also include sounds of the same pitch, but differing in their indices for other parameters. E.g., material V in bars 37–39 has all the pitches with two different sounds, and B flat even with three (see also materials II and VI).

Section XI is most important, since here Boulez for the first time, beginning with his works of the 50s, builds a form on a free development of its elements.

The presentation of four forms of the general series creates the coda of the second cycle or of its section XII. It is dispersed, the series I and R are presented in bars 25–34, and the series IR and O in bars 91–94. The series I and R sound simultaneously with the sound A natural in bar 29 in common, hence E flat is emphasized in both series, as it sounds separately; a mirror symmetry is produced in the distribution of the number of sounds and intervals to the centre of A natural (in Ex. 91 the register position of the sounds is not given).

Ex. 91

It is interesting that the series I and R, which seem to be the embodiment of the highest order in the composition, are presented during the greatest deformation of complete non–defective series, which is to a great extent due to the wish to veil the forms of the general series. Thus, bars 25–34 have three functions:  1) the ending of section X,  2) transition to section XI,  3) coda. The fact that section XI is surrounded by forms of the general series shows that it is of special importance and is somewhat opposed to the preceding development.

In bars 91–94 Boulez alternates parts of the series IR and O (see the score appended). Those four fragments of two series can be considered blocks by the sound distribution in them.

| | IR | O | IR | O |
|---|---|---|---|---|
| series | IR | O | IR | O |
| number of sounds | 5 | 7 | 7 | 5 |
| duration | 12 | 12 | 10 | 9 |

Ex. 92

The left part of the last block is marked by dotted lines, as it is not noted in the score. As seen in Ex. 92, the presentation of the two main forms of the general series is similar to that of the blocks in the second half of movement 4 of *marteau*. Those four blocks finishing the second cycle can be compared with the final chords in classical music, in both cases there is a maximum stability.

We shall note briefly the general form of movement 6 in Ex. 93.

From the viewpoint of presenting fermatas and fragments there is a symmetry (linked to the tempos). There are 7 parts, out of which parts 1, 4, 7 have a uniform tempo, while in parts 2 and 3 there is a slowing down, and in parts 5 and 6 an acceleration. Thus the alternation of sections X and XI is veiled.

In the first section of movement 9 of *marteau* three series from section X are repeated; they are separated by fermatas. Fragments of the series F sharp from bars 21–24 of movement 6 are presented in bars 1, 3–4, 7, 8 with some changes; in bars 3–4 and 7 fragments are repeated in retrograde form. In bars 9–11 of the finale the first series of movement 6 is partly repeated in R; then in bars 11–14 the E flat series and the beginning of the F sharp series are almost fully repeated, i.e. bars 17–20 of movement 6.

Now we shall discuss the second cycle as a whole. We begin with the total number of series per section (Ex. 94).

In sections I–X theoretically there should be 264 = 24×11 series, out of which almost half, 131 = 12×11-1 series belong to section VI.

The attacks in the percussion part are also defective; their duration in sections I–VI is 1, and in VII–XI it grows and comes to 12 at the beginning of section IX. The very alternation of different percussion instruments helps to emphasize the form sections and subsections, as mentioned briefly above, in the discussion of section IX.

Ex. 95 gives the number of sounds of the percussion instrument within each section. Only the sounds given in the score are counted here. E.g., if the attack of the percussion instrument coincides in two series, it is counted as one. Boulez places the series in such a way on purpose, so that there

| | Assez lent<br>court ⌢ | Tempo poco<br>più lento | plus<br>long ⌢ | Ancora<br>piu lento | long ⌢ | Toio<br>long ⌢ | Meno<br>lento | moins<br>long ⌢ | Ancora<br>meno<br>lento | très<br>court ⌢ | Toio |
|---|---|---|---|---|---|---|---|---|---|---|---|
| bars | 1-20 | 21-22 | | 23-24 | | 25-74 | 75-78 | | 79-91 | | 91-94 |
| Ex. 93 | | | | | | | | | | | |
| sections | | I-V | VI | | VII | VIII | | IX | | X | |
| number of<br>series | | 55<br>(5 X 11) | 131<br>(16+19+12+39+45) | | 17 | (16?) | | (34?) | | 11 | |
| Ex. 94 | | | | | | | | | | | |

| sections | I–V | VI | | | | | VII | VIII | IX | X | XI | |
|---|---|---|---|---|---|---|---|---|---|---|---|---|
| movements | 2 | 2 | 2 | 2 | 4 | 4 | 8 | 8 | 8 | 6 | 6 | 9 |
| bars | 1–53 | 54–74 | 74–102 | 103–114 | 1–47 | 47–105 | 1–20 | 20–50 | 51–138 | 1–33 | 33–92 | 1–41 |
| number of attacks | 183 | | | 464 | | | 66 | 65 | 169 | 47 | 51 | 11 |

VI detail (number of attacks): 55, 99, 45, 132, 133

$17 \times 11 - 4$  |  $5 \times 11$  $9 \times 11$  $4 \times 11 + 1$  $12 \times 11$  $12 \times 11 + 1$  |  $6 \times 11$  $6 \times 11 - 1$  $15 \times 11 + 4$  $4 \times 11 + 3$  $5 \times 11 - 4$

$42 \times 11 + 2$

$98$

$9 \times 11 - 1$

Ex. 95

should be a certain number of coinciding attacks, and their total number should be 1056 = 96×11, i.e. it should be four times the number of series in sections I–X.[†] Movement 4 of *marteau* contains almost a quarter of the attacks 265 = 24×11+1.

The largest percussion part is movement 2, where in the "trio" and bar 104 Boulez has introduced in the published score additional attacks (as compared to the facsimile).

As we see in the example, the numbers in each section and subsection often divide almost evenly by 11. The following examples show that in many even smaller fragments the number of attacks is also linked with the number 11 (see those examples with the Schemes II and III).

| bars | 74–91 | 92–102 | 103–104 | 105–110 | 111–114 |
|---|---|---|---|---|---|
| number of attacks | 55 | 44 | 12 | 22 | 11 |

Ex. 96a (movement 2)

| bars | 1–4 | 5–8 | 9–16 | 16–35 | 35–47 | 47–63 | 63–72 | 73–85 | 85–90 | 91–105 |
|---|---|---|---|---|---|---|---|---|---|---|
| number of attacks | 11 | 11 | 24 | 56 (45+11) | 29 | 45 | 15 | 22 | 10 | 41 (30+11) |
| | | | 2X11+2 | 5X11+1 | 3X11−4 | 4X11+1 | 11+4 | 2X11 | 11−1 | 4X11−3 |

Ex. 96b (movement 4)

We should also mention that the number of attacks in section I is 42, and in VI it is 42×11+2, hence the ratio 1:11. In section VI the first two subsections relate to the other three as 14:28 = 1:2 (see Ex. 95). Each half of movement 4 in the number of attacks is almost equal to the sum of attacks in sections VII and VIII, and also the "trio" of movement 2 in the first edition of the score, where there are 133 attacks (no double attacks). The first and third subsections of section VI taken together are almost equal to the second subsection, and also to sections X plus XI.

It is worth noting that the number of attacks of different percussion instruments is also linked to the number 11. E.g., two bongos in bars 54–104 of movement 2 have 166 = 15×11+1 attacks; further in bars 104–114 the *tambour* has 33 attacks. In movement 4 *cymbalettes* (bars 1–63) have 177 = 16×11+1 attacks, then cloche double in bars 63–99 has 77 attacks, after which in bars 100–105 11 attacks of the triangle follow.

The duration of different sections and subsections is connected with other proportions (see Ex. 97).

As seen from Ex. 97, in many sections the number 11 plays an important part. The role of the numbers 7 and 19, however, should not be underestimated either. In Ex. 98a and 98b the duration of some short fragments is noted.

Thus, in movement 4 the number 7 is most important, while in movement 8 it is 11. The duration ratio of those movements is (7×114):(11×114) = 7:11. It is interesting that the duration of bars 102–114 in movement 2 is 114 (Ex. 97), which is the duration of the last fragment of movement 4 (bars 91–105, Ex. 98a). The whole of movement 4 almost equals in duration section IX. The duration of section VI

---

† E.g., in section XI, at the very end of bar 86, for the same purpose the attack of the percussion instrument required for the B flat series is skipped, thus the number of attacks in the reprise (bars 75–92) is 11.

Ex. 97 — Structural/durational scheme

| sections | I | II–IV | V | VI | | | | | VII | VIII | IX | X | XI | coda |
|---|---|---|---|---|---|---|---|---|---|---|---|---|---|---|
| movements | 2 | 2 | 2 | 2 | 2 | | 4 | 4 | 8 | 8 | 8 | 6 | 6 | 6 |
| bars | 1–11 | 11–40 | 40–53 | 54–73 | 74–102 | 102–114 | 1–47 | 47–105 | 1–20 | 21–50 | 51–138 | 1–33 | 33–91 | 91–94 |
| duration | 117 | 250 | 118 | 209 | 270 | 114 | 383 | 415 | 172 | 280 | 802 | 286 | 578 | 43 |

Grouped durations and their factorizations:

- 485 = $44 \times 11 + 1$ = $69 \times 7 + 2$
- 479 = $25 \times 19 + 4$
- 593 = $31 \times 19 + 4$ = $54 \times 11 - 1$ = $85 \times 7 - 2$
- $6 \times 19$ (= 114)
- 383 = $20 \times 19 + 3$ = $55 \times 7 - 2$
- 415 = $22 \times 19 - 3$ = $59 \times 7 + 2$
- 172 = $16 \times 11 - 4$ = $9 \times 19 + 1$
- 280 = $15 \times 19 - 5$ = $25 \times 11 + 5$
- 802 = $42 \times 19 + 4$ = $73 \times 11 - 1$
- 286 = $26 \times 11$
- 43 = $4 \times 11 - 1$
- 798 = $42 \times 19$ = $114 \times 7$
- 1254 = $66 \times 19$ = $114 \times 11$ = $179 \times 7 + 1$
- 907 = $82 \times 11 + 5$
- 1078 = $98 \times 11$ = $154 \times 7$
- 1391 = $73 \times 19 + 4$ = $199 \times 7 - 2$ = $126 \times 11 + 5$
- 4037 = $367 \times 11$

| bars | 1–4 | 5–8 | 9–16 | 16–35 | 35–47 | 47–63 | 63–72 | 73–85 | 85–90 | 91–105 |
|------|-----|-----|------|-------|-------|-------|-------|-------|-------|--------|
| duration | 28 | 36 | 77 | 146 | 96 | 121 | 61 | 79 | 40 | 114 |
| | 4X7 | 5X7+1 | 11X7 | 21X7−1 | 14X7−2 | 11X11 | | | | 6X19 |

Ex. 98a  (movement 4)

| bars | 51–67 | 67–71 | 71–138 |
|------|-------|-------|--------|
| duration | 153 | 44 | 605 |
| | 14X11−1 | 4X11 | 55X11 |

Ex. 98b  (section IX)

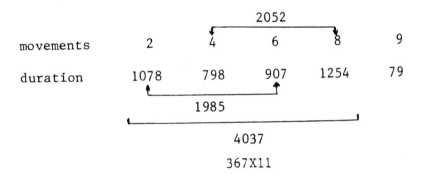

| movements | 2 | 4 | 6 | 8 | 9 |
|-----------|---|---|---|---|---|
| duration | 1078 | 798 | 907 | 1254 | 79 |

2052

1985

4037

367X11

Ex. 99

(1391) almost equals the duration of sections I–V plus the whole of movement 6 (1392). This is not by chance; in the first version of the second cycle movement 8 did not exist. Thus the duration of movements 2, 4, 6 reaches 2783 = 253×11 = 23×11×11.

The duration of whole movements of the second cycle of *marteau* seems to have been somewhat more important for the composer than the duration of individual sections, hence such clear proportions in the ratio, e.g., of movements 4 and 8, 2 and 4, 2 and 8. Ex. 99 gives the duration of four movements of the second cycle and the repetition of fragments at the beginning of the finale.

Finally, the duration of different fragments of movement 6 is mentioned in greater detail. The initial and the final sections are almost equal: 215 and 212 (Ex. 100).

The second cycle is based on the following five tempos† (see Ex. 101).

As seen in Ex. 101, there is a great break between tempos 3 and 4. It is not occasional, as the skipped tempo ♩ = 104 is used in the first cycle.‡ Thus both cycles of *marteau* have practically a common tempo scale (1+5 = 6 tempos). The presence of 5 tempos in the second cycle is not accidental, being in its general meaning linked to the five–part structure of the sections.

---

† In the new publication of the score (Philharmonia No. 398) tempos are usually slowed down.
‡ The first cycle is based on 2 variants of one tempo: ♩ = 104, ♩ = 208.

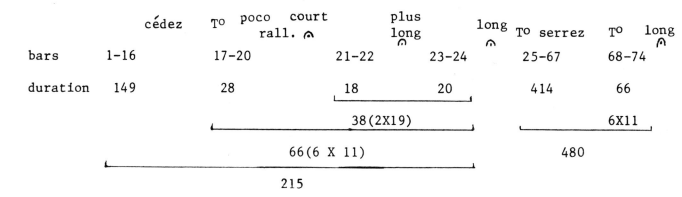

|        | cédez | T⁰ | poco court rall. ⌢ |        | plus long ⌢ | long ⌢ | T⁰ serrez | T⁰ | long ⌢ |
|--------|-------|-----|--------|--------|--------|--------|--------|-----|--------|
| bars   | 1–16  | 17–20 | 21–22 |        | 23–24  |        | 25–67  | 68–74 |        |
| duration | 149 | 28  |        | 18     | 20     |        | 414    | 66  |        |

38 (2X19)

6X11

66 (6 X 11)

480

215

| | moins long ⌢ | très court ⌢ | |
|---|---|---|---|
| bars | 75–78 | 79–91 | 91–94 |
| duration | 48 | 121 | 43 |

11X11   4X11–1

164 (15X11–1)

212

**Ex. 100**

|  | ♩ = | 63 | 76 | 92 | 120 | 132 |
|---|---|---|---|---|---|---|
| sections |  | X | I–V |  |  |  |
|  |  | XI | VII |  |  |  |

VI, VIII, IX

**Ex. 101**

Most sections are based on one tempo, if small accelerations and decelerations are not taken into account. A mobile, though directed tempo, which by means of *accelerando* and *ritardando* moves from one fixed standard to another, forms the basis of section VIII and partly of section IX.[†] In the second cycle, like in the other cycles of *marteau*, and also in his other works beginning with the 50s, Boulez presents the structures through the pressure of various tempos. Defective series stand in a special relation to the tempo change, for their parameters have only a part of the 12–step scale which

---

† The definition of a tempo is taken from op.cit., p.51.

varies all the time. Hence these structures can stand different tempos.[†]

We shall now discuss first the distribution of different serial objects, and then harmony. We shall make use of Boulez' term "diagonal distribution"[‡] to render the relations between the objects replacing the absent parts. Thus, the distribution (found on all levels):

1)  of sounds within polyphonous attacks;

2)  of attacks within a series;

3)  of series in a block (first half of movement 4);

4)  of different series in a group;

5)  of blocks of series in a group of series (distribution of distribution, second half of movement 4, see Scheme III);

6)  of 5 groups of series in a section.

The objects on all levels can begin simultaneously or follow each other, but that does not change the situation in which there is a diagonal distribution of these objects in principle. The diagonal distribution can be unconnected with a defective series, but usually is connected with a frequency "filtering". The diagonal distribution of objects on different levels is also an important stimulus for the transition to the aleatoric form. E.g., the 3rd movement of the Third Sonata consists of fragments which are diagonally distributed.

Harmony in the second cycle is produced either by the simultaneous presentation of several series, or by the compressed presentation of one series, where the attacks follow each other regularly and overlap (sections IX and X). All this results in the interpenetration of series and attacks (even when played by different instruments) and in the almost complete elimination of the role of intervals. In section VI only, with multiplication, the role of intervals increases, though it does not become a leading one. Those intervals are most clear in the first subsection (bars 54–74, movement 2); in other subsections, due to the coincidence of different multiplied structures of attacks, the role of intervals decreases. In the second cycle, in contrast to the first one, multiplication produces the distinction of intervals in connection with the fact that most attacks in all the series have one sound only. The multiplication of one–sound attacks by one interval, as a result of which the obtained second sound must follow simultaneously with the first (see Ex. 67a and 67b), produces the display of intervals.[§] The interpenetration and the audial mixing of series in many places of the second cycle lead to the elimination of the feeling of series as individual units of form, and instead in the perception of sound masses freely divided by fermatas, which creates the articulation of the form.

The series structure itself with varied sequence and structure of attacks helps to create an irregular harmonic density. Boulez varies the series distribution and makes different use of those features. The presence of negative attacks creates gaps in the harmonic density filled by the percussion instrument. Another phenomenon is the incomplete notation of sound durations widely used by Boulez. A special case can be found in bars 35–47 of movement 4, where Boulez notes sound endings only, which always have the shape of one semiquaver. Both those phenomena create an intermittence of sounding, which can be accepted as a characteristic feature of the second cycle. A feeling is created of a pointilistic texture, which does not exist in reality (this method was used by Boulez before, e.g., in *Structures I*).[¶]

---

[†]  See op.cit., p.142.
[‡]  Op.cit., p.119.
[§]  E.g., the major second is of great importance in the first half of movement 4.
[¶]  The varied alternation of polyphonous and one–sound attacks and their structure, the presence of negative attacks performed by the percussion instrument, and the incomplete notation of sound durations (with the respective instrumentation, of course) result in some listeners perceiving the music of the second cycle (sections I–VIII especially) as having a Far–East colouring, although we do not share that feeling.

In the second cycle the pitches are absolute and freely distributed in registers according to the composer's will. Nevertheless, Boulez distributes them mainly so as to avoid semitones. Hence even with multiplication to an interval of a minor second Boulez often uses really major sevenths and minor ninths (see, e.g., bars 69–74 of movement 2). On the other hand, in some cases Boulez distributes the sounds so that they form vertical 12–sound rows with features of symmetry with 2 (rarely more) axis intervals. Ex. 102 gives the pitches of bars 1–2 of movement 4.[†]

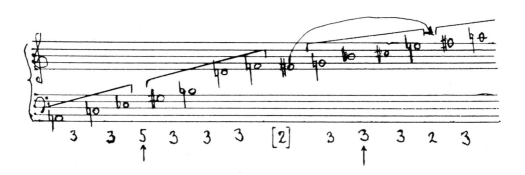

Ex. 102

There are two sounds F sharp and A natural here; with the transposition of one F sharp, as shown by the arrow, the row becomes mirror symmetrical, consisting of three diminished sevenths (vertical arrows denote the axis intervals). Boulez sometimes displays a mirror symmetric structure with a regular alternation of intervals 1 2 3 2 1 2 3, etc; in this case the centre of symmetry is any interval of 1 or 3. Ex. 103 presents the pitch row of a series for the voice in bars 13–24 in movement 6.

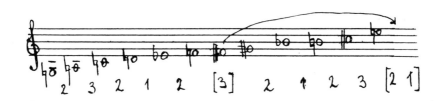

Ex. 103

A different symmetric structure is built, e.g., in the last series of movement 8 (bars 132–138). For this purpose the A natural sound must be transposed two octaves up. See also the pitch rows of other series.[‡]

Rows rather characteristic of Boulez are those in which two sections are formed with sounds of whole–tone scales with one or two transposed sounds; the deviating sound usually gives the row some originality. See Ex. 104, where the pitches are noted for the flute series in bars 3–10 in movement 8 (this row becomes mirror symmetric with the transposition of one sound).

We give also the first series of movement 6 (bars 1–2); with the transposition of the A natural or B natural sound the row becomes mirror symmetrical (Ex. 105).

---

† The following examples are given by the published score; in the facsimile some sounds of the vibraphone are in the upper register, being replaced by the lower in the publication. Boulez had to shift the sounds by several octaves, since he mistakenly considered the instrument to have a range higher by a fifth.

‡ These and other almost symmetric rows are not the result of an occasional pitch distribution.

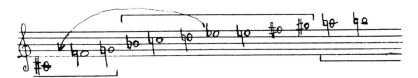

**Ex. 104**

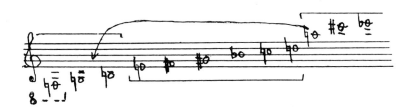

**Ex. 105**

Parts of whole–tone scales sometimes appear also horizontally in correspondence to those rows. E.g., in the vibraphone part in bars 11–13 of movement 8; with the flute in bars 1–3 and 106 in movement 2, etc. In the first half of movement 4, with frequency multiplication by one or two major seconds, there are chords of sounds of a whole–tone scale.

The alternation rhythm of the described vertical rows within the second cycle is different in accordance with the section. In section XI one row takes a rather long time, sometimes combining different materials. E.g, materials VI and IV in bars 80–81 contain pitches in the same registers (the following material II in bar 82 is partly connected with that). The ending of section X, which serves also as a transition to XI (bars 25–33), is built on one row on which the 4 series presented here are based (the two upper sounds are doubled, with the transposition of F natural the row becomes mirror symmetrical).

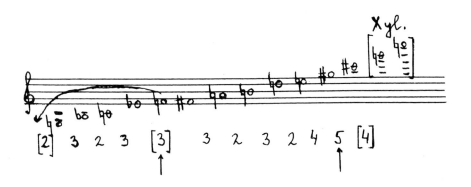

**Ex. 106**

Another example of the great length of one row is found in bars 51–58 of movement 6; symmetry is also formed with the transposition of one sound[†] (Ex. 107).

---

† B natural in the facsimile (bars 51–53, vibraphone) is three octaves higher; the same sound in bar 52 with the guitar seems to be in the lower register by mistake, since an octave is formed with a vibraphone sound. From the above examples the conclusion must not be drawn that most of Boulez' rows tend to symmetry.

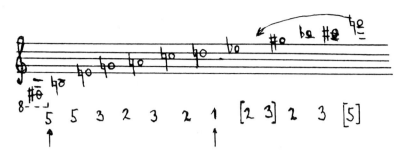

5  5  3  2  3  2  1  [2  3]  2  3  [5]

**Ex. 107**

The great duration of one row results in its pitches being perceived as relative. This, together with the slow tempo, also helps to create the quiet nature of the music in movement 6.[†] Thus the rows are to link the different defective series and partly to connect them on a general pitch basis. The alternation of 12–sound rows can generally be compared with the alternation of sustained harmonies in classical music, on the background of which some non–chord sounds are presented.

Series presentation should be considered the most important means of creating this or that harmony sounding; series structure, systems of transpositions and durations play a secondary part in this respect. E.g., there is no essential difference in the sounding of the harmony (if instrumentation is not taken into account) in sections IX[‡] and X; although the series structure differs in them, the alternation of compressed series results in a similar sound to a great extent. Similarly the harmony sounding in sections I–V and VII bears some resemblance too, despite the use of transpositions in the latter. Hence several harmonic spheres can be separated in the following sections: 1) I–V, VII; 2) VI; 3) VIII; 4) IX, X; 5) XI. As mentioned above, section VI is also subdivided into two spheres from the viewpoint of sound presentation in attacks (see Ex. 66, 67a, 67b).

Since the E flat sound is the first in the general series and the leading one for all the three cycles of *marteau*, while the C natural sound is at the basis of the general scheme for the series of the second cycle (Diagram IX), Boulez emphasizes them in section X (bars 24, 25), for which purpose, as mentioned, he changes the series sounds in attacks. The minor third created by those sounds[§] produces the impression of C minor tonality. Here several previous sounds in bars 21–22 can be perceived as a changed dominant seventh with a leading tone as the final sound. Thus there is a hint at a classical cadence, which in a varied form is repeated in bars 6–7 of the finale of *marteau*. In bars 24–26 of movement 5 in the vocal part the same minor third is presented with a long sustained C natural sound.[¶] Lastly, in movement 6 in material IX in the vocal part (see bars 55–56 and Ex. 90a) this minor third is presented in an ascending direction; like in bars 22, 24, the sounds B natural, C natural and E flat are found here. As mentioned, to emphasize this interval the duration of the C natural is disturbed and increased to a maximum. The duration sequence here is similar to that of the marked place in movement 5 (bars 24–26), but is presented in retrograde motion: 1, 12, 6. Thus an important detail creates the veiled unification of the two cycles.[*]

---

[†]  In movement 6 the middle register of the general range is mainly used. The upper one is used less often. This alternates with the rare "cool" sounds of the lower register of the guitar.

[‡]  Except bars 67–71 and 81–93, where series overlap.

[§]  In bars 24 and 25 there are two E flat sounds in each and three C natural sounds in each.

[¶]  There the word *la mer* is used.

[*]  This minor third is emphasized in a number of works by Boulez, e.g., in his *Sonatine* for Flute and Piano (1946), (where there is a special intruding tune), in his *Improvisations sur Mallarmé 1 and 2* (1958) (see the ending of the vocal part in *Improvisation 2*). These sounds may have a symbolic meaning; in bar 24 of movement 6 they sound with the words *s'est tu*.

The division of the octave into equal parts was already in use in the 19th century, but at that time, as well as later, in the 20th century, this meant the division of the pitch scale only. Hence modes came to be used which have a symmetric structure up to the "modes of limited transposition" of Messiaen. Boulez was the first to use the division of the 12–step scale, of durations and dynamics, into equal parts. His use of the general scheme for all the parameters (Diagram IX) is as natural and classical for serial music as the major scale for the preceding epoch. The second cycle of *marteau* is a unique example for basing the whole musical system on a newly treated chromatic scale (beginning with the C natural sound).

In contrast to the idea of the first cycle, the defective series was created because of the desire to use the 12–sound series in a new way (defectivization of the pitch structure was used very little). This was to a great extent linked with the fact that Boulez usually tried to veil the 12–sound objects with the help of their interpenetration and interlacing (exceptions, e.g., the flute part in bars 3–10 of movement 8 and other similar places; also the series alternation in section X, where they are better heard). Due to the interpenetration of the twelve–sound series not only listeners, but also investigators could not give a precise answer as to whether or not the composer was making use of them.

If the first cycle tended to use 12 sounds and more (within the range of each field), the second cycle used 12 sounds and less (this refers to all parameters); section VI, situated around the central movement of the first cycle, unites the two tendencies. Thus, beginning with *marteau*[†] two tendencies in their widest sense appear in Boulez' music. One tendency is to go out of the framework of a twelve–sound series, the other one is to use it in a new way. This can be observed in his further creations. Similar general trends can be found with some other serial composers.

We shall mention the similar features of both cycles of *marteau*; there is the following correspondence between the movements by function.

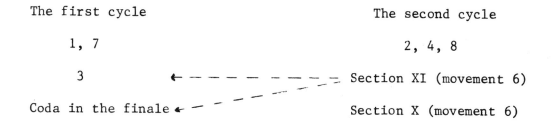

| The first cycle | The second cycle |
|---|---|
| 1, 7 | 2, 4, 8 |
| 3 | Section XI (movement 6) |
| Coda in the finale | Section X (movement 6) |

Ex. 108

The aim of the instrumental movements in both cycles is to present fully the main material. There is a certain correspondence between movement 3, where the main material is repeated selectively, and section XI, in which the series are presented in a dispersed way. This makes section XI even more close to the coda in the finale, where several harmonic fields are presented dispersed. On the other hand, section X corresponds to the coda of the finale, as in both cases the organization is based on secondary forms of the general series: I (first cycle) and IR (second cycle). The coda in movement 6, where the forms of the general series are presented, can really belong to the first cycle too. Both cycles are also connected by the following characteristics:

1) The use of one general series, which produces derived series of groups of frequencies. As a result 25 harmonic fields are created of $5 \times 25 = 125$ groups of frequencies in the first cycle, and in the second cycle 11 series (or fields) of $12 \times 11 = 132$ attacks.

---

† The trends of the first period of the creations of the 40s are not discussed here.

2) The use of frequency multiplication.

3) The number 11 for creating time proportions and 5 for inner form organization.

4) The use of absolute pitches and their control by means of twelve–sound rows.

5) An almost complete elimination of the role of intervals (with the exception of section VI in the second cycle).

Thus, although both cycles of *marteau* are directed in opposite ways, they complement each other and are two aspects of one very general organizational principle. That is why those techniques are often used together in Boulez' further works.

Directly after *marteau* Boulez applied the technique of a defective series in chapter I of *Structures II* (1956). There are two small fragments here, bars 105–120 and 170–185, where 11 defective series (3+3+5) are presented in the former, and 13 (7+6) in the latter. This ensemble of 24 series differs in the general idea of parameter organization from *marteau*. As different from *marteau*, in this creation the main role is played by sections organized by means of the multiplication technique, and a secondary one by sections with defective series. The second chapter of *Structures II* (1961) is also composed on the basis of both those techniques, combining them with the aleatoric form. Finally, serial technique similar to the second cycle of *marteau* (12–sound series with 12 attacks of various density) was used in one of the still unpublished movements of the Third Sonata (1957).[†]

---

† Op.cit., p.40, Ex.4.

*Chapter III*

# Analysis of the Third Cycle

## MOVEMENT FIVE

We shall analyse briefly the structure of movement five of *marteau*, which occupies the central position in the composition. It consists of six sections which can be combined in two groups. One includes sections I, III, V; the other one, sections II, IV, VI. The two groups are different in their characteristics, as can be seen in Ex. 109.

| Sections | Bars | Tempos | Performers |
|----------|------|--------|------------|
| I | 1–15 | Assez vif | instruments |
| II | (15)16–30 | Plus large | voice and instruments |
| III | 30–62 | Assez vif | instruments |
| IV | 62–89 | Plus large | voice and instruments |
| V | 89–109 | Assez vif | instruments |
| VI | 110–117 | Plus large | voice and instruments |

Ex. 109

A characteristic peculiarity of sections II, IV, VI is the presence of a texture where the instruments are opposed to the voice. When the voice takes part, the instruments usually have a common rhythm, the same dynamics, modes of attack, durations, at the same time differing from the voice.

Section III

Section VI

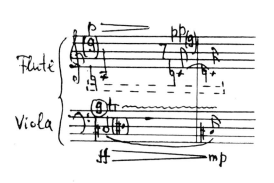

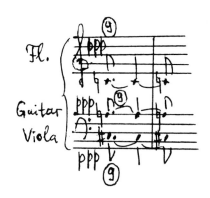

a)  bars 60–61

b)  bars 111–112

c)  bars 59–60

d)  bars 111–112

e)  bars 59–61

f)  bars 112–114

**Ex. 110 (a–f)**

This means that the instruments keep almost all the time a homophonous texture, e.g., in the shape of blocks (see bars 18–30).[†] In all the sections of movement 5 where the voice does not take part, the instruments play contrapuntally, with different frequency groups.

---

†  It is interesting that this fragment bears some similarity to movement 4 (*Eine blasse Wäscherin*, bars 1–8) of Schoenberg's *Pierrot Lunaire* (1912). Here too three instruments play with the same rhythm and dynamics, while opposed to the voice. There is also a resemblance in the blocks being created by the connection of the melodic lines. The use of two similar instruments is also of interest: the flute and the violin by Schoenberg, the flute in G and the viola by Boulez. There is also a certain similarity of tempo, which is relatively free. The metronome mark varies between ♩=60 and ♩=92 with Schoenberg, between ♩=50 and ♩=76 with Boulez.

In movement 5 Boulez seems to use a fixed serial system which includes frequency groups. The number of frequencies in each group does not exceed 12; the frequencies are usually not repeated within one group. The duration of each group is not more than 12 semiquavers. Many groups are repeated in variations within movement 5; there are also similar groups. From this viewpoint movement 5 is closer to the first cycle than to the second one in its serial organization. Boulez may have used here the same general series as in the first and second cycles of *marteau*, though in a different way.

Thus, note a certain similarity of the endings of sections III and VI (i.e., of half of movement V and of the whole movement).[†]

Let us compare bars 59–62 and 111–114. See Ex. 110 giving the respective groups of both sections, with the figures and dotted lines pointing out the assumed duration in semiquavers.

**Ex. 110g**  (bars 61–62)

**Ex. 110h**  (bar 114)

Compare also Ex. 111 with Ex. 110a and 110b.

**Ex. 111**  (bars 104–105)

The material of the flute and viola in bar 14 is compared to the finale of movement 5 (bars 111–114). Ex. 112 gives part of bar 14; it is divided into three groups of sounds. A comparison of group a with Ex. 2d, of group b with Ex. 110b, of group c with Ex. 110h shows a literal coincidence in sounds and registers.

And finally, Ex. 113a and b give a group of sounds which is repeated with a similar rhythm.

Other examples could be mentioned.

In movement 5 of *marteau* Boulez uses for the first time a pitch organization where the vertical structure of a series is of great importance. In such a series the order of appearance of a sound plays

---

†   A characteristic feature of movement 5 is the complete absence of fermatas, which distinguishes it not only from all the other movements of *marteau* but probably also from almost all the other works of Boulez. Instead of fermatas there are several caesuras. The absence of fermatas is an attempt to produce a more flowing, unfolding form, and is also to contrast movement 5 with movement 4 which is built on the alternation of short fragment separated by fermatas.

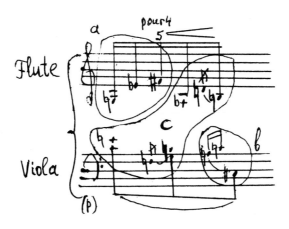

**Ex. 112** (bar 14)

**Ex. 113a** (bar 15)                    **Ex. 113b** (bar 77)

no leading role, while the vertical disposition of the sounds is the main structural procedure. Therefore the interval structure of the series in the vertical plays the main part (see Ex. 114, where figures show the number of semitones in the intervals). This example makes it clear that the series has a mirror symmetrical structure with two central intervals shown by arrows.

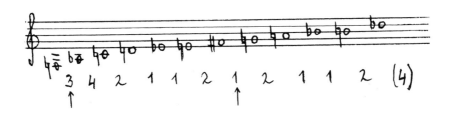

**Ex. 114**

As mentioned in the analysis of the first cycle of *marteau*, this series is a borrowing from the 1st movement of Boulez' cantata *Le soleil des eaux* (1948).[†] For the first time it sounds in *Soleil* in bars 12–13 in the voice part, being then repeated in bars 15–16. See Ex. 115a and b; here the arrow points out how one sound changes its place. Compare Ex. 115 to 114.

This series (Ex. 114) sounds first on the viola (the first 12 sounds in bars 1–3). The series is used 12 times taking up the whole of section I in movement 5, and 11 times in the finale of the movement.

---

†   It is also used in bars 40–42 of movement 3 of *marteau*.

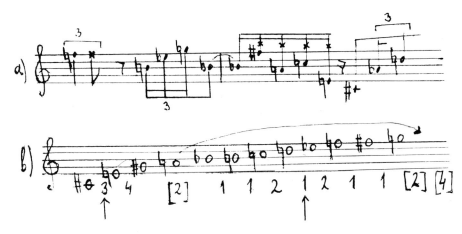

**Ex. 115** *Soleil* (bars 12–13)

(In the appended score with analysis those series are separated and their transpositions are mentioned.) All the transpositions in section I form a large scale series with the same structure as that of the series itself (compare Ex. 116 with Ex. 115).[†] The series transpositions are conducted similarly in the finale of the movement (bars 97–117).

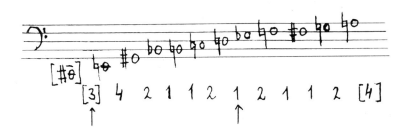

**Ex. 116**

Boulez chose purposefully the lowest section of the sound range for the series transpositions. The highest transposition of the series from the sound A natural reaches the sound F natural in the second octave. Therefore Ex. 117 shows the whole sound range of the music, where those transpositions of the series are used, with the sound A natural as centre.

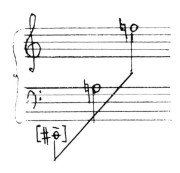

**Ex. 117**

---

† The sound C sharp really sounds three octaves higher, as the lowest sound of the guitar is E natural.

Another characteristic of Boulez' serial system deserves mentioning. Here the large plane is often opposite in direction to the small one, while the structure is the same. Thus, in *Structures Ia* the series transpositions are conducted with the use of the series structure, but taken in inverse form. A similar phenomenon is observed in the analysis of the *marteau* finale. In movement 5 such a structure is not observed, since the series has a mirror–symmetrical structure. Hence it can only be assumed that the series of Ex. 116 (large plane) is an inversion of the series in Ex. 114 (small plane).

In Diagrams I and II the series transpositions are given. The arrows show where the sounds should have been if there were no deviations from the required series structure. The omitted sounds are marked in square brackets, the superfluous sounds, in round ones. The name of the series transposition is marked by the lower sound; the respective bars are also pointed out, and sometimes the instruments as well. In Diagram II the additional series of bars 79–80 is also given. Ex. 118 shows the sequence of transpositions by their lower sound at the beginning and at the end of movement 5 (i.e., as in both Diagrams). The sound groups which are similar for both sequences are given in brackets.

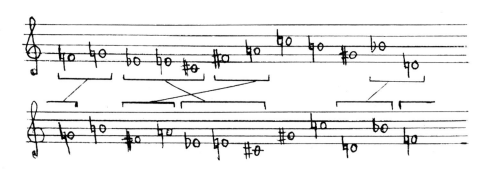

**Ex. 118**

Ex. 118 shows that movement 5 begins and ends with the same transposition (F natural). At the beginning of the movement it is performed by the viola, at the end, by the voice. The use of the F natural transposition in the finale of movement 5 may be linked to the fact that F natural is the lowest sound in the vocal range. It is important that the measure of this vertical series is linked to the vocal range. It is not by chance that this series is used for the first time in *Soleil* in the voice part (see Ex. 115a).

This series transposition has one more peculiarity. When transposing the sound B natural an octave lower (in Ex. 119 it is put down in round brackets), the series acquires a mirror–symmetrical structure with the central sound E flat.

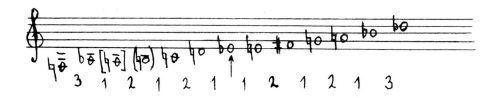

**Ex. 119**

The whole system connected with the vertical structure of the series and its transpositions is an additional means of pitch organization in movement 5. This system is to control just the register position of sounds which become relative pitches. It is not directly related to any other parameter, such as durations, etc. On the other hand, the main role of the general organization of all the parameters seems to remain with the general series.[†]

The harmony of movement 5 is characterized by the following. First, it is based on twelve–tone vertical rows, one of which is the series, mentioned above, that is used at the beginning and at the end of movement 5. The other rows are built in the process of the development of the music and have approximately the same range as the main series (i.e., from one and a half to two octaves), while having no essential differences in structure from the main series.

Secondly, differing from the harmony of the first and second cycles as well as from the previous compositions of Boulez of the 50s, the interval of a minor second (along the vertical and along the horizontal) is often found in movement 5. Thus, minor second trills are used. This singles out movement 5 from the whole cycle.

A characteristic feature of the material of movement 5 is the use of trills, which were almost absent from Boulez' compositions of the beginning of the 50s (see *Structures I*, the first and the second cycles of *marteau*). This brings this movement closer to such Boulez compositions of the 40s as *Le soleil des eaux* and the Second Sonata (1948). It is noteworthy that movement 5 of *marteau* begins with a trill (sounds B natural and A natural), which also opens the second material of *Soleil* (bars 5–7). In both cases the same register is used, almost the same duration and dynamics. Further in *Soleil* the sounds are B flat, G sharp, F sharp, D natural, and C natural. The same sounds (with the exception of G sharp) follow the trill in the viola part in movement 5 also. It is interesting that in the Second Sonata (bar 116) Boulez uses a trill with the same sounds and the same dynamics (*fortissimo*). In all the three cases the trill begins with the weak part of the bar, and in movement 5 even with an upbeat(!), which points to its traditional origin.

Let us note the temporal proportions of movement 5 in semiquavers (Ex. 120).

| sections | I | II | III | IV | V | VI |
|---|---|---|---|---|---|---|
| duration | 115 | 89 | 227 | 205 | 162 | 69 |
| | 5X23 | 4X23–3 | 10X23–3 | 9X23–2 | 7X23+1 | 3X23 |
| | | 431 | | | 436 | |
| | | 19X23–6 | | | 19X23–1 | |
| | | | 867 | | | |
| | | | 79X11–2 | | | |

Ex. 120

The duration of sections I, III, V is 504 = 46×11–2; the duration of sections II, IV, VI is 363 = 33×11. The duration of the central sections III and IV (432) is almost equal to the duration of the surrounding sections I, II, V, VI (435).

---

[†] See Ex. 2 on p.39 in *Boulez on Music Today*, where the composer gives an example of an almost exact general series from *marteau* transposed by a tritone, which has the vertical structure from movement 5 of *marteau* (except that the sound B natural is moved up an octave). It is noteworthy that even in Ex. 5 (p.41) in the same book Boulez unites the series of his Third Sonata with the vertical structure of the series in movement 5 of *marteau* (the transposition of the sound C natural is used). See also Ex. 39a (p.107), where with the sounds G natural and B natural placed an octave higher the same vertical structure is obtained with the transposition of D sharp.

In movement 9 of *marteau* fragments of movement 5 are repeated; the duration of some of them in movement 9 is linked with the Fibonacci rows (34, 55, 89) (Ex. 121).

| bars in movement 5 | 62–66 | 63–68 | 83–89 | 83–86 |
|---|---|---|---|---|
| bars in movement 9 | 15–16 | 17–21 | 21–26 | 27–30 |
| duration in movement 9 | 12 | 34 | 55 | 29 |

89

130

**Ex. 121**

Quotations in the *marteau* finale are repeated in the following way. The composer repeats only the two fragments (the initial and the final one) of section IV where there is a text. First in bars 15–16 of movement 9 the viola gives the voice material of bars 62–66 of movement 5, while the voice recites the respective text. Then in bars 17–21 the material of bars 63–68 is given, each motif being usually reversed. In bar 21 the viola plays the motif which in bars 67–68 of movement 5 was produced by the voice (the word *sauvage*). Thus in bar 21 the viola finishes the voice part begun in bars 15–16. In bars 21–26 the material of bars 83–89 is produced in a reversed and condensed shape. In bars 27–28 the viola presents the voice part of bars 83–84 of movement 5, where the text *Homme l'illusion* was used. It is worth mentioning that all the quotations from the voice part are played by the viola in the finale pizzicato. It should also be mentioned that the sounds E flat, A natural, and G natural in bars 28–30 repeat the motif of movement 5 (bars 85–86) of the voice part with the word *imitée* (see Ex. 122a and 122b). The durations of the three sounds are the same in both cases (with the exception of A natural, which is a little shorter in movement 9). The dynamics and tempo are similar. It is important that in bar 29 of movement 9 at the point of the motif sounding the voice pronounces the word *imitée*.

**Ex. 122a**  Movement 5 (bars 85–86)

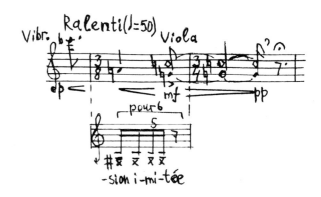

**Ex. 122b**  Movement 9 (bars 28–30)

Movement 5 seems to be the most important one from the viewpoint of the poetic text, which will be discussed in greater detail in the analysis of the finale. The form of movement 5 is more clearly and noticeably linked with the form of the text than the forms of movement 6 and even 3 of *marteau*.

Thus, sections II and VI are completely based on the presentation of the text, while in section IV a portion of the text is given at the beginning and another one at the end of the section. In section VI portions of the text are connected with several characteristic motifs. The first two motifs are parts of the respective series having a vertical structure. Each motif consists of three sounds or three syllables of text. Further in bars 114–117 the voice develops the last series, where there are three motifs (of 6 different sounds, 3 and 3). It is interesting that here the twelve–tone series is linked to 12 syllables of the text, though without complete coincidence of sound and syllable.

In movement 5, in contrast to movements 3 and 6 of *marteau*, the technique called *Sprechgesang* (semi–singing, semi–recitation) is used to some extent. This technique, which connects *marteau* with Schoenberg's *Pierrot Lunaire* and with Boulez' two cantatas of the 40s, will be used to a greater extent in the *marteau* finale, with the repetition of the same text.

Thus movement 5 occupies the central position in *marteau*. Its importance lies also in its contrast with the other two cycles of *marteau*. Ex. 123 displays a certain symmetry in the position of movements of the cycles with the centre in movement 5.

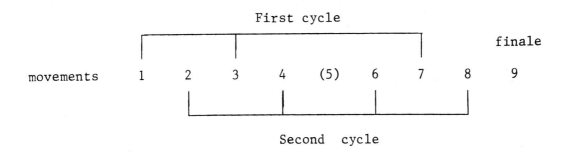

**Ex. 123**

Finally, movement 5 is also distinguished by the longest pause after it: *arrêt très long*, the longest interval between *marteau* movements.


## MOVEMENT NINE

The finale of *marteau* consists of three large sections: 1) bars 1–41; 2) bars 42–163; 3) segmented into a number of small fragments placed both within the second section and after it, namely, bars 88–95, 100–102, 128–143, 154–158, 164–188.[†] In the first section variations of quotations from the central movements of all the three cycles (i.e., movements 3, 5, and 6) are presented together with the text of movement 5. The second (main) section of the finale includes a voice part without text. It is based on materials similar from the viewpoint of organization to movements 6 and 5 of *marteau*. In the third section only the flute and percussion instruments participate; it is the coda both of movement 9 and of *marteau* as a whole.

Now comes a more detailed discussion of the first section.[‡] The quotations from the previous movements follow in reversed order, i.e., first from movement 6, then 5, and then 3. As mentioned above in the analysis of the three cycles, different fragments of those quotations also follow each

---

† The finale of *marteau* practically unites all the three cycles. The third section is discussed in the analysis of the first cycle of *marteau*, therefore no special discussion of it will be given here.

‡ In the analysis of all the three cycles of *marteau* all the quotations were mentioned which are to be found in the first section of movement 9. For this reason they are not repeated here.

other in a reversed order or in inverted form. This is the expression of the opposition of the small and large planes, when the same material is directed differently. That is a characteristic feature of Boulez' thinking. It is noteworthy that later too, in his composition *Don* from the cycle *Pli selon pli*, quotations from other movements of the cycle are also presented in a reversed order, i.e., from the third *Improvisation* first, then from the second, and then from the first.

Both in the first section of the *marteau* finale and in the respective section of *Don* there is a collage, i.e. a mingling of heterogeneous elements. In the first section of *marteau* the quotations are partly united by a common text. In the first section, in connection with the use of quotations, Boulez practically mixes together three different texts with the text from the third cycle as the main text. Boulez uses special fragments from three cycles also probably because of their textual direction, with the purpose of uniting the texts to some extent, of throwing light on the texts of the first and second cycles through the prism of the text of the third cycle. In bars 1–8 of movement 9 the text of the third cycle alternates with the almost complete instrumental material of bars 21–24 of movement 6 where the text is used. Thus the text fragment of the third cycle through the marked instrumental material combines with the text fragment of the second cycle.

| The third cycle | The second cycle |
|---|---|
| *J'écoute marcher dans mes jambes*<br>*La mer morte vagues pardessus tête* | *(Le marcheur*<br><br>*s'est tu)* |

In movement 9 the repetition of the second couplet from the text of the third cycle adds emphasis to its importance. In bars 15–16, and also 27–29 of movement 9 there seems to be a double "reading" of the text; on the one hand, the text is recited by the voice, on the other, instruments (the viola especially) play the musical material of movement 5 connected with the same text.

| The third cycle (movement 9) | The third cycle (movement 5) |
|---|---|
| *Enfant la jetée promenade sauvage*<br><br>*Homme l'illusion imitée* | *Enfant la jetée promenade*<br>*sauvage* (bar 21,mov.9)<br>*Homme l'illusion imitée* |

In bars 31–41 of movement 9 texts of the third and first cycles seem to alternate, as in bars 35–39 of movement 9 the material of bars 38–42 of movement 3 is presented. Only one word *la tête* coincides.[†]

| The third cycle | The first cycle |
|---|---|
| *Des yeux purs dans les bois*<br>*cherchent en pleurant*<br><br>*la tête*<br><br>*habitable* | <br><br>*(Je rêve)*<br>*la tête*<br>*(sur la)* |

Thus, each couplet in the text of the third cycle combines in turn with the text of the second, third, and first cycles, which divides the first section of movement 9 into three fragments ("spheres of influence") (bars 1–14, 15–30, 31–41).

---

† See also the remarks on the repetition of a fragment of movement 3 in the *marteau* finale in the analysis of the first cycle.

Studying the first section of movement 9 is important for understanding the symbolics of the text of the three cycles as understood and expressed by Boulez.

The first section will be discussed in greater detail later; now our aim is to analyse the second section of movement 9. This main section as well as a number of fragments of the first section are based on one series, which has a vertical structure[†] and is used 48 times (8 times in the first section and 40 in the second). The presence of a series with a vertical structure brings movement 9 closer to movement 5. A vertical series can exist in two forms only: the original and its inversion (O and I), since the sequence order of its sounds in time is free, in contrast to a series with a horizontal structure, which can exist in four forms (O, I, R, RI).[‡] Ex. 124a shows the vertical series O, and Ex. 124b shows its inversion (I)[§] (the figures here represent the size of the intervals).

Ex. 124a

Ex. 124b

In the second section of movement 9 the composer makes use of three kinds of material. The first one is based on a scheme for all the four parameters (pitch, duration, dynamics, modes of attacks), which is used for the second cycle of *marteau* (see Diagram IX for the second cycle) and is some kind of agglomeration of sound "points". The second material consists of blocks, which resembles the material of the even sections of movement 5 of *marteau*. The third material consists of sound groups (or short "lines") and is similar to the material of the odd sections of movement 5. Fragments made of "points" are built of series which we will denote as O1 and I1; fragments made of blocks are built

---

†   For the sake of briefness we shall call it simply a vertical series.

‡   It should be remembered that the series of twelve attacks existing in the second cycle of *marteau* are used in two forms only, the original and the retrograde form (O and R).

§   In Ex. 124b and similar further ones the sound D flat is given in brackets, as in reality it is five octaves higher; that results from the lowest sound of the guitar being E natural, as mentioned above in the analysis of movement 5 of *marteau*.

of series which will be denoted as O2; fragments made of "lines" consist of series I2. Thus, "points", "blocks", "lines" are three contrasting materials which create the main section of movement 9.[†] There is a specially great contrast between the series O1 and I1 ("points") and the series O2 and I2 ("blocks" and "lines").

Each of the series O1, I1, O2, I2 is presented in all twelve transpositions, thus creating an ensemble of 48 series (24 series O and the same number of I). The series O1 and O2 move along the pitches of series I, and the series I1 and I2 move along the pitches of series O. Thus, the opposite direction of the small and large planes is observed again with the same structure, which is typical of Boulez.

Diagram I displays all the 48 transpositions with the notation of their place in the score; the main transposition tones and series forms are also noted. The Diagram shows that different transpositions cannot usually find room within the general sound range of the instruments in *marteau*; therefore a part of the sounds is in such cases moved from the upper register into the lower one and vice versa.

In the first and second sections of movement 9 the sound E flat occurs in two registers only, in the lower and the upper one (see Ex. 124a and 124b), regardless of the transposition used or quotation from the previous movements of *marteau* (exceptions: bars 25 and 37, quotations from movements 5 and 3 of *marteau*). Thus the sound E flat has two pivot centres from each of which one of the four series begins. The transpositions of the series O1 begin from the lower position of the sound E flat and move creating on the large plane the series structure I (Ex. 125a); the transpositions of the series I1 begin from the upper position of that sound and move producing the series structure O (Ex. 125b); the transpositions of the series O2 begin from the upper position of E flat and move

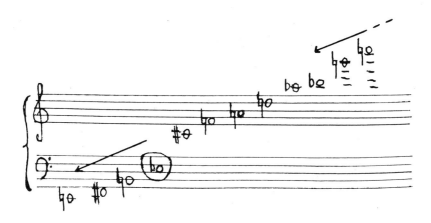

Ex. 125a

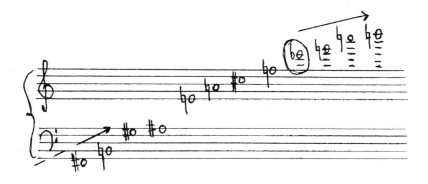

Ex. 125b

---

†   The contrast of lines and blocks was shown in the analysis of movement 5 of *marteau*. Such a contrast can be seen already in movement 1 of the Second Sonata by Boulez (1948). The contrast of points and blocks can be found in movement 3 of his Third Sonata (1957).

Ex. 126  Pitches of all 48 transpositions

creating the series structure I (Ex. 124b); and last, the transpositions of the series I2 begin from the lower position of the sound E flat and move creating the series structure O (Ex. 124a).

Ex 126 displays a sound system in which the pitches of all the main tones of all the 48 transpositions are noted. This example shows that the system of transpositions encompasses the whole sound range of instruments, from the imaginary sound D flat to F natural, with the central note A natural. The figures above tell the number of times the pitch is used, and the figures below note the intervals between pitches. This pitch scheme is absolutely mirror–symmetrical for all indices.

It should be noted that connecting the main tones of the 24 transpositions of the series O1 and O2 results in a sound system consisting of two twelve–tone rows (see Ex. 127a, where the rows are separated by lower brackets, while the brackets above show wholetone sections in one of the rows). A similar effect is obtained by connecting the transpositions of series I1 and I2 (Ex. 127b).

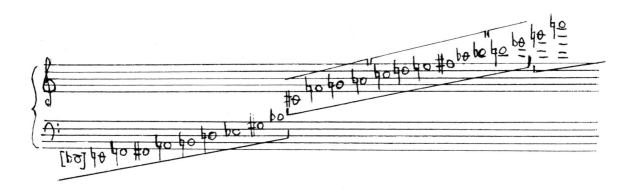

**Ex. 127a**   (transpositions of series 01, 02)

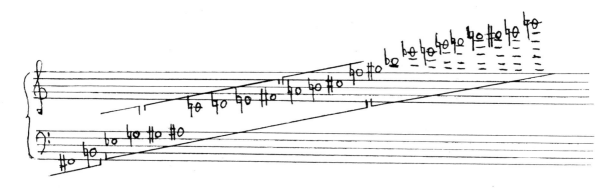

**Ex. 127b**   (transpositions of series I1, I2)

Diagram I gives all·the 48 transpositions of the vertical series. Beside each transposition the respective bars in the score, the main sound of the transposition, and the form of the series are shown. The omitted sounds are noted in square brackets, the superfluous sounds, in round brackets. If a sound is in a wrong register, an arrow points to where it should be.

Ex. 128 shows the sequence of transpositions in the first and second sections of movement 9. The main sound of each transposition is in the same register as in the music. The respective bars in the

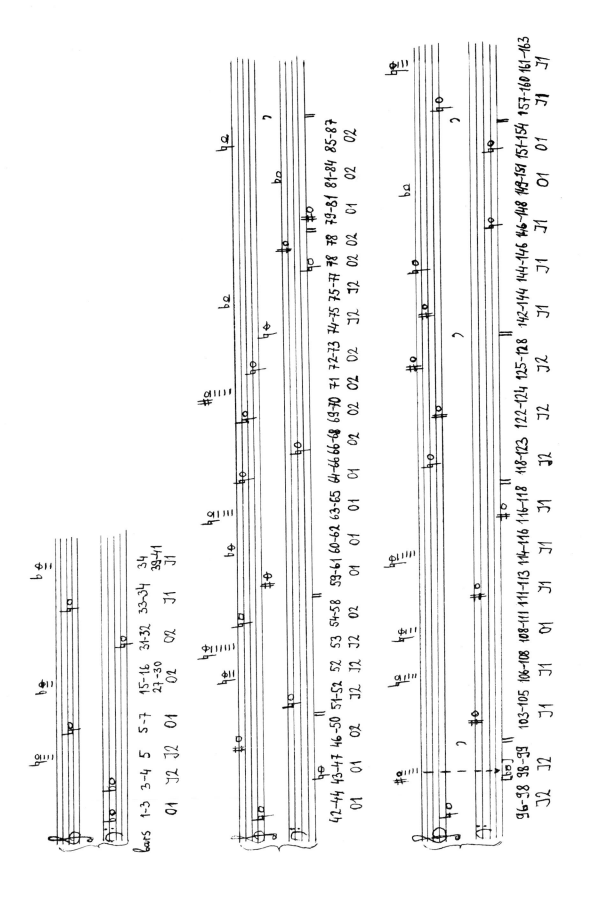

Ex. 128

score and the kind of series are also given. This example shows that the first section uses only the most important 8 transpositions, from E flat and A natural, each of the four kinds of series appearing twice (now with the transposition E flat, then A natural). If all the eight pitches are connected, the result will obviously be a symmetrical structure (Ex. 129).

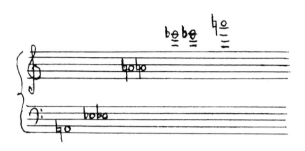

Ex. 129

In the second section of movement 9 the transpositions follow each other more or less freely, though restricted by certain regularities, which will be mentioned further. Such a movement on a large plane corresponds to the order sequence of sounds within a series, which is also more or less free.

The second section of movement 9 can be divided into five subsections for two reasons.

1)   The subsections are separated by fragments of the third section of movement 9.

2)   At the end of a subsection a kind of series is produced for the last time, or at its beginning a kind of series is produced for the first time.

Thus, there are five subsections (in Ex. 128 they are separated by caesuras).

1)   Bars 42–87 series O2 finish, and the third section of movement 9, the coda begins (22 series in all);

2)   bars 96–99, the second fragment of the coda is presented, then series I1 begin (2 series in all);

3)   bars 103–128, series O2 finish, then the third fragment of the coda sounds (9 series in all);

4)   bars 142–154, series O1 finish, then the fourth fragment of the coda sounds (5 series in all);

5)   bars 157–163, the ending of series I1 and of all the second section, after which comes the final fifth section of the coda (2 series in all).

The second section of movement 9 can also be divided into two large subsections:

1)   bars 42–87, after which comes the first fragment of the coda (22 series);

2)   bars 96–163, after which the second section of movement 9 ends (18 series).

Boulez himself uses double bar lines to subdivide the second section of movement 9 into 9 fragments (see Ex. 128, where short double lines are put between bar numbers). When passing from one material to another (e.g., from "points" to "blocks" or "lines") a double bar line could obviously be used. Boulez, however, uses it when such a change happens between bars[†] (otherwise there would have been 15 fragments instead of 9).

It should also be noted that in the second half of the second section (bars 96–163) the material of "lines" is comparatively little used, and the material of "blocks" is absent altogether. Thus, the closer to the conclusion of movement 9, the more the material of "points" is used, which creates an essential contrast to the material of the coda.

Let us discuss the materials in greater detail. As mentioned above, the material of "points" is based on the same general scheme for all the parameters as the material of the second cycle of *marteau* (see Scheme IX for the second cycle). Therefore when carrying out the pitch transposition of series O1 or I1, the other parameters are "transposed" simultaneously and similarly. It is not by chance that in the first section of movement 9 only transpositions of E flat and A natural are used. These transpositions belong to sound scales with the sounds F sharp and C natural respectively equal to one both in duration and dynamics, i.e., being essentially privileged, since on each step of the chromatic scale their indices for all the parameters coincide. Thus, as in the second cycle of *marteau*, the first sound of any transposition is at a distance of a minor third from the first sound of the chromatic scale to which it belongs. The difference from the second cycle is that to find the respective chromatic scale, the minor third should be built up, and not down from the initial sound of the transposition.

It is probably correct to see the series O1 and I1 as consisting of separate sounds ("points") which are not united in groups and whose sequence is not bound by any serial scheme.

Ex. 130 shows the number of attacks in the series O1 and I1 counted by the beginnings of sounds and by their endings. If the number of attacks is not established precisely, the other possible figure is given in brackets. The number of attacks with the series O1 and I1 should probably be divisible by 11. The number of attacks counted by the sound endings in series O1 is often 11, and in series I1 it varies from 4 to 10. It is interesting that the transposition of series I1 in bars 111–113 uses a special sound alternation. First it consists of two sounds produced in turn, then the other sounds follow, going from the longer to the shorter sound (with the exception of G natural); the duration of those sounds stops simultaneously.

It should also be mentioned that in the transpositions of series O1 and I1 the groups of sounds produced by each instrument separately usually follow each other without overlapping and are connected by legato.

The series O1, I1 and O2, I2 have in common not only the same structure of the vertical series and the same principle of pitch disposition of transpositions, but also the same scale of durations and dynamics.

This means that the duration of any block in the transpositions of series O2, as well as the duration of any sound or group of sounds in the transpositions of series I2 can be from one semiquaver to twelve semiquavers (similar to what is observed in movement 5 of *marteau*). In a similar way the dynamic scale of series O2 and I2 has 12 steps and goes from *fortissimo sforzando* to *pianissimo* (similar to what is found in the second cycle of *marteau*, and also in series O1 and I1). Modes of attacks in series O2 and I2 are analogous to those in movement 5.

Each series O2 corresponds in dynamics to a series I2 with the same main sound of transposition (usually it is in different registers for series O2 and I2). See Ex. 131 where the pairs of transpositions with the same dynamics are noted. This example shows that in each transposition of series O2 and I2 only two dynamic steps are used as a rule (additional dynamic steps for transpositions of O2 and I2 are also noted). Ex. 131 shows that different dynamic steps are not used the same number of times, and *forte* is not used at all. Ex. 131 displays the fact that the given pairs of series are never side by side, so that the repetition of the dynamics should not be noticed. That is another explanation

---

[†]  Practically he does not always do that; e.g., a double line is absent between bars 53 and 54, despite the change of material.

Ex.130 (number of attacks)

| | | Series O1 | | | | Series I1 | |
| --- | --- | --- | --- | --- | --- | --- | --- |
| bars | trans-positions | number of attacks taken by beginnings of sounds | number of attacks taken by endings of sounds | bars | trans-positions | number of attacks taken by beginnings of sounds | number of attacks taken by endings of sounds |
| 42–44 | f natural | 9(10) | 11 | 103–105 | b flat | 11 | 5 |
| 43–47 | e natural | 12 | 12 | 106–108 | c natural | 9(10) | 7 |
| 59–61 | c sharp | 8 | 11 | 111–113 | g sharp | 11 | 4 |
| 60–62 | a flat | 10 | 11 | 114–116 | d natural | 9(10) | 9(8) |
| 63–65 | c natural | 7 | 11 | 116–118 | f sharp | 8 | 8 |
| 64–66 | d natural | 9 | 11 | 142–144 | c sharp | 6 | 10(?) |
| 79–81 | f sharp | 8 | 11 | 144–146 | f natural | 9 | 9(8) |
| 108–111 | g natural | 7 | 11 | 146–148 | b natural | 6 | 8 |
| 149–151 | b flat | 10 | 12 | 157–160 | e natural | 8 | 7 |
| 151–154 | b natural | 10(9) | 8 | 161–163 | g natural | 7 | 8 |
| | | 90 attacks in all | 109 attacks in all | | | 84 attacks in all | 75 attacks in all |

**Ex. 130**  (number of attacks)

of the sequence of transpositions given in Ex. 128.

Unlike the transpositions of series O1 and I1 with 12 sounds only, the transpositions of series O2 and I2 can have a much greater number of sounds. Ex. 132a and 132b show how many series and additional sounds each transposition of series O2 and I2 really includes. Ex. 132a points out that 20 series are used and 24 additional sounds which can be said to produce two more "series", 22 series in all. With the addition of 2 series from the first section of movement 9 the total will be 24 series. Ex. 132b points out that 14 series and 46 additional sounds[†] are used, which can be said to produce almost 4 "series" more (minus two sounds); 18 series in all. With two series from the first section of movement 9 added the total will be 20 series. Thus, the transpositions of series O2 and I2 in the first and second sections of movement 9 have really 24+20 = 44 series (instead of 24 found in series O1 and I1). Let us take an example. On the transposition of series O2 (bars 54–58) there are 3×12 = 36 sounds. The first block has 7 sounds here, 5 missing sounds from the fourth block can be added (see bars 54–55 and 58); the second block consists of 12 sounds (bar 56); and finally, the eleven–sound block in bar 57 can be completed by adding the sound G sharp from bar 56.

---

† The sounds of the chromatic scale are not used the same number of times here.

| Series 02 bars | transpositions | Series I2 bars | dynamics main dynamic degrees | supplementary dynamic degrees for special bars |
|---|---|---|---|---|
| 46–50 | f sharp | 122–124 | *ff* *p* | *ff* *f* –I2 |
| 54–58 | e natural | 52 | *mf* *pp* | |
| 66–68 | d natural | 96–98 | *ff* *p* | *mf* –02 |
| 69–70 | c natural | 74–75 | *mp* *p* | |
| 71 | c sharp | 98–99 | *mp* *pp* | *pp* –I2 |
| 72–73 | g natural | 51–52 | *ff* *pp* | *mf* –I2 |
| 78(beginning) | f natural | 53 | *mp* *pp* | |
| 78(end) | a flat | 125–128 | *ff* *f* | |
| 81–84 | b flat | 75–77 | *mf* *mf* | *mp* –02 |
| 85–87 | b natural | 118–123 | *mf* *mp* | *mf* *p* –I2 |

Ex. 131

As mentioned above, the material of the series in O2 consists of blocks only. Diagram II gives all the blocks in movement 9 (with the exception of quotations). First 5 blocks are noted, which are found in the first section of movement 9 in the series I2 and I1, then the following 44 blocks of the second section.

As seen in Diagram II, in the second section the transpositions of series O2 have 40 blocks, besides this the transpositions of series I2 have 4 blocks. Thus, there are 49 blocks.[†] It is possible that each transposition of series O2 must consist of 4 blocks, as 40 blocks are placed in 10 transpositions. See, e.g., the transpositions of series O2 in bars 55–58, 66–68, 69–70, 71, 72–73, 85–87. Each of those transpositions has 4 blocks, two of them usually having the same dynamic degree and the other two another one. It should be noted that even two transpositions in bar 78 consist of four sound groups, each of them played by a separate instrument; two groups have the same dynamic degree, the other two another one. Nevertheless, e.g., the transposition in bars 46–50 consists of 9 blocks. In Diagram II bar lines separate the transpositions, beside them the bars are noted. The sounds in brackets could really be included in the block, but they sound a little earlier or later. The encircled figures denote the number of sounds in a block, i.e., its density. Diagram II shows that the density can vary from 1 to 12.

---

† It is not always possible to state precisely the presence of a block, as its duration is not always clear and, besides that, any block can include a different number of sounds. Therefore the number 49 is approximate. From the viewpoint of serial organization there should probably be 48 blocks.

| | Series 02 | | Series I2 | |
|---|---|---|---|---|
| bars | number of twelvesound series per transposition | bars | number of twelvesound series per transposition | |
| 44–50 | 3 | 51–52 | 1 | |
| 54–58 | 3 | 52 | 1 | |
| 66–68 | 1(+ 7 sounds:g♮,a♭,a♮,b♭ b♮,c♯,f♮) | 53 | 1 | |
| | | 74–75 | 2 | |
| 69–70 | 2(+ 3 sounds:b♭,d♮,e♭) | 75–77 | 1(+ 9 sounds) | |
| 71 | 3(+ 2 sounds: e♮,a♮) | 96–98 | 1 | |
| 72–73 | 2(+ 3 sounds:f♯,a♮,c♯) | 98–99 | 2 | |
| 78(beginning) | 1 | 118–123 | 2(+ 21 sounds) | |
| 78(end) | 1 | 122–124 | 1(+ 2 sounds) | |
| 81–84 | 2(+ 6 sounds:f♮,b♭,b♮, c♮,c♯,d♮) | 125–128 | 2(+14 sounds) | |
| 85–87 | 2(+3 sounds:f♯,b♭,c♮) | | | |
| | 20 series + 24 sounds | | 14 series + 46 sounds | |
| | 22 X 12 sounds or 22 "series" in all | | 18 "series"(+ 2 sounds) in all | |

Ex. 132a                                             Ex. 132b

As mentioned above, the material of the transpositions of series I2 is similar to the material of the odd sections of movement 5. But the material of movement 9 is essentially transformed with the use of other data for all the parameters. E.g., another vertical series is used, other dynamics, etc. Even so a direct similarity can sometimes be observed. E.g., the last transposition of series I2 in bar 125 has a trill on the sounds E flat and C sharp. A similar trill, also played by the viola in the same register and with a similar dynamic, can be found in bars 60–61 at the end of the first half of movement 5. However, this trill is put down in movement 9 in reversed form, as it begins with E flat instead of C sharp; the dynamic is also put down in reversed form. Similarly in bars 126–127 of movement 9 there is a trill in the sounds A natural and B natural with which movement 5 started (which "borrowed" that trill from *Soleil* and the Second Sonata). In both cases it is played by the viola in the same register and with similar dynamics. Similarly the trill is written here in reversed form beginning with the sound A natural, and the dynamic development also has a reversed form. This trill was obviously put down in bars 126–127 with the last development of the transposition of series I2, thus hinting at the beginning of movement 5.

Another example. The sound group with the viola in bar 116 of movement 9 resembles the sound group with the voice in bar 30 of movement 5, where the word *tête* is used. The similarity here is in sound, rhythm and dynamics. In both cases four sounds are played legato, the central sound is D natural, and the last one is C natural, which is in the same register (see Ex. 133). Other examples could be added.

Each transposition of series I2 consisting of 12 sounds should probably include four sound groups, while two groups must have one dynamic degree and the other two another one. Each group should probably be played by a separate instrument. E.g., see the transpositions in bars 51–52, 52, 53. In bar 53 the sound F natural with the xylorimba and B natural with the vibraphone together build one group. The sound F natural should have been played by the vibraphone (Boulez even

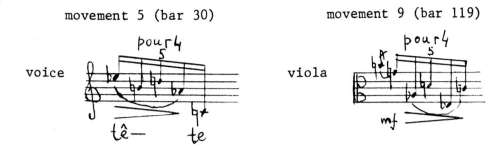

movement 5 (bar 30)    movement 9 (bar 119)

voice    viola

**Ex. 133**

wrote one crescendo sign for both instruments), but this instrument cannot produce the sound F natural in this very high register. In this transposition two sound groups are played *mezzo piano*, and two others, *pianissimo*. In bars 98–99 two identical pitch transpositions are separated by a dotted line. Here both transpositions include approximately four groups each, two of which are played *mezzo piano*, and the other two, *pianissimo*.

Now we return to the analysis of the first section of movement 9. As mentioned above, it consists of quotations and eight series. At the beginning quotations are partly the material for the series (see bars 1, 3, 7), but mainly the material of these series is unlike the three mentioned materials of the second section. It consists of different sound groups, which have dissimilar characteristics and are sometimes repeated in varying forms. There is a possibility that changed material of movement 5 is used here, as in bars 27–34 and 40–41 the tempo of movement 5 is used. It is possible that those peculiar "motifs" are small quotations from earlier compositions of Boulez since, as already mentioned, the first section of movement 9 is a collage.

Let us mention some sound groups. In Ex. 134a such "motifs" in the xylorimba part are noted. They are united by the same timbre, similar register, dynamics, rhythm. Ex. 134b shows that if these sound groups are united, the result will be an incomplete series of 8 sounds, with the first and third "motifs" having the same interval structure and being placed at a tritone distance.

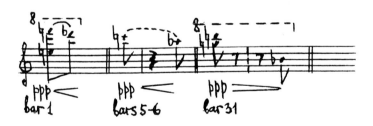

**Ex. 134a**

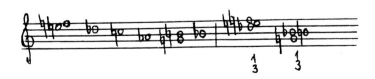

**Ex. 134b**

Ex. 135a and 135b show two other similar sound groups also played by the xylorimba. The group in bar 34 is similar to the group played by the flute in bar 114 in movement 5 (the sounds are A flat, D natural, E natural; compare Ex. 135b and 135c). In both cases those sound groups are played simultaneously with the part of the voice, which has the text *cherchent en pleu–(rant)*.

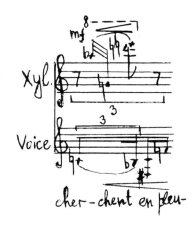

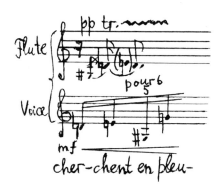

**Ex. 135a**  Movement 9 (bar 7)      **Ex. 135b**  Movement 9 (bar 34)      **Ex. 135c**  Movement 5 (bar 114)

In bar 29 of movement 9 the sounds F natural and G natural with the xylorimba resemble the "motif" of those sounds with the vibraphone in bar 30 of movement 8 of *marteau*. In movement 8 the sounds of this motif have an unusual connection. In both cases the other instruments also produce the sounds A natural and F sharp. A characteristic detail of bars 29–30 of movement 9 is the playing of the sounds by all instruments *mezzo forte* with an accent.

A quite independent material in the first section of movement 9 belongs to the part of the voice, which in many respects is opposed to this part in movement 5.[†] It has a great role in shaping the material of the eight series in the first section.

The sound E flat is played in the first section in turn by the guitar, viola, vibraphone and xylorimba with different dynamics and long duration. This sound is played 7 times (see bars 1–2, 3–5, 5–6, 15–20, 27–29, 32–33, 40–41). In bars 32–33 and 40–41 this sound is produced by the vibraphone simultaneously with the part of a percussion instrument. That may be a hint that it is the turn of the percussion instrument to produce that sound, but the vibraphone has to take its place. For series 1–4 E flat is played in the lower register (bars 1–7), and for series 5–8 in the upper one (bars 15–16, 27–30, 31–32, 40–41). The long duration of this sound can to some extent be compared with the long sounds with the percussion instruments in the coda of movement 9.

Next comes the discussion of the harmony in movement 9. Ex. 124a shows the interval structure of the vertical series. A characteristic feature here is the absence of the semitone (the minor third is also absent, but its derivative, i.e. the major sixth is used instead). Therefore semitones are absent from the harmony of the second section of movement 9. Unisons are used rarely, with overlapping transpositions.

On the other hand, Ex. 136 shows the series to consist of two sections (denoted by brackets) the sounds of which can form two whole tone scales (if the place of B natural is changed as shown by the arrow). Moreover, the upper three sounds of the series form an augmented triad, which produces a similarity between this vertical series and the general series of *marteau*. The lower six sounds of the series form two minor sixth chords which are at a distance of a major seventh (in Ex.

---

† That is what Boulez said in an interview. See U. Stürzbecher, *Werkstattgespräche mit Komponisten*, p.51.

136 they are noted by dotted brackets), and the sounds E natural, A natural and D flat form a major six–four chord. These chord characteristics of the vertical series are not emphasized in the harmony of movement 9; a much greater role, however, is played by other features, which will be clarified later.

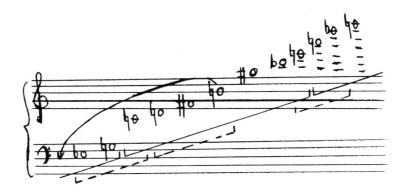

Ex. 136

The vertical series of movement 9 can have been derived in some way from the general series of *marteau*. It is interesting that at the end of the first half of movement 4 (at the end of bar 44) there is an eleven–sound block which in its interval structure resembles somewhat the vertical series of movement 9.[†] In Ex. 137 brackets point out the coinciding interval groups taken in one of the rows in inverted form; the important fact is that both rows have the same range from E flat to F natural. Thus, the block in movement 4 hints at the beginning of movement 9.

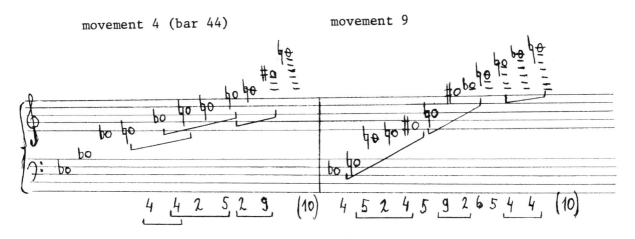

Ex. 137

The temporal organization plays an especially prominent part in forming the pitch structure of the vertical series. Ex. 138 makes it clear that the pitch structure of the series is produced with due regard for the temporal basis connected with the series O1 and I1. In Ex. 138 the duration of each

---

† The block structure of bar 44 is quoted from the published score. In the facsimile edition the sound B flat with the vibraphone is three octaves higher (which is obviously impossible to play).

sound in semiquavers is noted by encircled figures; the transposition of series I1 is moved three octaves up for greater vividness.

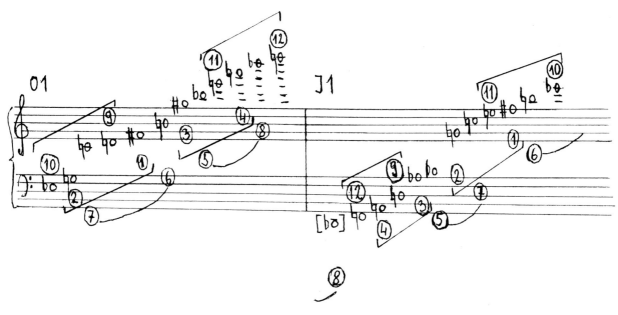

Ex. 138

In Ex. 138 all the durations are divided into three groups:  1) short, i.e., 1–4;  2) middle, 5–8;  3) long, 9–12. The distribution of sounds within those groups has features of mirror symmetry (which is shown by brackets); series I1 is less mirror–symmetrical from this viewpoint. An important point is the regular distribution of long sounds through the whole range of the series, which promotes greater stability of the series as a whole. The long sounds seem to form the basis of the vertical structure of the series with the shorter sounds on their background. Usually the longer the sound, the greater its part in building vertical structures.

Despite the presence of a single vertical series, the role of intervals is considerably weakened, none of them being dominant.

As seen in Ex. 128, the alternation of the main tones of the transpositions often happens with great interval leaps. Usually two neighbouring transpositions have only a few sounds in the same register (e.g., see Diagram I). It should be added that in contrast to the first section of movement 9, in the second section the transpositions of series O1 and I2 having the sound E flat in the same lower register never stand next to each other; the same is valid for transpositions of series O2 and I1 having E flat in the upper register (see Ex. 128). Thus, the pitches often move from one register to another one and the development as a whole is rather dynamic. That expresses one of the principles of transposition alternation.

Diagram III gives all the pitch structure of the transposition of series O1 and I1 within the second section of movement 9. Lines (usually curves) divide the transpositions; the main tone of each transposition is noted in brackets. The figures under each vertical pitch structure note its duration in semiquavers. If the duration is 5 or more, the figure is encircled. Lower still the interval composition of three–sound structures is noted; the assumption is that the sounds of those structures are noted in a contracted way (the figures render the interval in the number of semitones). The figure placed within the vertical structure notes its density (i.e., the number of sounds). This density index is encircled when it is 5 or more. Diagram III shows that there are 235 different vertical structures in all. Further a table is presented displaying the line of structural density and the number of times each is used (Ex. 139).

| density | 1 | 2 | 3 | 4 | 5 | 6 | 7 | 8 | 9 |
|---|---|---|---|---|---|---|---|---|---|
| number of times | 31 | 70 | 83 | 31 | 13 | 2 | 1 | 2 | 1 |

Ex. 139

Ex. 139 makes it clear that three–sound structures are most often used, after them come two–sound ones. Hence the rarefied density of vertical structures with series O1 and I1, which produces the respective character of the music. Most of the three–sound structures (57 out of 83) have one interval (two more rarely) which equals 1 (i.e., a minor second the sounds of which are in two different registers; see Diagram III). Ex. 140 presents all the possible three–sound structures (the figures note the number of semitones). One can see that most structures have no minor second. The prevalence in the abovementioned series of three–sound groups with a minor second is one of the characteristic features of modern harmony.

Ex. 140

Thus, Diagrams II and III present numerous pitch structures which are transposed parts of the same structure of the vertical series.

It is also noteworthy that each transposition of any of the four series is a separate field (independent of the number of sounds used) both from the viewpoint of pitch and from that of other parameters.

The next point is the discussion of the tempo organization in movement 9 and in the whole of *marteau*. Movement 9 has no independent tempo; it uses the tempos of all the other movements of *marteau*. In the first section of movement 9 the tempo of quotations are used: here a quarter is 63 (quotations from movement 6 and series 1–4), 50 ⟵ 60 ⟶ (72) (quotations from movement 5 and series 5–8), 104 (quotations from movement 3). In the second section the transpositions of series O1 are performed in the tempos of 63 and 76, and the transpositions of series I1, in the tempos of 92, 120, 132 (all those five tempos are borrowed from the second cycle of *marteau*). The transpositions of series O2 sound in tempos 100 ←— 120 —→ 152, i.e., two times faster than the similar material of the even sections of movement 5, and series I2 in tempos 66 ←— 80 —→ 120 (i.e., tempos of the odd sections of movement 5). The coda of movement 9 is performed in the tempo of movement 3 (104).

Ex. 141 presents the general interrelation of tempos in the whole of *marteau* (the proportions are noted by brackets and figures above them). This example shows the following.

1) The often used correlation of tempos is 1.2, which is 10 times less than 12. This connects a part of the tempos of the second and third cycles.

2) The second and third cycles have two tempos in common (76 and 120).

3) A correlation of tempos equal to 1.5 is also used, though it is of less importance than 1.2. The correlation of tempos which is 2 is used within the first and third cycles (e.g., 208:104 = 2, 100:50 = 2, etc.).

If the correlation of tempos were 1.2 everywhere, the second cycle would have had approximately the following tempos: 63 76 92 (110) (132), and the third cycle would have had 50 ←— 60 —→ (72), 66 ←— 80 —→ (96). Boulez, however, changed the tempos mentioned in brackets to avoid a monotonous sequence of tempos of one proportion. Hence the additional correlation 1.5.

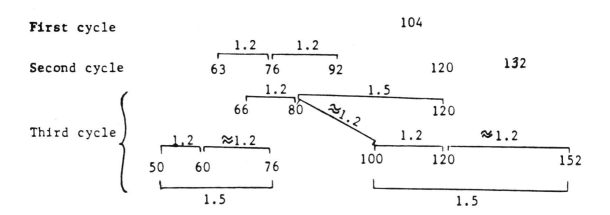

Ex. 141

The proportions of the form of movement 9 should be mentioned. Ex. 142a presents the proportions of the first section. The first subsection (bars 1–14) connected with the presentation of the quotations from movement 6 has a duration of 114, which was found before in the second cycle of *marteau* (movements 2 and 4). The central part of the second subsection (bars 17–26) with the quotations from movement 5 has a duration of 89 and equals the duration of the second section of movement 5. The duration of the third subsection (bars 31–41) is 117 and equals the duration of the first section of the second cycle of *marteau* (i.e., bars 1–11 in movement 2 of *marteau*). The duration of the first and third subsections (bars 1–14 and 31–41) is 114+117 = 231 = 21×11. And lastly, the duration of the whole first section (361) is almost equal to the duration of sections II, IV, VI of movement 5 of *marteau* (363). That is not a mere coincidence, since the text is the same in both cases, hence Boulez decided to keep to a similar duration.

Ex. 142b presents the proportions of the second section. Its first half (bars 42–87, to the beginning of the third section) is about equal to the second half (450 and 457). The whole duration of the second

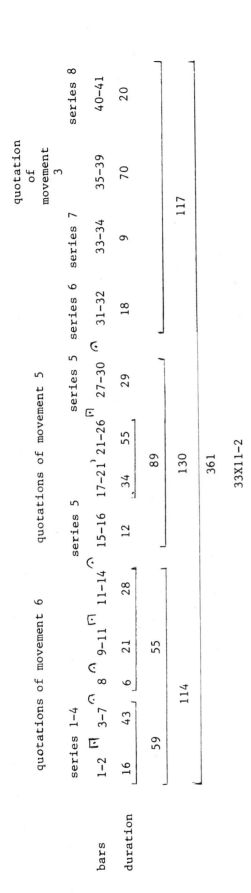

Ex. 142a  Movement 9 (the first section)

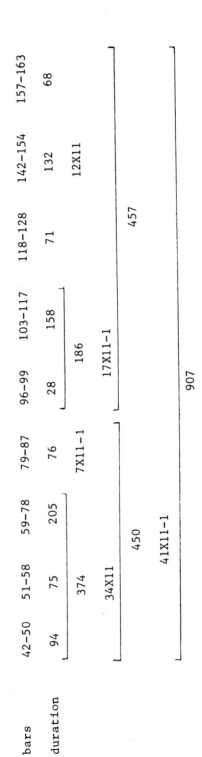

Ex. 142b  Movement 9 (the second section)

section (907) is approximately equal to the duration of movement 6 of *marteau*.

Webern was among the first who began to place the sounds of a series in such a way that they should occupy certain registers, and thus the vertical series acquired a special structure. E.g., see the series at the beginning of the Concerto, op. 24 (1934) (bars 1–3), which has a mirror–symmetrical structure along the vertical with two central intervals (Ex. 143). In the second presentation of the series (bars 4–5) the sounds are in the same registers. Thus the pitches become relative. E.g., see also movement 2 of his Variations for Piano, op. 27, and other compositions.

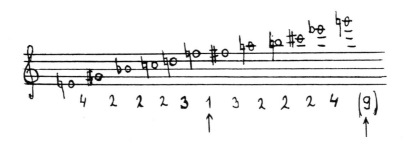

**Ex. 143**   Webern, Concerto op. 24, movement 1 (bars 1–5)

Boulez must have started using vertical rows and relative pitches with the Second Sonata and *Soleil* (1948). In his paper *Proposals* Boulez quotes such an example from movement 2 of the Second Sonata.[†] However, in *marteau* only (movements 5 and 9) Boulez creates for the first time a serial organization where a series having a vertical structure is transposed for all 12 pitches and produces the whole vertical structure of the music. Taken on its own, such a serial technique, due to its great simplicity, has features of narrowness and therefore must obviously be combined with another kind of serial technique (as done already in *marteau*). This technique is most convenient for combining several heterogeneous materials, as Boulez did in movement 9 (since also the second section of the finale of *marteau* can be considered a collage). Boulez seems to have used this technique in *marteau* only, and in his composition *...explosante–fixe...* (1971, work in progress) created a similar technique, where transpositions of a vertical series can be found as well.

---

†   Boulez, *Notes of an Apprenticeship*, p.65.

# Conclusion

## Some General Conclusions on the Development of Music in the 20<sup>th</sup> Century, on Boulez' Serial Organization and Harmony

Before the general discussion of serial organization and its use by Boulez, a very brief and sketchy review should be supplied of the historical development of music, comparing it to some natural phenomena.[†]

When two–part music appeared in the Middle Ages, only consonances were used, especially perfect ones. Gradually music became richer and richer: complex contrapuntal textures appeared, then (from the 17th century on) harmonic functionality and tonality. The latter was essentially regular in the sequence of harmonic functions according to the formula T-S-D-T for the small plane of the composition and T-D-S-T for the large plane. This formula is a movement in one direction (forward or backward). Then the development of musical language went to the later period of Wagner and Liszt, Debussy, Scriabin, and early Schoenberg. Hence it became very difficult to follow this formula of harmonic functionality, though it was preserved, because the impression was that one chord could be followed by any other (and therefore the feeling of the abovementioned formula as the main regularity was lost).

Consider this analogy: first a river is very narrow, then it grows wider and wider, until at the mouth it becomes so wide that the opposite bank cannot be seen, although it is there. A river has one direction only: forward or backward.

Finally tonal music became so complex that the above formula stopped controlling it, and so–called atonal music appeared. This music (Schoenberg and his school) had no unidirectional formula, since after one chord any other could follow. Schoenberg discovered the basic regularities of the organization of such music for the first time.

In our analogy: the river has flowed into the sea, which has a huge number of directions, none of them more important than any other one. An example is a composer such as Berg, who composed atonal music with features of tonality. He can be said to have been "navigating" in the sea not far from the river mouth. On the other hand, Webern was the first to discover that the sea (as opposed to the river) has a greater depth. His "ship" was small and was partly under water (therefore the public left it almost unnoticed and did not protest). Thus Webern was the first to try penetrating into the depth of the imaginary sea.

---

[†]   This comparison is very general and should be understood as one of many possibilities.

The new generation of composers (Boulez, Stockhausen, etc.) was the first really to make use of the sea depth, having discovered its fundamental laws. Thus, they began moving along the diagonal, so to say, in the multidirectional space and combined organically all the musical parameters (so–called serial music appeared). Those who remained on the sea surface became mainly imitators of Schoenberg.

The openness of the aleatoric form with these innovative composers was the result of using the multidimensional core which in its development produced such a form. The openness or multidirectionality of the aleatoric form is as natural as the unidirectional form was for many years of musical history.

In our own times the sea has become a well–studied object and too cramped for the huge number of composers in it. Next comes the ocean, which relatively few try to penetrate today. Even if they get there, they usually swim by the rules of the sea they have studied, just instinctively feeling that the ocean has laws of its own. This "ocean" is the widest and deepest space that can be imagined now. It has an almost infinite number of pitches (instead of the former twelve), durations, and gradations of dynamic and timbre.

We shall consider only that new music which has parameters belonging to the "ocean" and at least some features of new organization.

Some regularities should be mentioned which control the historical development of music. One of them is the usually sharp transition from one object to the maximum number of objects possible at the present stage of development, with which the leading role of that one object is eliminated. This one object is not absolutely one, it is understood as one entity in a wider sense. Further the mentioned maximum number of objects also comes to be understood as one large object, and a sharp leap happens to a much greater number of objects, the maximum possible at a new higher stage of development. That is the expression of the explosive process of development.

Some examples. In the traditional harmonic system there is only one type of chord, which consists of thirds. Composers were using this type of chord in multiple ways, building it with two, three, four different thirds, taking its derivative, etc. Having exhausted many possibilities, composers did not move to using chords of seconds or fourths, quite the reverse. They started using all the possible sound combinations (new chords), thus moving from one type of object to an enormous number of them (i.e., from the river to the sea). Thus the old type of object lost its exclusive role, and all the sound structures acquire an equal chance of being used in composition.

Thus,

| tonal music: | atonal music: |
|---|---|
| chord of one type of structure (from 3 to 5 sounds) | chords of all possible structures (from 2 to 12 sounds) |

By our times thousands of different pitch structures built of 12 sounds have been used in atonal music. Now (in the "ocean") we have an almost infinite number of various pitch structures, since instead of 12 pitches there exists an enormous number of them.[†] Another example. After the serialization of one parameter in dodecaphonic music a transition has appeared at the same time to the serialization of all the parameters in serial music. Finally, after many years of using almost entirely harmonic sounds with the same inner structure,[‡] in new music (in the ocean) we pass on to an almost infinite number of varied structures of sounds usually called in–harmonic, and also to sounds of aleatoric structure (i.e., noises). On the other hand, in harmonic sounds the lower partial is the strongest and most important one, which determines the pitch of the given sound, while in

---

† We are not solving here the problems of psychoacoustics, which studies the number of pitches really distinguished by an average listener.
‡ The omissions of overtones are not taken into account here.

in–harmonic sounds often all the partials are more or less important for the perception of pitch. Thus, after the full power of one object we move to the power of many objects, which are formally of approximately equal importance. We repeat: this regularity is based on the explosive nature of the historical development of music together with the physical nature of music.

Everything said above about the development of music points to the conclusion that jumping a stage in the historical process is inadvisable. Such an omission of a stage leads to a simplified, conservative and narrow understanding of innovation and produces a confusion in the explanation of the development of music, though at a first glance this or the other composer may seem ultra–modern. For example, Hába, Wyschnegradsky, Partch and others tried to use quartertones and other microintervals, dividing the octave into different numbers of equal intervals. At the same time their musical language remained in many cases less developed than that of Webern and other composers, who developed the musical language essentially on the basis of the twelve–tone chromatic scale.[†] On the other hand, their understanding of new music (i.e., of the "ocean") remained narrow, since without understanding the main law of the development of musical language and by attempting to omit a stage, they naturally apprehended this new, far stage in accordance with their *t r a d i t i o n a l* notion of the development of music. Thus they wanted to divide the octave into a great number of equal intervals instead of coming to the conclusion that new music  1) does not need a pitch scale consisting of equal intervals;   2) if equal intervals are still used, any interval can be divided into any number of equal parts, the initial interval not necessarily being the octave;   3) after using a tempered system and 12 pitches, new music does not have 24 or 75 pitches following, but a huge, almost infinite number of them. This attempt to omit a stage also resulted in the wrong understanding of many other phenomena, e.g., of the role of instruments in new music. Such composers as Boulez, Stockhausen, Xenakis, Berio were more consistent in their ideas about the development of music and did not attempt to omit a historical stage in their compositions.

The undulatory nature of the development of music is also to be pointed out, as it is clearly expressed in the 20th century. This wavelike nature can be explained by the gradual upsurges and slumps in the development of music, where one generation of composers essentially develops and enriches the language of music, and the next generation just widens the ideas translated into reality by the previous generation. Thus, one generation makes a leap to a new stage, and the next one mainly fills in the gap, partly going back. For example, the generation of composers born in the 70s and 80s of the previous century (Schoenberg, Bartók, Stravinsky, Webern, Varèse, Berg) made this leap (in their case from tonal to atonal music). The composers after them, born in the 90s and at the beginning of the 20th century (Prokofiev, Honegger, Milhaud, Hindemith, Eisler, Krenek, Shosta-kovitch) were mainly between atonal and tonal music, coming closer to the one or to the other. After that another sharp leap in development is observed; this time made by composers born mainly in the 20s of the 20th century (or somewhat earlier or later). They are Boulez, Stockhausen, Xenakis, Nono, Berio, Ligeti, Babbitt, Cage, Feldman. This leap consists in an even greater development of the musical language and the creation of new types of musical organization. It can probably be stated by now that the next generation of composers, born at the end of the 30s, in the 40s and at the beginning of the 50s, have practically not moved much forward. They either used freely some ideas of the already known serial system or went back to quasi–tonality, though often using the newest electronic technology.[‡] Thus, it should be mentioned that from about 1907 to the end of the 20s there was a gradual upsurge in the development of music, then from the 30s to the end of the

---

[†]  A similar phenomenon is the wish to use different noises in the music of the beginning of the 20th century, which is characteristic of the Italian futurist composers.

[‡]  This is not the place for a more detailed discussion of the subject.

40s there was mainly a slow descent; then from the end of the 40s to the end of the 60s there was another ascent followed again by a descent. These ups and downs of innovation influence most composers. Thus, the mentioned composers born in the 70s–80s of the previous century composed their music in the 30s and 40s of the 20th century almost without any innovations in principle.[†] The mentioned composers born in the 20s and making many discoveries in the 50s and 60s, stopped making essential innovations in music in the 70s.

Let us have a few quotations. In his paper on the music of the 1930s Elliott Carter says the following:[‡]

> 'By the time Schoenberg came to this country [USA–L.K.] in 1933 the earlier period of interest and even enthusiasm for the musical *avant–garde* both of America and Europe had passed. Enthusiastic support to these, as was given by Huneker and Rosenfeld in their criticisms of the early 20s and by Stokowski at Philadelphia Orchestra concerts, had given way to the views of a new generation, which looked back on this music as "old–fashioned modernism".[§] Conductors were following the lead of Koussevitzky in hailing neo–Classicism and populism as the vital new trend.'

On the other hand, Boulez remarks:[¶]

> 'However, after an adventure that had taken him [Stravinsky–L.K.]—like Schoenberg—such a long way, there came this regression, this fear of the unknown and the desire to organise the world in a reassuring way. The same thing happened with painters too. For example, when one compares the Kandinsky of 1911, 1912 and 1913—which was his most extraordinary period—or the Mondrian of 1914 and 1915 with the same painters from 1930 to 1940, one can see the urge towards discipline, the will to tame a world that had a dangerous tendency towards chaos, by reference to masters of the past.'

But, however important the historical events of the 30s and 40s, this is not the essence, as the wavelike process is not necessarily linked with historical events.

Let us discuss an important principle of musical organization.[*] It is the correlation in the music of the repetition and non–repetition of different objects. The wider the sound field with the transition from the "river" to the "sea", and then to the "ocean", the greater the number of objects that can be used and the less need there is to repeat the objects. A change occurs here in the correlation of repetition and non–repetition. With the development of music old forms of repetition disappear and are replaced by new ones. With each transition to newer music a tendency appears towards the non–repetition of many objects, as a result of which objects are re–arranged, old objects are replaced by new ones, and a new type of repetition, not used before, appears. Thus, repetition never disappears from music, it changes and decreases.[**] For example, with the transition from tonal to atonal music, the only possible and continuously repeated type of chord built of thirds is replaced by chords of different structures, i.e., a tendency appears to use different chord structures instead of repeating one. On the other hand, a tendency appears not to repeat a sound before playing all the other sounds. This resulted in the production of the twelve–sound series, which destroyed the old type of repetition, on the one hand, and introduced a new type, on the other hand, since the whole composition was built now of a series which had one structure repeated all the time. The elimination of octave doubling of pitches results in the pitches being repeated in the same registers,

---

[†]   Webern was an exception. It is interesting that Stravinsky at the beginning of the 50s, when an ascent started in musical development, also started looking for something new. It should be noted that the dates of the beginning and the end of historical musical periods are approximate.
[‡]   E. Carter, *Current Chronicle*: New York [Edward Steuermann].
[§]   Something similar can be heard also today from the representatives of the young generation of composers with reference to the music of the previous generation.
[¶]   Boulez, *Conversations with Célestin Deliège*, p.107.
[*]   This principle is not a law, but a trend.
[**]  Practically the old forms of repetition go on being partly used together with the new ones.

thus producing a new type of repetition. Furthermore the following takes place in serial music.

1) Composers carry out the serialisation of all the other parameters in order to avoid the old types of repetition;

2) composers begin to use series consisting of all (i.e., different) intervals with the purpose of avoiding the repetition of any interval;

3) to avoid repeating one serial structure, permutations of objects within internal structure of series are used, derivative series being produced;

4) instead of the limited number of forms of classical music, a huge number of different forms is produced; then aleatoric compositions are born, in which the form changes with every performance.

However, due to the desire to get rid of old types of repetition, in serial music too a new type is born, which is a similar serial organization of all parameters. Different parameters can be organized by means of the same progression, the same row of numbers, the same structure of the series, and also a similar way of deducing the derived objects can be used. This new type of repetition is much less noticeable than the historically preceding types; nevertheless, it must be eliminated in new music (the "ocean"). In the new music the serial system disappears with the general series as its basis. Instead of it use is made of a great number of different, much more complex organization systems, including to a different extent regulated random processes. Thus, a huge number of non–repeated objects is used in the new music.

As seen from the given examples, the principle of non–repetition can be said to devolve from the explosive nature of the development of music.

Finally, mention should be made of three historical stages in the development of music.

1) Vocal music. Man is the source of sound, performer and composer.

2) Instrumental music. The instrument operated by man is the source of sound. Man is the performer and composer.

3) Electronic–computer music. The electronic device or computer operated by man is the source of sound. The electronic device is the performer. The computer is man's assistant in composing the music.[†]

None of the three stages is eliminated in the transition to a new stage; it goes on developing, influencing the new stage and being influenced by it.

Now we pass on to a more detailed discussion of serial thinking in music. First let us mention very briefly the origin of serial organization, though it is still difficult to state it precisely. An enormous role belongs to the late works of Webern who was gradually approaching the creation of serial organization. The American composer M. Babbitt (born 1916), who also had an education in mathematics, seems to have been the first to apply serialization of two (or more) parameters. At the end of the 40s he composed his first works with elements of serial organization, namely, *Three Compositions for Piano* (1947), and *Composition for Four Instruments* (1947–48). A great influence on Babbitt's creation of a serial system was the study of musical systems undertaken by J. Schillinger, and also the late works of Schoenberg.[‡]

---

[†]  The problem of the three stages is mentioned for the specific purpose of emphasizing the importance of the computer in the organization of the new music.

[‡]  That is what Babbitt told the author during their meeting in Jerusalem in the summer of 1977.

In 1949 Messiaen composed *Quatre études de rythme* for the piano, the second of which is *Mode de valeurs et d'intensités*. In this étude Messiaen used 36 pitches, 24 durations, 12 modes of articulation and 7 dynamic steps. This piece is really modal and only just approaches serial organization.

The Belgian composer Karel Goeyvaerts (born 1923) was a student of Messiaen and Leibowitz and studied very carefully the late works of Webern. Without being acquainted with the abovementioned composition of Messiaen's, but under the influence of Webern he composed in 1951 his *Sonata for Two Pianos*, which had an almost totally serial organization. This composition, as well as *Mode de valeurs* by Messiaen and the later music of Webern, had a great influence on Stockhausen, who, being influenced by them, soon composed his *Kreuzspiel* (November 1951), where he produced a serial organization.[†]Boulez created his *Structures Ia* for two pianos(April 1951) where he borrowed the pitch series from Messiaen's *Mode de valeurs*. Boulez points out that in this composition he wanted"to use the potential of a given material to find out how far automatism in musical relationships would go".[‡]

The serial organization of instrumental music is based on the general uniform chromatic scale of pitches with the semitone as the smallest interval.[§] This pitch scale influences the other three sound dimensions, as well as additional parameters. Therefore, to avoid discrepancy between the various dimensions, a serial composer strives to produce similar scales for durations, dynamics, and also for the most complex dimension, the timbre. The pitch scale has 12 steps within the octave, the scales of the other dimensions can also be linked to the number 12, though that is not obligatory. What is more important is the link of parameters through progressions and scales. The chromatic pitch scale within the octave is logarithmic. Boulez regularly uses a duration scale with an arithmetic progression of 12 steps,[¶] which corresponds to the twelve–step logarithmic pitch scale within an octave.[*] As a rule, Boulez uses the number 12 for scales on which three dimensions are based, namely, pitch, duration, dynamics.[**] With Stockhausen the duration scale is usually based on a geometric progression or the Fibonacci row progression. The geometric progression of durations seems to him to correspond to the seven octaves in the pitch sphere.[***]

The dynamic scale of both composers is evidently logarithmic, since, though in instrumental music this scale is not measured, both composers and performers seem as a rule to treat it as logarithmic. E.g., the 12–step dynamic scale of Boulez is evidently to be understood and performed as a logarithmic one, leading from loud sounds to soft ones.

Boulez' tempos are not always connected with the same scale,[****] while Stockhausen often uses the logarithmic scale of tempos (see *Zeitmasze, Gruppen*, Piano Piece V, etc.).

All the scales mentioned above can be considered basic. The serial composer bases on them series of different structure. Boulez built a classification of musical spaces.[†] His various "striated spaces" result in producing different scales.[‡]

Finally, it should be mentioned that nature has unilinear scales for the three main dimensions of sound: frequency, duration, amplitude; however, the unilinear scale is absent for the most complex parameter, timbre. The frequency scale consists of the transition from low to higher frequencies

---

†   See more details about the appearance of serialism in R. Toop, *Messiaen/Goeyvaerts, Fano/Stockhausen, Boulez*. It is still difficult to say today with any precision which composition influenced another and to what extent, and also what was the chronological sequence of these compositions.

‡   Boulez, *Conversations with Célestin Deliège*, p.55.

§   The quartertone scale of 24 pitches is a widened variant of the twelve–sound chromatic scale. Serialists use it very rarely, e.g., Boulez in *Polyphonie X* and *Improvisation sur Mallarmé 3*.

¶   See *Boulez on Music Today*, p.52, Ex. 11, and *Notes of an Apprenticeship*, pp.165–6.

*   Such a discrepancy cannot be considered a drawback, as the use, e.g., of the techniques of duration multiplication results in a complex system of durations of frequency groups.

**   See the chromatic scale in Ex. 57.

***  See Stockhausen, *...how time passes...*, his composition *Gruppen*, etc., Henck's analyses of Piano Pieces IX and X.

****In a number of compositions Boulez does not mention the tempo by the metronome (*Eclat, Cummings ist der Dichter*).

†   *Boulez on Music Today*, pp.87–88.

‡   Different space types with Boulez are really scales.

(and vice versa); the duration scale includes the transition from short to long durations; the amplitude scale comprises the transition from small to greater energy. The timbre is produced by the data of all the three mentioned sound dimensions. Hence there is an infinite number of scales of timbre.

On the basis of the chromatic pitch scale Boulez produces the twelve–tone series which is general or universal,[†] the so–called "mother" of serial organization. With Boulez the general series is usually, so to speak, synthetic, as it consists of a series denoting pitch, duration, dynamics and modes of attacks. That was shown in the analysis of the second cycle and finale of *marteau*. This characteristic feature probably distinguishes Boulez from other serialists. The pitch structure of Boulez' series is usually partly symmetric with isomorphic figures (*marteau*, Third Sonata) and therefore differs from the fully symmetric series of Stockhausen (*Gruppen, Kontakte*, etc.) or Nono (*Il canto sospeso, Varianti*, etc.),[‡] which usually comprise all the intervals. Although in the serial music of Boulez the pitch structure of the general series is most important for building the pitch structure of a composition, its role is much less than in dodecaphonic music (which will be shown later). With Stockhausen the pitch series can be basic, influencing the structure of many other parameters (as in *Gruppen*), but it can also play a secondary, less important role, when the number row of proportions becomes primary (as in Piano Piece X[§] and many other works).

The general series in itself, however, cannot produce a developed serial organization. That requires the presence of a number row (usually simple), so to say, a "father" of the serial organization, which in connection with the series, gives the possibility of producing derivative series. The number row by means of number permutation produces derivative number rows, as a result of which permutations of sounds or of other objects appear as also do the different combinations of sounds into groups (multiplication technique as described by Boulez).

The generation of derivative series is connected with the use of transpositions and permutations. Practically any transposition already contains a permutation of objects, i.e., transposition is object permutation with the initial interval structure of the series preserved. Hence the transition from usual transpositions with the dodecaphonists to special types of transpositions used by serialists was a natural process. Permutations can be both simple and complex (the simplest type is rotation, i.e., rotary permutation). Series transpositions, like rotation, are restricted to 12. Permutations can be interrelated or based on statistics. Thus, the following types of permutations can be mentioned:

1) transposition;

2) rotation;

3) permutation with the derivative series deduced on the basis of a certain principle and therefore interrelated;

4) permutation based on a law of statistics.

Both Boulez and Stockhausen use transpositions and permutations of pitches, durations, and other objects to deduce derivative series; for Boulez, however, especially produced transpositions seem to be of greater importance, while permutations seem more important for Stockhausen. As an example of Boulez' use of pitch transposition and permutation the 2nd movement of the Third Sonata[¶] can be taken. A characteristic feature of Boulez is serial transposition where on a large plane the structure of the series in inversion is preserved; thus any transposition system devolves from the series structure itself. E.g., see *Structures Ia*, the third cycle of *marteau*, etc.[*] The same refers to a

---

[†]   Boulez calls it "initial", or "basic", or "original" (see *Boulez on Music Today*, pp.35,45). In p.104 (op.cit.) he calls it "fundamental" and "generalised".
[‡]   Both composers also produced series which are not fully symmetric.
[§]   See, e.g., Henck's *Karlheinz Stockhausen's Klavierstück X*.
[¶]   See *Boulez on Music Today*, p.74, Ex. 29a.
[*]   See also op.cit., pp.38–39, Ex. 1,2.

duration series as well.

Thus, in a developed serial composition by Boulez instead of one series an ensemble of series is really used, which is linked to the general series by a certain hierarchy. Hence the general series does not usually take any direct part in building a composition, though it can appear in the music (as shown in the analysis of movement 6 of *marteau*). Boulez (like Stockhausen, and also probably like Nono and Babbitt) often uses one series for several compositions, since their serial organizations usually vary, and the presence of one series connects those works.

Here is Boulez' definition of the series, where he speaks also of its ability to create an "ensemble of possibilities":

> 'The series is—in very general terms—the germ of a developing hierarchy based on certain psycho–physiological acoustical properties, and endowed with a greater or lesser selectivity, with a view to organizing a F I N I T E ensemble of creative possibilities connected by predominant affinities in relation to a given character; this ensemble of possibilities is deduced from an initial series by a F U N C T I O N A L generative process (not simply the consecutive exposition of a certain number of objects, permutated according to restrictive numerical data). Consequently, all that is needed to set up this hierarchy is a necessary and sufficient premise which will ensure the t o t a l   c o h e s i o n[†] of the whole and the relationships between its successive parts.'[‡]

Thus the functional process of creation is understood as a strictly consecutive deduction of derivative objects, as a result of which they are inseparably linked with the resulting hierarchic system. The deduction of objects (or of an "ensemble of possibilities") by means of "a f u n c t i o n a l generative process" is one of the most characteristic features of the serial thinking of Boulez. Thus, the composer shows the generation of sound complexes by multiplication and adds that these complexes are generated "in the most functional way possible, in that they obey a logical, coherent structure".[§] That may be one of the primary reasons for Boulez coming to the directed aleatoric form.

In contrast to Boulez, Stockhausen used to a great extent the statistical method of producing a serial organization, which, in his works of the 60s especially, resulted in a much less manageable aleatoric form. Stockhausen says on the subject:[¶]

> 'My K l a v i e r s t ü c k XI[*] is only the relatively late result of a development which in my case began as early as 1953 under the influence of seminars about information theory and phonetics held by Prof. Dr. Meyer–Eppler at Bonn University. There we made scientific studies of chance operations as essential areas of modern information theory; as is well known, phonetics operates with statistical methods in the area of sound analysis, with mathematical principles of statistical average; "chance operations" were our daily bread. Gradually I then transferred these methods into musical composition, at first still invisibly, since the notations still looked deterministic, but I already used statistical criteria for permutations, frequency distribution.'

The statistical method of generation is understood as the deduction of objects by means of statistical laws, which can mean, e.g., a more or less free disposition of objects within a certain period of time. In this case the saturation density of this formal section is decisive and can be studied with

---

†   Our emphasis. L.K.
‡   *Boulez on Music Today*, pp.35–36. See also the next two sentences of Boulez.
§   Op.cit., p.39.
¶   See Faas, *Interview with Karlheinz Stockhausen*, p.191.
*   Composed in 1956.

the help of the laws of statistics operating with the notion of the average value. In such a case a composer does not usually think of the given form section as divisible into smaller structures.[†]

Boulez also speaks of statistics when discussing "amorphous time":[‡]

'Amorphous time can vary only in density according to the statistical number of events which take place during a chronometric global time–span; the relationship of this density or an amorphous time–span will be the index of content.'

Boulez also seems to have generated some form sections statistically. E.g., see *Structures II*, (*Chapitre 2*) and *Don*. On the other hand, it is essential that with Boulez the functional method of generation can result in a musical form p e r c e i v e d statistically. This is not unreasonable, as often a complex serial texture can be first perceived statistically. In *marteau* the most outstanding example of this is the first half of movement 4, where the listener perceives the form as consisting of sound structures of different density separated by fermatas. A similar idea can apply to the multiplication technique (e.g., movements 1 and 7 of *marteau*).

Here are some more quotations from Boulez, where the new features of his serial organization are shown. Boulez is against reducing the whole serial organization to one "global structure", which was characteristic of Schoenberg in the sphere of pitch. He writes:[§]

'It would surely be illusory to try to link all the general structures of a work to one and the same global generative structure, from which they would necessarily derive in order to assure the cohesion and unity, as well as uniquity of the work. This cohesion and uniquity cannot, in my opinion, be obtained so mechanically; the principle of allegiance of structures to a central authority seems rather to resort to Newtonian "models", contradicting the developments of present–day thought.'

Further Boulez develops his idea:[¶]

'A generalised series is indispensible to the creation of elementary morphologies, the first plans of development, but it ought not to remain the only reference in the course of composition; this basic series will enable us to formulate objects which, in their turn, can be the basis of serial generation.'

Then he points to the difference of his serial organization from that of Webern and Berg, who developed Schoenberg's idea to the point of producing serial ensembles.[*]

'In comparison with the practice of Webern or Berg, we are no longer dealing with serial ensembles but with partial, local structures, having their own independence, while retaining their filiation with the global structure. A global structure will create a cascade of local structures directly dependent on itself.'

In this respect it is noteworthy that the developed hierarchic serial organization used by Boulez (and other serialists) is based, as with dodecaphonists too, on a series the elements of which (e.g., frequencies) are formally equal (i.e. there is no hierarchy). A similar thing happens in series and scales of other parameters. The presence of hierarchy in the pitch sphere was characteristic of tonal music, while in the serial music of Boulez there is a hierarchy of structures.

---

[†]  See also W. Meyer–Eppler, *Statistic and Psychologic Problems of Sound*, K. Wörner, *Stockhausen* (pp.96–101), H. Eimert and H.U. Humpert, *Das Lexikon der elektronischen Musik* (pp. 324–325).
[‡]  *Boulez on Music Today*, pp. 88–89.
[§]  Op.cit., p.99.
[¶]  Op.cit., p.104.
[*]  Op.cit., p.105.

The type of serial organization is a method of generating and developing a serial organization, due to which a united coherent organism is produced. With Boulez each type of serial organization has its method of deducing derivative series or other organisms from the general series and the hierarchy of system elements appearing after that. With Stockhausen the characteristic types of serial organization seem to be those in which serial organization appears and develops from a numeric row of proportions. It is still too early to make a classification of types of serial organization, since many works of serial music both by Boulez and by other composers have not yet been analysed. Each serial composer has probably produced several types of serial organization which he then used with different changes (as if directing them differently), developed and united with other types of serial organization. Mention has already been made of three types of serial organization produced by Boulez in the three cycles of *marteau*; to them should be added the organization which uses circular permutation of the series sounds (movement 2 of the Third Sonata). Other serial organizations are found in *Improvisations sur Mallarmé*, in *Rituel*, and in some other works.

We shall now point out the common features characteristic of many serial organizations by Boulez. Based on the general series and the numeric row used to produce the organization, the following hierarchy of the system elements appears:

1) frequency (a sound consisting of partials is usually meant here):
   a) sound of definite pitch,
   b) sound of indefinite pitch;

2) group of frequencies (sonority, element of the field), includes no more than 11 frequencies:
   a) simple (non–multiplied),
   b) complex (multiplied);

3) field, includes several groups of frequencies:
   a) simple (non–multiplied), includes 12 sounds,
   b) complex (multiplied);

4) domain,[†] consists of several fields;

5) the whole serial system, includes one or more domains;

6) constellation,[‡] consists of several serial systems.

All these elements are interrelated, however, not all of them are present in each serial system. E.g., the existence of fields does not have to produce a domain; a field can consist of frequencies not united into groups. The conditional term "constellation" denotes the presence of several serial systems (different or more similar) in one composition; at the same time one general series is used, which unites them (*Structures I*, *marteau*, The Third Sonata,[§] *Structures II*, etc.). Many of the elements mentioned refer not only to pitch, but also to durations, dynamics, timbre. Thus, Boulez speaks about fields of duration, of time, of amplitude, of resonances, about defined and non–defined chronometric fields.[¶] It should be noted that some elements mentioned have names which do not correspond directly to real physical phenomena, but are musical–psychological conceptions of physical terms.

All the elements mentioned above are the components of serial form with Boulez. The field is one of the most essential elements of the given hierarchy. In his research on musical technique Boulez discusses in detail this element of the system and gives a field classification.[*] In Boulez' serial system,

---

†   The term is ours. L.K.
‡   The term is ours. L.K.
§   The name "Constellation" given to the 3rd (central) movement of the Third Sonata can, in our opinion, refer to the Third Sonata as a whole.
¶   *Boulez on Music Today*, pp.55,88,96,98,51 respectively. In p.64 Boulez shows the dynamic fields.
*   Op.cit., pp.108–109 (Table 1 especially), 39,41,44.

derivative series are fields of frequencies or of frequency groups (as shown in the analysis of the three cycles of *marteau*). The group of frequencies and the field are the most important new elements of composition, which lead to the generation of the new serial form.

For his part Stockhausen speaks of "time–fields" and other fields in his paper *...how time passes...*. His understanding of this phenomenon is different from that of Boulez, though he too cannot think of his music without fields, groups and phases for different dimensions. The assumption would be valid that since the second half of the 50s all serial composers have been using such phenomena as the group and the field, although their treatments of those phenomena are not the same. In the music of the 60s created by younger composers and having no serial organization, the field is also often the most essential element of form. Thus, until the elements of musical form were radically changed, the new form was not created.

In the first half of the 20th century the musical language underwent a cardinal change, but the forms were not really changed. The appearance of an essentially new form took place in the second half of the 20th century, only with the creation of serial organization and the new turn in the development of the musical language. It can be said that the most important achievement of the generation of the above composers born in the 20s lies in the field of form.[†]

As shown in the analysis of *marteau*, form depends to a great extent on the chosen type of serial organization, which builds its basis. However, serial form is not equated with a certain type of serial organization on which it relies, as the composer directs the chosen type of organization in his own way and creates the form he wants. At the same time he can make some changes, e.g., in the dispositions of the formal sections, abbreviations, insertions, etc. For example, as shown above, the first cycle of *marteau* and the first half of *Tombeau* are based on the multiplication of frequencies, using the same general series, numeric row of proportions and derivative series. Nevertheless the forms of those compositions are different.

Only a richly worked out serial form can be opposed to the developed classical form. It is still early to produce a classification of serial forms. It can also be assumed that the making of a classification will not really explain the essence of serial form, as this or that classification of chords does not clear up the principles of atonal harmony. There is a huge number of serial forms in contrast to their limited number in classical music, since each serial composition really has its own, unique form. Serial music has a unity of form and material, which makes it essentially different from the preceding dodecaphonic music.

As shown in the analysis of *marteau*, serial form (like the other parameters) must be calculated also from the viewpoint of temporal proportions connected by measuring the formal sections by means of a selected measuring unit (e.g., a semiquaver). This promotes the building of a proportional correlation of sections and thus the strengthening of the form. For the serial composers this parameter is most important (for Stockhausen it is the essential one), and their perception of form influences the calculation of the form. Through it the composer gains a better formal control. Boulez seems to take, as a rule, one number as a measurement unit on which the calculation is based (e.g., 11 in the first cycle of *marteau*); in some cases, besides the one basic number, some parts of the form can also be measured with the help of other numbers, as seen in the analysis of the second cycle of *marteau*. The calculation of formal sections in Boulez' works is usually complicated, with interwoven indices of different formal sections. On the large plane, however, the proportions can be simple. For example, as analysis shows, movement 1 of *marteau* relates to 7 as 2:1; movement 4 relates to 8 as 7:11. Boulez uses the row proportions of Fibonacci very rarely, as compared to their frequent use by Stockhausen. The temporal calculation of the form agrees with the computation of other parameters. Moreover, the same number or proportion can be used to calculate several parameters.

---

† Here one could also refer to Cage, whose most characteristic compositions are related to his special approach to form, of course not serial, but connected with indeterminacy, pure chance, and even "negative", like in the piece 4'33" (tacet) for any instrument(s) (1952).

For example, the number 11 in the second cycle of *marteau* is also used to count the attacks with the percussion instruments, the number of series and the sections in the whole of the second cycle. With Boulez the proportions of formal sections are usually not connected directly with the duration scale on which the serial organization of the composition is based (e.g., see the analysis of *marteau*), while such a link is most typical of Stockhausen (e.g., see Piano Piece IX).[†]

It is also essential to point to the presence of a conflict in serial organization. However paradoxical it may be, a similar serialization of many parameters, which eliminates the incompatibility between different dimensions of a sound present in dodecaphonic music, results in a conflict of those parameters. The reason is that the data of one parameter which are obtained as a result of the generating process, must be correlated with the data of all the other parameters. In the process of creating music the composer strives to solve this "confrontation" of parameters, which builds the inner dynamics of serial organization and form. The composer can, to a greater or smaller extent, develop or muffle the dynamic nature of the serial form in accordance with the required nature of the music. Besides, some types of serial organization seem to produce greater dynamics of form and of the very nature of the music. For example, the form based on the technique of frequency multiplication is innerly dynamic, as the multiplication process is one of the most active types of generation, as a result of which frequency groups of different density are formed. Hence the inner dynamic of the first cycle of *marteau*. On the other hand, the technique of the filtering of frequencies results, e.g., in the second cycle of *marteau*, in the forming of twelve–tone series of frequencies, the alternation of which, even varied, results in a more static form.

Boulez displays a general interest in producing static structures with little evolution within a composition, and also in building up a contrast by opposing materials of different nature. This is seen in *marteau*, in the Third Sonata, in *Rituel*, and in many other works. In one of his lectures Boulez said that he likes to build complex objects which do not undergo any deep changes.[‡] One can observe that within the first and second cycles of *marteau* there are neither essential changes of the material nor clearly expressed climaxes. That does not mean that in the serial music of Boulez there is no development, but it is not like the classical (in its wide sense) development of elements, which was still found, in his Second Sonata. One of the characteristic types of development in Boulez' music is the following: Boulez creates a complex system including a number of various elements; in the process of material development the elements replace each other, but all of them are really equal in value (i.e., none of them is more dynamic than another), they have little inner development, they replace each other kaleidoscopically and are "attracted" by the central system generating them. The first and second cycles of *marteau* are typical examples.[§] That does not mean that dynamic forms with a more intense inner development are absent from the serial music by Boulez. Movement 5 of *marteau* can serve as an example. If there are no contrasting dynamic elements in the first and second cycles, they are present in movement 9 due to the presence of the material of movement 5. Static elements, however, are stronger and occupy a greater place here as well.[¶] In his later compositions a greater contrast between static and dynamic elements can sometimes be observed (e.g., see *Eclat*).

Finally, beginning with *marteau*, Boulez decided to reject the extreme automatism of serial organization and began to control it more flexibly. He says the following about *marteau*:[*]

'There is in fact a very clear and very strict element of control, but starting from this strict control and the work's overall discipline there is also room for what I call local indiscipline: at the overall level there is

---

† Stockhausen produces temporal proportions of the form from the very outset of his work at a composition.
‡ May 1980, IRCAM, Paris.
§ Because of their very fast tempo movements 1 and 7 of *marteau* are, of course, perceived as much more dynamic music than movement 3 and the second cycle. The fast tempo, however, is rather an outward sign of dynamics.
¶ After the last "charge" of dynamic elements (bars 118–128) leading to a distinctive climax, a rather long quiet comes.
* Boulez, *Conversations with Célestin Deliège*, p.66.

discipline and control, at the local level there is an element of indiscipline—a freedom to choose, to decide and to reject.'[†]

What Boulez calls "local indiscipline" should be understood as free choice and manipulations with elements of the serial organization. Nothing alien is introduced into the system, therefore there is no contradiction to the serial system. This was displayed to a great extent in the analysis of *marteau*. Thus, Boulez achieves free choice by a gradual movement from the global structure to the most peripheric ones. Boulez speaks of "justified freedom"[‡] and adds, "...it is essential to discover to what extent we can make a transition from strict to free writing".[§] Further he mentions:

'A progressive loosening of the vice–like grip of strict writing will finally lead to complete freedom—freedom, of course, within general structural principles.'[¶]

Finally Boulez writes:

'The play of structures implicitly suggests a scale of relationships going from the chance of automatism to the chance of choice...'[*]

It should be also mentioned that Boulez often builds some sections or movements of a composition in strict correspondence to the serial scheme, while other sections are constructed much more freely. In *marteau* (also possibly in his later works) the transition from strictness to greater freedom usually takes place at the end of cycles. E.g., if movement 3 is built strictly, its "double" in the coda of movement 9 is much more free. In the second cycle, from movement 8 to 6 a gradual transition to greater freedom takes place. Finally, the *"double"* of movement 5, movement 9 (its first section especially) is composed much more freely than the original. On the other hand, strict and more free sections can alternate. This is seemingly the case in *Cummings ist der Dichter*, where the strict sections are performed in a *Moderé* tempo, and the freer ones in *Libre*. Besides, some deviations from the schemes in *marteau* and other works of Boulez are due to technical reasons (e.g., range limitations of instruments, over–complicated part for some instrument, etc.). It should not be forgotten that deviations from the schemes due to this struggle of parameters are possible.

Our next point is a short discussion of harmony. By harmony we mean on the wide plane the whole pitch system, and on the narrow one the presence of vertical structures linked in a special way. In his theory of harmony Boulez strives to link the two planes, which will be seen further. Boulez produces a classification of textures, where polyphony is evidently the main one. He subdivides the latter into counterpoint and harmony, which is in its turn subdivided into functional and non–functional. According to Boulez both those kinds of harmony lead to multiplied harmony.[**] Boulez obviously uses here almost fully the traditional terminology applied to his serial music, while displaying the link between tonal and serial music.

Boulez explains:[***]

'If it depends directly on the figures implied by the series, harmony will be functional and will embrace the collectivity of vertical relationships; when it is not functional and is subject to such accidents as grouping,

---

†   In his lecture in May 1980 (IRCAM, Paris) Boulez mentioned his liking for semi–automatic structures.
‡   *Boulez on Music Today*, p.104.
§   Op.cit., p.105.
¶   Op.cit., p.106. See also the following text by Boulez.
*   Op.cit., p.106. Stockhausen speaks about a gradual transition from strictness to freedom: "It can be a profitable working method for a composer to select a series of degrees of freedom for a work." ("...how time passes...", p.38).
**  See *Boulez on Music Today*, p.119, Table 4.
*** Op.cit., pp.118–119.

each relationship or group of relationships will obey individual criteria. Finally, if harmony, whatever its nature, is linked with new functions of density (fixed or variable) in order to produce "mutations", the totality of relationships (functional, or having individual criteria) will be modified individually. As with counterpoint, any vertical relationship of points, figures or structures, can be considered as harmony.'

Thus, the first kind of harmony includes the vertical structures built of series fragments. The so–called principle of chromatic supplement is used here. The dodecaphonic works of Schoenberg, Berg, Webern, the early works of Boulez (*Sonatine* for Flute and Piano, the First and Second Sonatas, etc.) can serve as examples. The second kind really includes any sound combination not based on a series structure. E.g., the harmony in the second half of *Tombeau*, in the so–called "free" parts of *Rituel*, etc. Multiplied harmony was explained in the analysis of the first cycle of *marteau*; it is found in every case of frequency multiplication. See also the first half of *Tombeau*, the "Blocks" in movement 3 of the Third Sonata, *Structures II, Eclat, Domaines*, etc. Multiplied harmony is functionally linked in a new way with the series which has generated it.

Since Boulez understands as harmony the vertical relations between sounds, structures, etc., then all textures, including monody which is complex in structure,[†] can also be studied from the viewpoint of vertical structures.

Boulez adds:[‡]

'Vertical relationships can be conceived as basic material, as an intermediary factor in the elaboration of complex objects, or as a control in working with complex objects. The vertical dimension cannot be treated identically in all three cases, since each demands special treatment, according to the laws of organisation, which are derived, of course, from a basic but organically specific law.'

In the above quotation we find the existence of three stages, the second of which is intermediate, which is characteristic of the thinking of Boulez.

Boulez explains what made him look for new ideas in harmony.[§]

'What worried me increasingly in my own early works and, for instance, in the works of Schoenberg was the absence of control over vertical structure. Harmonic encounters took place more or less by accident. Melodic lines had reached an extreme degree of refinement, but side by side with them were harmonic relationships that not only lacked refinement but were the result of pure chance.'[¶]

Further Boulez speaks about Webern's invention in movement 5 of the Second Cantata (Op.31), which allows unity of the vertical, horizontal and diagonal aspects of the composition. Then he points out his achievement:[*]

'...in my most recent works practically all the pitches are deduced from each other by means of harmonic systems such as those which can be multiplied by each other. I believe it is impossible to write in two different dimensions following two different sets of rules, and that one must in fact follow laws that apply reciprocally to the horizontal and the vertical.'

Thus, multiplication of harmonic systems may be the most essential achievement of Boulez in the field of harmony. And its invention took place at the beginning of the 50s with the composition of the first cycle of *marteau*.

---

† See op.cit., p.137 (Ex. 57).
‡ Op.cit., p.27.
§ Boulez, *Conversations with Célestin Deliège*, p.90.
¶ This refers also to many other composers contemporary to Boulez.
* Op.cit., pp.90–91.

Finally, Boulez says:[†]

'The harmonic vocabulary, too, should obey a law of evolution rather than a statistical generalisation. The textures evolve, but the way in which they are arranged is at least as important as their density.'

"A law of evolution" can be understood here objectively and subjectively. Boulez obviously has in mind the objective meaning of what is said, i.e., the necessity of evolution. On the other hand, he has his own understanding of that law, where the essential part belongs to the functional generation of derivative objects on the basis of a series. Generally, in the wide sense, due to his essential striving for functional generation and evolution Boulez differs from Debussy, who usually tried to avoid the functional method of thinking. From the general viewpoint the ideas of Boulez on harmony link him to Wagner. The latter strove to develop in a new way the functional relations of chords in tonally organized music and to create a harmonic hierarchy, where the highest power belongs to tonics, but where there are also local centres with local control. One should also remember the peculiar unity of the melodic principle and harmony in Wagner's music, similar to that of Boulez, who developed the idea considerably.

The approach of Boulez to harmony comes from the structure of pitch organization in his works. The special attention paid by Boulez to the vertical aspect ("extremely close attention to the vertical aspect")[‡] was historically necessary after many years of unclearness on the subject. On the other hand, to a great extent it is also the expression of the deeply personal interest of Boulez in this parameter, which is characteristic of his style. His care for the control of the vertical aspect results in an almost complete absence of aleatoric freedom in this dimension.

The given quotations and theoretical works of Boulez lead to the conclusion that pitch organization is usually most important in his music, that this organization is probably the starting point of the organization of his compositions, and then it influences the organization of other parameters (such as durations). That distinguishes Boulez from Stockhausen, who, both in the organization of his compositions and in his theoretical works, usually stresses the basic importance of temporal proportions.

The main feature should be mentioned which links the harmony of the serialists to the music of the first half of the 20th century.

Serial instrumental music has not used a single essentially new vertical structure that was not built or could not be built in the music of the composers of the first half of the 20th century (that refers also to the cluster, and to quartertone intervals). That is explained by the fact that the same chromatic pitch scale has been in use all that time, therefore the production of essentially new pitch structures was impossible. Besides, octave doubling was usually absent from all pitch structures. In spite of the progressive nature of the ban on octave doubling, there is some contradiction between the absence of octaves from the music and their presence in the tempered tuning itself with octaves as its basis. This contradiction is resolved with the transition to electronic music.

Now we will mention some new characteristics.

1. Density, one of the most essential parameters of serial music,[§] is very seriously controlled by means of various serial techniques. Boulez subdivides density into fixed and mobile.[¶] To the former, belongs the density of each of the "variations" in *Structures Ia*; to the latter, the multiplication technique generating groups of frequencies of varying density, where each group has its own density and number of attacks. The latter, like the duration of frequencies within a group, influences

---

†   Op.cit., p.92.
‡   Op.cit., p.92.
§   The notion of density can refer to all sound dimensions, and not to pitch only.
¶   See op.cit., pp.38–39. Boulez speaks of "fixed and mobile density of generation". The latter is his invention.

the density of vertical structures; thus, the fewer attacks a group of frequencies has, the more saturated are its vertical structures. In the second cycle of *marteau* the density of each series of frequencies is also mobile; mobile density is also found with the overlapping of several different series. Since in the second cycle the multiplication of any series is produced by means of some interval or group of intervals, a fixed transformation by means of density appears (see section VI in the second cycle and Schemes 2 and 3, where the change of density is clearly demonstrated).[†] It should also be mentioned that in *marteau* mobile density is, as a rule, seemingly contained within certain limits in each section; hence the greatest contrast is produced with the transition to another section, and especially to another movement (e.g., from movement 3 to 4). Besides, to avoid overburdening the texture, Boulez marks the duration of a note as a short sound plus a pause already in *Structures Ia*. This is also widely used in the second cycle of *marteau* (e.g., see movements 2 and 4).

Unlike Boulez, Stockhausen uses statistical processes for the organization of density.[‡]

2. Tessitura plays an important part in the serial music of Boulez. With a developed system Boulez controls the pitch fixity in certain registers, pitch mobility, and also the linking of different pitch structures.

Boulez writes that tessitura

'can evolve from total fixity to total mobility, the index of fixity covering a more or less restricted field. The i n d e x  o f  f i x i t y is the ratio between the number of fixed frequencies and that of mobile or semi–mobile frequencies...'[§]

Several pitches form a field which can be fixed or mobile (with all the intermediate stages) in accordance with the index of fixity, i.e., the fixity of the pitches in the register.
Further Boulez adds[§] that

...functions of tessitura can maintain direct organic relationships with the serial functions, and can, as a result corroborate them [the main section of movement 9 of *marteau*. L.K.]; but they can also be completely independent, mechanically applied, and can impose their own outline pattern, and thus tend to "erase" or erode the serial functions [movement 5 of *marteau*. L.K.].'

3. The existence of a greater or smaller harmonic tension depends on the size of the pitch field along the vertical. If the pitches build a wide field, the harmonic tension is smaller than with the same pitches in a narrow field. This feature connects serial music with traditional music. The difference lies only in the interval composition of the vertical aspect (this will be discussed further). A maximum tension produces a cluster of semitone intervals. Therefore the cluster plays the part of a noise in serial music. Boulez (like many serialists) uses the cluster restrictedly, e.g., in his Third Sonata, in *Structures II* (*Chapitre 2*), and in some other compositions. Boulez does not object to using the cluster (like other kinds of noise); however, he is against using it out of the hierarchic system. Boulez writes:[¶]

'Now that we have an organism like the series, whose hierarchy is no longer based on the principle of identity by transposition, but, on the contrary, on localised and variable deductions, noise can be integrated

---

† See op.cit., p.108, where Boulez gives examples of transformation by means of density.
‡ E.g., see Henck, *Karlheinz Stockhausen's Klavierstück X*, p.29.
§ Op. cit., p.111. See also pp. 112–115, where the composer gives a detailed description of the parameter. In p.115 he shows that the notion of tessitura can refer to pitch, duration, dynamics.
¶ Op.cit., p.42. See also pp.43–44.

more logically into a formal construction, provided that the structures responsible for it are based on its own criteria.'

Thus Boulez really speaks about a transition scale from sound to noise. Such a scale is also produced in the works of Stockhausen, e.g., in his Piano Piece X.[†] In summing up one can say that one of the typical features of instrumental music by the serial composers is the serialization of noises which can be considered one of the extreme achievements of serial music. At the same time usual sounds can be in such conditions that they will be perceived as colorful noise, or, vice versa, the sounds of instruments with an indefinite pitch could be perceived as having quasi–pitch (e.g., see the coda of movement 9 of *marteau*, *Gruppen* and other works by Stockhausen).[‡]

4.   The reasons of the lessening of the leading role of intervals in serial music by Boulez were discussed in the analysis of *marteau*. With other serialists the role of intervals also diminishes considerably. This is connected with the break from the thinking of the dodecaphonists, Webern especially. As mentioned in the analysis of *marteau*, the different serial techniques of Boulez lead to the elimination of the leading role of intervals, although they allow the composer to lay special stress on separate intervals, such as, e.g., in bars 54–102 of movement 2 of *marteau* or in *Structures II* (*Chapitre 2, Première et Deuxième pieces*). With Stockhausen the diminishing role of intervals is connected to a great extent with the use of statistical processes in the permutation of the series. The mixture of different intervals can be considered to be one of the characteristic features of the music of Boulez and other serialists.[§] The above does not mean indifference to intervals and their chaotic use; the latter is rather found in compositions with an absolutely automatic serial organization or based on total chance.

5.   Now the role of the minor second in serial music will be discussed. We begin with Webern, with whom a very rare (usually veiled) use of the minor second along the vertical is one of the most characteristic features of his music, both tonal (see *Entflieht auf leichten Kähnen*, op.2, 1908), atonal (beginning with op.3, 1908), and dodecaphonic especially.[¶] Webern rejected (probably by instinct) the use of the minor second along the vertical plane before leaving octave doubling and tonal organization. The use of the minor second along the horizontal becomes more rare in his later works. See, for example, his *Variations for Piano* (op.27, 1936), where there is not a single minor second along the vertical plane, while there are a few along the horizontal plane, or *String Quartet* (op.28, 1938), and other works.[*]

Boulez seems to have instinctively limited the use of the minor second already in his early works of the 40s (e.g., see movement 1 of the Second Sonata).[**] From 1951 to 1954, during the period of composing strictly serial works, Boulez and Stockhausen exclude completely the appearance of the minor second both along the vertical plane and along the horizontal plane (it appears as a rare exception, sometimes accidentally). E.g., in *Structures I*[***] there are no minor seconds along the vertical or the horizontal planes, with the exception of one, which must have got in by chance into *Structures Ib* (bar 168). There are almost no minor seconds either in *Oubli, Signal, Lapidé* (for a mixed

†   See Henck, *Karlheinz Stockhausen's Klavierstück X*.

‡   In *Gruppen* such instruments even perform series.

§   The mixture of different objects in general is one of the most characteristic features of serial thinking. That does not mean that the opposite process is impossible in serial music; vice versa, it can be used as a contrast.

¶   One of the rare exceptions is, e.g., movement 5 of *Six Bagatelles for String Quartet* (op.9, 1913), as well as the third piece out of *Four Pieces for Violin and Piano* (op.7, 1910), where the minor second is used for the finest straining of tension (with very low dynamics). In op.6 the minor second is also used to stress the sharp character of the music.

*   In his later works Webern uses the minor second along the horizontal, often for special purposes, such as creating a *lamento* character. See movements 3 and 5 of the Second Cantata (op.31, 1943).

**   It is interesting that even with Messiaen in *Mode de valeurs et d'intensités* (1949) the minor second happens rarely along the vertical, but often along the horizontal.

***   In this composition even major seconds and minor thirds are relatively rarely used along the vertical.

chorus, 1952). See also the works of Stockhausen: *Kontrapunkte* (five minor seconds only), Piano Pieces I–VIII, except VI (one minor second in Piece I, none in II–IV, in V and VIII one in each, several in VII). *Zeitmasze* (here the number of minor seconds grows a little; still they do not play almost any special part, with the exception of e.g., bars 338–349, 279 and a few others, where the character of the music is somewhat intensified). It is interesting that the avoidance of the minor second at that time seems to belong to Boulez and Stockhausen only (they were most faithful to Webern's ideas and brought the development of that trend to its peak), while Italian serialists Nono and Berio used this interval rather often.

Beginning with *marteau*, the transition to the use of the minor second can be observed. In the first cycle this interval is almost absent, in the second cycle (especially in bars 54–102 of movement 2) it is present, though not to a great extent, but then in movement 5 there are quite a few minor seconds (especially in the shape of trills). In Stockhausen's *Piano Piece VI* (1954–55) some sections often use minor seconds along the vertical. In *Piano Piece IX* this interval plays a very important part, being in the structure of the main chord. Thus, since about the late '50s both composers lift the ban from the minor second, but still they use it rather for special purposes than more neutrally, like other intervals. E.g., in movement 3 of the Third Sonata the minor second is used in *Blocs* only and only along the vertical, while *Mélange* and *Points* do not have a single semitone. In the following twenty years it is generally characteristic of Boulez to use the minor second mainly along the vertical plane, probably with the purpose of producing sharp chords typical of him, these chords sometimes approaching noise in their sounding (see movement 3 of the Third Sonata, *Structures II*, *Eclat*, *Rituel*, etc.), or with the purpose of some sharpening of the soft character of the music (*Improvisations sur Mallarmé 1,2,3*).

Since the late '50s, with the spread of clusters the minor second begins playing a great part in the music of Ligeti, Penderecki and many others. In some works of Ligeti the minor second is the most important and even almost the only interval. E.g., see *Atmosphères* and movement 1 of the Concerto for Cello with Orchestra. The use of the minor second in different ways is characteristic of him, as well as of Penderecki (e.g., along the vertical only; see the beginning of movement 2 of the above Concerto).

The avoidance of the minor second by Webern, Boulez and Stockhausen is due to that interval having a striking sharpness, which makes it stand out from the other intervals. Avoiding that interval is not a law of serial music, but a historical trend. Thus, the full chromatic system was used, while semitones were avoided, which resulted, in a wider sense, in a special sound world and style. The absence of the minor second softened the music to some extent and increased its abstract character. The latter quality may have been especially important for Boulez and Stockhausen. The avoidance of semitones resulted in a special register disposition of sounds. As mentioned in the analysis of *marteau*, with Boulez this caused the formation of vertical twelve–sound rows, which often consisted of sections of a wholetone scale.

Thus, after the serial harmony of the beginning of the 50s with its avoidance of semitones, a so to say anti–Webern "explosion" took place, where the minor second became almost the basis of harmony. Both these extremes contrast modern harmony to the more traditional one (including even Schoenberg). It is not accidental that the avoidance of semitones was historically the initial tendency, and their exclusive use the following one, since the former trend is less noticeable and softens the harmony to some extent, while the latter one leads to sonorities close to colorful noise.

Thus, we have discussed some features of the serial organization of Boulez and of his harmonic thinking. We shall make a preliminary attempt at summarizing the most essential characteristics of the serial thinking and organization of the two most important serial composers, Boulez and Stockhausen. We bear in mind the relatively dominant features, leaving out the secondary cases where the composers behave differently, or even in the opposite way.

| *Boulez* | *Stockhausen* |
|---|---|
| 1. Basic role of the general series (linked with the numerical row) in building the serial organization. | Basic role of the numerical row for building the serial organization. |
| 2. Functional methods of generation. | Statistical methods of generation. |
| 3. A somewhat greater role of pitch organization which probably influences the organization of duration. | A somewhat greater role of temporal organization. |
| 4. Pitch series of partly symmetrical structure with isomorphic figures. | Usually completely symmetrical series (often of all intervals). |
| 5. Arithmetic progression of durations. | Geometric progression of durations. |
| 6. Interest in the use of transpositions. | Interest in the use of permutations. |
| 7. Multiplied harmony. | Harmony based on the series and its permutations. |
| 8. Limited aleatorics ("prepared chance"[†]). | Unlimited aleatorics based on serial organization or serial thinking at least ("statistical chance"[‡]). |
| 9. Usually many–movement works. | Usually one–movement works. |
| 10. Interest in static evolution. | Interest in dynamic evolution. |

In addition the difference should be mentioned in the philosophical concepts which to some extent influenced the serial method of thinking of the two composers. To a great extent Boulez was close to the general philosophical ideas of Louis Rougier (as well as the physicist L. Brillouin and some others),[§] while Stockhausen was guided by the ideas of the physicist Werner Meyer–Eppler.

It should also be noted that the serial music of Boulez is more abstract in nature than that of Stockhausen, which in itself has little connection with the differences of serial organizations, but results from the general musical thinking of the two composers.

Serial organization had an influence (sometimes great) on the music both of younger composers born in the 30s, and on the composers who, for some reasons, joined the *avant–garde* only in the mid–50s (like Ligeti). Many of the composers started composing some music with serial organization (or under its great influence). The main achievement of those composers usually lies in the renewal of sonorous features of music. At the same time they have fewer inventions in the field of form. The influence of serial music varies with them and is the following:

*1. The use of series.*   In spite of the new achievement in musical sonority, the pitch material (as well as durations and other parameters) can be connected with the series, which appears periodically in veiled form or not (sometimes in its four main forms and transpositions). In such cases there is a return to Schoenberg, but in contrast to the latter, the series builds only a part of the pitch material (less often all of it). Such compositions are essentially non–serial, but quasi–dodecaphonic. Often a sequence of 10–12 different sounds is used instead of a series (since there is a trend towards non–repetition), which resembles a "free atonal" organization. With all this the organization of compositions can have many new characteristics. See some works of Penderecki, Globokar and many others.

---

† Boulez, *Conversations with Célestin Deliège*, p.105.
‡ Op.cit., p.84.
§ See *Boulez on Music Today*, pp.30–32, and others. Rougier probably must have played an important part in the philosophical development of Boulez.

*2. The influence of the general ideas of serialism on building a more or less independent organization without using a series.*   One of the most clear examples is the music of Ligeti, who modified the serial principles. Ligeti writes that he took from serialism, for example, the principle of choice and systematization of elements and operations. The composer points out that his methods of composing remained serial in a very wide sense, but without the use of series.[†]

Thus, on a large plane the development of musical language and its organization towards serialism can be presented as follows:

1)   1908/9–1923, the period of so–called free atonality;

2)   1924–1951, dodecaphonic organization;

3)   1951–1965,[‡] serial organization.

The relatively short period of development of serialism may be tentatively explained by the following causes:

1)   Inner causes:
    a)   serialization of all the parameters complicates greatly the organization;[§]
    b)   the complexity of serial organization makes difficulties in creating the composition and does not always give the desired results;[¶] it does not allow any considerable deepening and developing of the serial system, though formally it is not limited;
    c)   serialism is the last stage in the development of music with the series as the basis of material, and the last stage in the development of a phenomenon can be very intense and short.

2)   Outer causes:
    a)   the development of technology and the use of electronic devices, whose enormous sound field and other parameters do not directly correspond to serial organization;
    b)   an interest by the younger generation of composers in new inventions in the sound of music itself at the expense of simplifying the organization of other parameters.[*]

All these causes have influenced to various extents the shortening of the period of development of serialism. The development was very stormy, bright, changing considerably the previous concepts of musical thinking and organization and influencing essentially the further development of music.

---

[†]   See Ligeti, *Fragen und Antworten von mir selbst*, p.513.
[‡]   Practically the main development of serialism finished about the mid–60s.
[§]   It also usually prevents singling out one parameter at the expense of the others. Therefore many composers attempted to find other ways of organizing music.
[¶]   This is one of the reasons of incompleteness of some Boulez' compositions and his dissatisfaction with some of his compositions.
[*]   Hence the decrease of the number of composers writing serial music.

# Bibliography

## I Books and Articles by Pierre Boulez

*a) Books*

*Boulez on Music Today*, Faber, London, 1971, trans. by Susan Bradshaw and Richard Rodney Bennett, originally published
    as *Musikdenken heute–1*, Schott, Mainz, 1963 and *Penser la musique aujourd'hui*, Gonthier, Paris, 1963
*Notes of an Apprenticeship*, Knopf, New York, 1968, trans. by Herbert Weinstock, originally published as *Relevés d'apprenti*,
    Seuil, Paris, 1966
*Werkstatt–Texte*, Propyläen, Frankfurt and Berlin, 1972
*Anhaltspunkte*, Belser, Stuttgart and Zurich, 1975
*Conversations with Célestin Deliège*, Eulenburg, London, 1977, originally published as *Par volonté et par hasard: entretiens
    avec Célestin Deliège*, Seuil, Paris, 1975

*b) Some Articles not Published in Notes of an Apprenticeship*

*Sonate, que me veux-tu?*, in Perspectives of New Music, Vol.1, No.2, 1963, pp.32–44
*Style ou idée?*, in Musique en jeu, No.4, Seuil, Paris, October 1971, pp. 4–14
*Über meine 'Structures pour deux pianos'*, from the unpublished article *Nécessité d'une orientation esthétique*, Addendum to
    the record of *Structures* I, II, Wergo No. 60011
*Mahler aktuell?*, in Gustav Mahler in Wien, ed. S. Wiesmann, Belser, Stuttgart and Zurich, 1976
*Through Schoenberg to the Future*, in Journal of the Arnold Schoenberg Institute, Vol.2, No.2, February 1978, pp.121–125

## II Interviews with Pierre Boulez

Bornoff, Jack, *Music, Musicians and Communication: Five Interviews*, in Cultures: Music and Society, Vol.1, No.1, Off Print,
    Unesco and la Baconnière, 1972
Fleuret, Maurice, in Le Nouvel Observateur, Paris, 5 January 1976, pp.64–66, 68
Hall, Barry, in Music and Musicians, September 1965, London, pp.18, 25
Jack, Adrian, *Boulez Answers Some Questions*, in Music and Musicians, November 1973, London, pp.32–36

Jameux, Dominique, *Pierre Boulez: sur Polyphonie X et Poésie pour pouvoir*, in Musique en jeu, No.16, Seuil, Paris, November 1974

Mayer, Hans, *Der Interpret von der Objektivität der Partitur*, in Wille und Zufall, Belser, Stuttgart and Zurich, 1977

Oesch, Hans, in Melos/Neue Zeitschrift für Musik, No.4, Schott, July–August 1976, Mainz, pp.293–296

Peskó, Zoltán, *Musical Aspects in Today's Musical Theatre*, in Tempo, No.127, London, December 1978, pp.2–9, originally published in Melos, Schott, Mainz, September–October 1973

Schmidt, Felix and Hohmeyer, Jürgen, *Sprengt die Opernhäuser in die Luft*, in Der Spiegel, No.40, Hamburg, 25 September 1967

Stürzbecher, Ursula, in Werkstattgespräche mit Komponisten, Gerig, Cologne, 1971, pp.46–57

Tomek, Otto, *Lösungen für unsere Zeit finden!*, in Neue Zeitschrift für Musik, No.2, Schott, Mainz, 1971, pp.62–68

# III Works on Pierre Boulez

Baron, Carol K., *An Analysis of the Pitch Organization in Boulez's 'Sonatine' for Flute and Piano*, in Current Musicology, No.20, 1975, pp.87–95

Bowen, Meirion, *Boulez—the Medium and the Message*, in Records and Recording, No.203, August 1974, pp.16–19

Bracanin, Philip, *The Abstract System as Compositional Matrix: An Examination of Some Applications by Nono, Boulez and Stockhausen*, in Studies in Music, No.5, University of Western Australia Press, Nedlands, Western Australia, 1971 (an analysis of Boulez' *Structures Ic* is published here), pp.99–109

Bradshaw, Susan, *...explosante-fixe...*, in Tempo, No.106, London, September 1973, pp.58–59

Bradshaw, Susan and Bennett, Richard Rodney, *In Search of Boulez*, in Music and Musicians, London, January and August 1963, pp.10–13; 14–18, 50

Brenneke, Wilfried, *Boulez* in Die Musik in Geschichte und Gegenwart, ed. F. Blume, Supplementary Vol.15, Bärenreiter, Kassel etc., 1973, pp.1007–13

Chanan, Michael, *Boulez's Eclat/Multiples*, in Tempo XCV, London, Winter 1970/71, pp.30–33

Cross, Anthony, *The Significance of Aleatoricism in Twentieth-Century Music*, in The Music Review, Vol. 29, No. 4, 1968, pp.305–322

Cross, Anthony, *Form and Expression in Boulez' Don*, in The Music Review, Vol. 36, No. 3, August 1975, pp.215–230

Derrien, Jean-Pierre, *Dossier: Pierre Boulez*, in Musique en jeu, No.1, Seuil, Paris, November 1970, pp.103–132

Fink, Michael, *Pierre Boulez: A Selective Bibliography*, in Current Musicology, No.13, 1972, pp.135–150

Fuhrmann, Roderich, *Pierre Boulez: Structures I*, in Perspektiven Neuer Musik, ed. D. Zimmerschied, Schott, Mainz, 1974, pp.170–187

Gerlach, Reinhard, *Pierre Boulez und Stéphane Mallarmé. Ein Fragment über das Artifizielle*, in Über Musik und Sprache, ed. R. Stephan, Schott, Mainz, 1974, pp.70–92

Griffiths, Paul, *Boulez*, Oxford University Press, London etc. 1978

Grimm, Jim, *Formaspekte der 2. Klaviersonate von Boulez*, in Schweizerische Musikzeitung, No.4, July–August, 1972

Häusler, Josef, *Einige Aspekte des Wort-Ton-Verhältnisses*, in Die Musik der sechziger Jahre, ed. R. Stephan, Schott, Mainz, 1972, pp.65–76

Häusler, Josef, *Klangfelder und Formflächen: Kompositorishe Grundprinzipien im II. Band der Structures von Pierre Boulez*, Addendum to the record of *Structures I, II*, Wergo No. 60011

Heinsheimer, Hans, *New York, Abschied von Boulez*, in Melos/Neue Zeitschrift für Musik, No.3, Schott, Mainz, 1977, pp.239–240

Jack, Adrian, *Boulez Premiere*, in Music and Musicians, London, April 1975, pp.10–11

Jack, Adrian, *Modern* in Music and Musicians, London, June 1975, pp.49–51

Koblyakov, Lev, *Analysis of Boulez' Structures Ia*, Jerusalem, July 1974, not published

Koblyakov, Lev, *P. Boulez' 'Le marteau sans maître': Analysis of Pitch Structure*, in Zeitschrift für Musiktheorie, Döring, Herrenberg, 1977, No.1, pp.24–39

Kohn, Karl, *Current Chronicle: Los Angeles*, in The Musical Quarterly, XLIX, 1963, pp.360–69

Ligeti, György, *Pierre Boulez: Decision and Automatism in Structure Ia*, in Die Reihe, No.4, 1960, pp.36–62

Ligeti, György, *Some Remarks on Boulez' 3rd Piano Sonata*, in Die Reihe, No.5, 1961, pp.56–58

Northcott, Bayan, *Boulez's Theory of Composition*, in Music and Musicians, London, December 1971, pp.32–36

Oesch, Hans, *Isorhythmische Strukturen im Orient und Abendland*, in Melos, No.1, Schott, Mainz, 1970, pp.12–14

Peck, Agnès, *Parole, silence et musique: René Char et Pierre Boulez*, in Musique en jeu, No.5, Seuil, Paris, November 1971, pp.138–140

Peyser, Joan, *Boulez. Composer, Conductor, Enigma*, Schirmer, New York, 1976

Philippot, Michel, *Pierre Boulez Today*, in Perspectives of New Music, Fall–Winter, 1966, pp.153–160

Piencikowski, Robert T., *René Char et Pierre Boulez. Esquisse analytique du 'Marteau sans maître'*, in Schweizer Beiträge zur Musikwissenschaft, No.4, ed. J. Stenzl, Haupt, Bern and Stuttgart, 1980, pp.193–264

Schaeffer, Pierre, *A la recherche d'une musique concrète*, Seuil, Paris, 1952, pp.190–91

Schiffer, Brigitte, *Pierre Boulez: 'Notations'*, in Schweizerische Musikzeitung, No.5, September/October 1980, pp.315–17

Scriabine, Marina, *Pierre Boulez et la musique concrète*, in La Revue Musicale, No.215, Paris, 1952, pp.14–15

Stahnke, Manfred, *Struktur und Ästhetik bei Boulez. Untersuchungen zum Formanten 'Trope' der Dritten Klaviersonate*, Wagner, Hamburg, 1979

Stephan, Rudolf, *Bemerkungen zu Pierre Boulez' Komposition von René Chars 'Klage der verliebten Eidechse'* (1969), in Zur musikalischen Analyse, ed. G. Schuhmacher, Wissenschaftliche Buchgesellschaft, Darmstadt, 1974, pp.441–51

Stockhausen, Karlheinz, *Music and Speech*, in Die Reihe, No.6, 1964, pp.40–64

Stoianowa, Iwanka, *Pli selon pli: portrait de Mallarmé*, in Musique en jeu, No.11, Seuil, Paris, June 1973, pp.75–98

Stoianowa, Iwanka, *La Troisième Sonate de Boulez et le projet mallarméen du Livre*, No.16, Seuil, Paris, November 1974, pp.9–28

Stoianowa, Iwanka, *Verbe et son 'centre et absence'*, in Musique en jeu, No.16, Seuil, Paris, November 1974, pp.79–102

Stoianowa, Iwanka, *Narrativisme, téléologie et invariance dans l'oeuvre musical: à propos de 'Rituel' de Pierre Boulez*, in Musique en jeu, No.25, Seuil, Paris, November 1976, pp.14–31

Sutton, D.R., *Pli selon pli*, in Music and Musicians, December 1976, London, pp.28–31

Trenkamp, Anne, *The Concept of 'Alea' in Boulez's 'Constellation–Miroir'*, in Music and Letters, Vol.LVII, No.1, London, January 1976, pp.1–10

Young, Lynden De, *Pitch Order and Duration Order in Boulez' Structure Ia*, in Perspectives of New Music, Vol.16, No.2, Spring–Summer 1978, pp.27–34

## IV Literature about Other Modern Composers and Modern Music in General

Carter, Elliott, *Current Chronicle: New York. [Edward Steuermann],* in The Musical Quarterly, Vol.52, No.1, January 1966

Eimert, Herbert and Humpert, Hans Ulrich, *Das Lexikon der elektronischen Musik*, Bosse, Regensburg, 1973

Faas, Ekbert, *Interview with Karlheinz Stockhausen Held August 11, 1976*, in Interface, Vol.6, 1977, pp.187–204

Harvey, Jonathan, *The Music of Stockhausen*, Faber, London, 1975

Henck, Herbert, *Karlheinz Stockhausen's Klavierstück IX*, in Musik und Zahl, ed. G. Schnitzler, Verlag für systematische Musikwissenschaft, Bad–Godesberg, 1976, pp.171–200

Henck, Herbert, *Karlheinz Stockhausen's Klavierstück X*, (Second Edition), Neuland Musikverlag Herbert Henck, Cologne, 1980

Ligeti, György, *Metamorphoses of Musical Form* in Die Reihe, No.5, pp.5–19

Ligeti, György, *Fragen und Antworten von mir selbst*, in Melos, No.12, Schott, Mainz, 1971, pp.509–516

Meyer–Eppler, Werner, *Statistic and Psychologic Problems of Sound*, in Die Reihe, No.1, pp.55–61

Stockhausen, Karlheinz, *... how time passes...* in Die Reihe, No.3, pp.10–40

Toop, Richard, *Messiaen/Goeyvaerts, Fano/Stockhausen, Boulez*, in Perspectives of New Music, Fall–Winter 1974, pp.141–169

Toop, Richard, *Stockhausen's Konkrete Etüde*, in The Music Review, November 1976, pp.295–300

Wörner, Karl H., *Stockhausen: Life and Work*, Faber, London, 1973

# Comments

## Comments on the First Cycle

### General Remarks

1. Dotted lines circle certain sounds that seem to belong to two adjacent groups. As a rule there is a rest in one of these groups at that moment.

2. Certain group designations in the score are given in round brackets since their origin is not quite clear. Possibly it results from specific deviations from the multiplication pattern or from confusion of different groups; misprints are also possible. Some cases are considered below.

3. Groups of main fields are given in square brackets.

4. Roman figures note the number of the domain.

5. In the 1st movement of *Marteau* the letter unifying several groups shows the vertical field.

### Movement 1

1. Group ca of domain III includes an alien E flat (as sounding)[†]; see bar 31, a grace note in the flute part, and bars 91–92 in the vibraphone part. Boulez seems to have included E flat in this group in his scheme by chance. When using Diagram I for *Tombeau* an extra E flat is also included in the group ca. See bars 84–85 for the piano in *Tombeau*.

2. In the first half of bar 57 group eb is evidently used. In the flute part instead of A natural there should be G natural (misprint in the score, see the original publication).

3. In bar 84 from the point of view of field and group alternation there should evidently stand group ed. Sound D sharp is missing and in the flute part there should be F natural instead of A natural.

---

† All the sound designations for the flute are given as they are denoted in writing, unless stated otherwise.

4.  In bar 90 of the flute part sounds F sharp and G natural are used to duplicate the guitar and viola sounds; no such group exists independently in domain III.

## Movement 3

1.  In bar 8 (group bd) F natural sounds twice instead of C natural.
2.  In the second half of bar 37 (group de) of the flute part there should be A flat instead of A natural.

## Movement 7

1.  In the first part of bar 16 there evidently should be group bc; the vibraphone then should have E flat instead of E natural.
2.  In bar 19 of the guitar part, instead of G sharp there should evidently be G natural which would also complement the simultaneously sounding vibraphone group.
3.  In bar 25 of the flute part there is supplementary C natural (as sounding) as a grace note.

## Coda of movement 9

1.  In bar 135 groups bd and bc are mixed up; instead of A natural there should be A flat.
2.  In bars 154, 155, 158 there is F sharp sounding complementarily as a grace note.
3.  In bar 166 there should be A natural instead of F natural.
4.  Groups bc and db (grace notes only) are brought together in bar 167. Instead of the first C sharp there should be C natural; evidently, it does not appear here to avoid conflict of octave with a clearly sounding C natural, which complements group db in bar 168.
5.  Bars 168–169 (almost entirely) display group bb; the missing sound F sharp appears at the beginning of the next group dc. Besides, there are three superfluous sounds: A flat, F natural, E natural. The given passage is similar to the conclusion of movement 1 of the First Sonata by Boulez.

# Comments on the Second Cycle

## I  COMMENTS ON SCHEMES

1.  The length of the arrows renders the duration of series, where 1 mm along the horizontal in the scheme scale equals one semiquaver in duration.
2.  If the arrow points right, that means that the series is presented in original motion (O); if the arrow points left, the retrograde motion of the series is assumed (R).
3.  Vertical dotted lines in Schemes I and IV are drawn from the end of a series to the beginning of the next series, if the latter begins without break.

## Scheme I

1.  The beginning of each section is marked by a short vertical line put over the Scheme.

2.  The series C sharp (bars 33–36 and 43–45), D natural (bars 36–39), and E natural (bars 36–40) are presented on two levels. Hence in the Scheme two parallel lines are drawn connected by a diagonal dotted arrow.

3.  The C sharp series in section III is divided into two parts presented in bars 24–26 and 30–32.

## Schemes II and III

1.  Each multiplied series is marked by two, three or four lines in accordance with the number of simple series it includes. The distance between these lines along the vertical depends on the multiplication intervals, where a semitone equals 1 mm (along the vertical). The numbers alongside with the series also mark the multiplication intervals.

2.  In Scheme III two B flat series in bars 81 and 84 are marked by small crosses; the composer shortened their duration by two semiquavers.

## II COMMENTS ON TABLES OF SERIES

We present Tables of series for section I–IX of the second cycle, since without them it is almost impossible to distinguish the series, even with the score where all these series are specifically marked and with the schemes.

1.  Before each series its main data are noted above. The initial numerals are the numbers of bars. The encircled numbers mark the durations, the next numbers mark the dynamics. Then the series "name" and its direction (O or R) are noted. After that the transpositions are given, their pointers corresponding to simple series moving down from above. The multiplication intervals are noted after that (the numerals marking the number of semitones). Sometimes the symbols "." or "+" are given pointing to the fact that in the appended score a series is marked by dots or crosses alongside with duration data for easier identification. In sections VIII and IX the numbers are also noted representing the duration selected for a uniform sequence of attacks. If the arrow alongside it is directed to the right, the uniform sequence of attacks is determined by their beginnings; if the arrow is directed to the left, their sequence is determined by endings of their durations.

2.  Alongside each sound of a series its duration is noted (in a circle, if the sound has a full duration in the score; in brackets if the sound duration is noted partly). With multiplied series the duration marking refers to several sounds. Rhythmical figures render the attacks of the percussion instrument. The dynamic markings under them are the same as in the score, although in some cases the attacks of the percussion instrument serve two or more series. Hence the dynamic markings do not always reflect the dynamic level of a series.

    If a sound is absent for some reason, it is given in square brackets and there is an arrow on its left. If the skipped sound is not in the range of the required duration of another simultaneous series, it is also noted in square brackets, but the arrow is on its right. If the sound is in the facsimile score only, alongside it the marking "or" is given. In multiplied series, for better structure understanding, there is a notation even of repeated sounds which are rejected in the multiplication process and are absent in the score; they are noted without square brackets.

In sections VIII and IX, if an attack is not presented at the required time, the symbol "$\sim$" is noted under it.

Two kinds of two–level series are found in sections IV and V, and also in bars 103–114 of section VI:

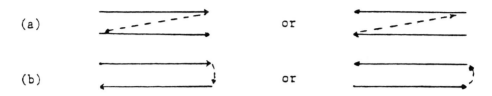

In case (a) the series direction (O or R) can be determined, as both its parts have the same direction. In case (b) both directions can be taken into account (or the direction of the series part beginning first can be given preference to). See Schemes I and III.

3. To the right of the series a control scale is given, where the correlation of duration and dynamics can be found, which is shown by horizontal lines with brackets. In multiplied series the scale is created by the upper sound of each group of sounds. If there are deviations in the sphere of dynamics, the dynamic step theoretically required is marked below in brackets. In some places arrows show two dynamic steps, which should switch places.

# III COMMENTS ON THE SCORE WITH ANALYSIS

The present score should be studied with the Tables of series.

1. The duration of a note is marked by an encircled number over the note usually. If the duration is not fully noted, the number is in brackets and there is a dotted line (under the note usually), which shows the assumed duration.

2. Section VI.
   a) With multiplication, if the attack sounds are presented by one instrument and have a simultaneous attack (bars 54–74 of movement 2), they are noted as said in point 1.
   b) If the sounds of one attack are presented by different instruments simultaneously, they are united by one vertical bracket, while the attack duration is noted once over the upper sound in the score and there is a dotted line under it. Hence if the duration of the given sound is fully noted, there is no dotted line, although the other sounds of that attack may be noted incompletely.
   c) If the sounds of one attack are presented in turn, (bars 103–114 of movement 2; bars 47–105 of movement 4), the duration is noted once with the first sound. If the sounds of one attack are distant from each other, a diagonal bracket unites them. This is of special importance in the second half of movement 4, where the sounds of the same attack can be presented by different instruments.

3. In sections I–V, VII and partly VI (bars 105–114 of movement 2) before the series beginning there is a short vertical line "|" (as the composer himself sometimes marked it).

4. The figures in square brackets mark a skipped attack.

5. Some series are marked by dots or crosses in accordance with the series in the Tables. In the "reprise" of section XI the D natural series is marked by dots, E natural by crosses, and B flat by dots.

# Appendix

Music Diagrams

| sections | series | direction | bars | instruments | durations | dynamics | index of dividing |
|---|---|---|---|---|---|---|---|
| I | f♮ | 0 | 1–3 | Fl., Xyl. | ①–④ | 9–12 | 3 |
| | g♮ | 0 | 1–3 | Alto, Xyl. | ①–④ | 9–12 | |
| | f# | 0 | 4–5 | Xyl. | ①–③ | 10–12 | 4 |
| | d♮ | 0 | 4–5 | Alto | ①–③ | 10–12 | |
| | c# | 0 | 5–6 | Xyl., Alto | ① | 12 | 12 |
| | b♮ | 0 | 6–8 | Fl. | ① ② | 11 12 | |
| | e♭ | 0 | 6–8 | Xyl. | ① ② | 11 12 | 6 |
| | g# | 0 | 6–8 | Alto | ① ② | 11 12 | |
| | b♭ | 0 | 8–11 | Fl. | ①–⑥ | 7–12 | |
| | e♮ | 0 | 8–11 | Xyl. | ①–⑥ | 7–12 | 2 |
| | d♮ | 0 | 8–11 | Alto | ①–⑥ | 7–12 | |
| II | f♮ | 0 | 12–18 | Xyl. | ④–⑥ | 7–9 | 4 |
| | g♮ | R | 13–18 | Alto | ④–⑥ | 7–9 | |
| | a♮ | 0 | 11–18 | Xyl. | ⑤–⑧ | 5–8 | 3 |
| | f# | 0 | 12–18 | Alto | ⑤–⑧ | 5–8 | |
| | c# | 0 | 16–21 | Fl. | ①–⑥ | 7–12 | 2 |
| | e♭ | R | 19–22 | Xyl. | ④ | 9 | |
| | g# | R | 19–22 | Xyl. | ③ | 10 | 12 |
| | b♮ | R | 19–25 | Xyl. | ⑦ | 6 | |
| | e♮ | R | 19–21 | Alto | ① ② | 11 12 | |
| | b♭ | 0 | 19–23 | Alto | ③ ④ | 9 10 | 6 |
| | d♮ | R | 19–24 | Alto | ⑤ ⑥ | 7 8 | |
| III | g♮ | R | 22–26 | Xyl. | ①–⑥ | 7–12 | 2 |
| | f♮ | R | 22–26 | Xyl. | ①–⑥ | 7–12 | |
| | f# | 0 | 21–25 | Alto | ⑤ ⑥ | 7 8 | 6 |
| | d♮ | 0 | 23–26 | Alto | ③ ④ | 9 10 | |
| | c# | R | 24–26, 30–32 | Fl. | ④–⑥ | 7–9 | 4 |
| | b♮ | 0 | 25–32 | Xyl. | ⑤–⑧ | 5–8 | |
| | e♭ | R | 26–29 | Xyl. | ①–④ | 9–12 | 3 |
| | g# | 0 | 27–30 | Xyl. | ①–④ | 9–12 | |
| | d♮ | 0 | 24–31 | Alto | ⑧ | 5 | |
| | e♮ | 0 | 25–31 | Alto | ⑤ | 8 | 12 |
| | b♭ | R | 26–29 | Alto | ② ←→ | 9 | |

| sections | series | direction | bars | instruments | durations | dynamics | index of dividing |
|---|---|---|---|---|---|---|---|
| IV | g♮ | 0 | 29–34 | Alto | ⑤ | 8 | 12 |
| | f♮ | R | 30–33 | Xyl. | ③ | 10 | |
| | f# | 0 | 30–33 | Xyl. | ①–⑥ | 7–12 | 2 |
| | a♮ | 0 | 31–34 | Alto | ①–⑥ | 7–12 | |
| | c# | OR | 33–36 | Xyl., Alto | ⑦ ⑧ | 5 6 | 6 |
| | b♮ | 0 | 33–37 | Xyl. | ④–⑥ | 7–9 | |
| | e♭ | R | 34–36 | Alto | ①–③ | 10–12 | 4 |
| | g# | 0 | 34–36 | Fl. | ①–③ | 10–12 | |
| | d♮ | 0 | 36–39 | Fl. | ⑤–⑧ | 5–8 | |
| | e♮ | R | 36–40 | Alto | ⑤–⑧ | 5–8 | 3 |
| | b♭ | R | 37–40 | Xyl. | ①–④ | 9–12 | |
| V | f♮ | 0 | 40–43 | Alto | ① ② | 11 12 | 6 |
| | g♮ | R | 42–47 | Xyl. | ⑤ ⑥ ←→ | 11 12 | |
| | f# | R | 40–43 | Alto | ② | 11 | 12 |
| | a♮ | R | 40–47 | Xyl. | ⑦ | 6 | |
| | c# | OR | 43–45 | Alto | ①②,5,⑧ | 5–8, 9–12 | 3 |
| | b♮ | 0 | 45–49 | Alto, Fl. | ①–⑥ | 7–12 | |
| | g# | 0 | 45–49 | Fl., Xyl.Alto | ①–⑥ | 7–12 | 2 |
| | e♭ | 0 | 46–49 | Alto, Xyl.Fl. | ①–⑥ | 7–12 | |
| | e♮ | 0 | 49–50 | Xyl., Alto | ①–③ | 10–12 | |
| | d♮ | R | 49–53 | Fl. | ④–⑥ | 7–9 | 4 |
| | b♭ | 0 | 51–53 | Xyl., Alto | ①–③ | 10–12 | |

| sections | f♮ / g♮ | f# / a♮ | c# | g# / e♭ / b♮ | d♮ / e♮ / b♭ |
|---|---|---|---|---|---|
| I | 3 | 4 | 12 | 6 | 2 |
| II | 4 | 3 | 2 | 12 | 6 |
| III | 2 | 6 | 4 | 3 | 12 |
| IV | 12 | 2 | 6 | 4 | 3 |
| V | 6 | 12 | 3 | 2 | 4 |

| series | durations | number of series | general number of series | index of dividing |
|---|---|---|---|---|
| f♮ | ①–⑥ | 2 | | 2 |
| | ①–④ | 2 | 8 | 3 |
| | ④–⑥ | 4 | | 4 |
| g♮ | ①–⑥ | 2 | | 2 |
| | ①–④ | 2 | 8 | 3 |
| | ④–⑥ | 4 | | 4 |
| f# | ⑤–⑧ | 5 | 10 | 3 |
| | ⑤ ⑥ | 5 | | 6 |
| a♮ | ①–③ | 5 | 9 | 4 |
| | ③ ④ | 4 | | 6 |
| c# | ①–⑥ | 5 | | 2 |
| | ④–⑥ | 4 | | 4 |
| | ① | 1 } | 12 | |
| | ② | 1 } 3 | | } 12 |
| | ③ | 1 } | | |
| g# | ①–④ | 4 } 5 | | 3 |
| | ⑤–⑧ | 1 } | | |
| | ① ② | 4 | 14 | 6 |
| | ③ | 3 } 5 | | } 12 |
| | ⑦ | 2 } | | |
| eb | ⑤–⑧ | 4 } 5 | | 3 |
| | ① ② | 1 } | | 6 |
| | ② | 1 } | 9 | |
| | ③ | 1 } 4 | | } 12 |
| | ④ | 1 } | | |
| | ⑦ | 1 } | | |
| b♮ | ①–④ | 3 | | } 3 |
| | ⑤–⑧ | 2 | | |
| | ① ② | 5 | 16 | 6 |
| | ③ | 3 } 6 | | } 12 |
| | ④ | 3 } | | |

| series | durations | number of series | general number of series | index of dividing |
|---|---|---|---|---|
| d♮ | ①–⑥ | 1 | | 2 |
| | ① ② | 2 | | |
| | ③ ④ | 2 } 6 | | } 6 |
| | ⑤ ⑥ | 2 } | 12 | |
| | ② | 1 } | | |
| | ⑤ | 3 } 5 | | } 12 |
| | ⑧ | 1 } | | |
| e♮ | ①–⑥ | 3 | | 2 |
| | ① ② | 2 } | | |
| | ③ ④ | 3 } 7 | | 6 |
| | ⑤ ⑥ | 2 } | 15 | |
| | ② | 2 } | | |
| | ⑤ | 1 } 5 | | } 12 |
| | ⑧ | 2 } | | |
| bb | ①–⑥ | 3 | | 2 |
| | ① ② | 2 } | | |
| | ③ ④ | 2 } 6 | | 6 |
| | ⑤ ⑥ | 2 } | 18 | |
| | ② | 3 } | | |
| | ⑤ | 3 } 9 | | } 12 |
| | ⑧ | 3 } | | |

indices of dividing

series   2   3   4   6   12

f♮ g♮
f# a♮
c#
g# eb b♮
d♮ e♮ bb

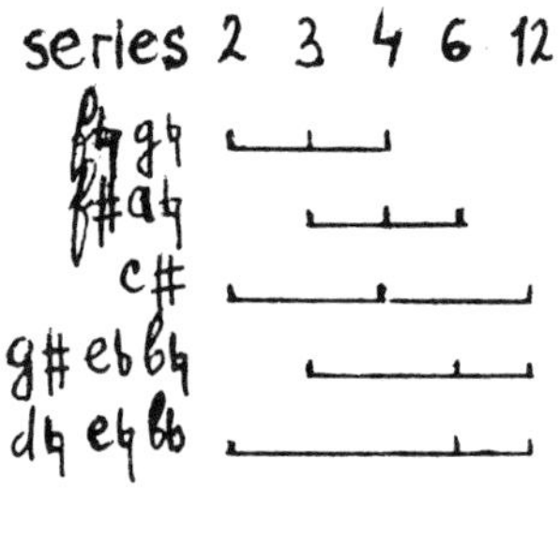

| series | bars | durations | dynamics | index of dividing | direction | intervals of multiplication | transpositions | instruments |
|---|---|---|---|---|---|---|---|---|
| f♮ | 54-56 | ①-④ | 5-8 | 3 | 0 | 3 | 5↓, 4↑ | Alto |
| | 57-59 | ①-④ | 5-8 | | R | 3 | 2↓, 5↓ | Xyl |
| | 59-64 | ④-⑥ | 4-6 | 4 | 0 | 2 | 6, 4↑ | Alto |
| | 59-64 | ④-⑥ | 4-6 | | R | 2 | 4↓, 6 | Alto |
| | 59-64 | ④-⑥ | 4-6 | | R | 2 | 0, 2↓ | Xyl. |
| | 59-64 | ④-⑥ | 4-6 | | 0 | 2 | 2↓, 4↓ | Xyl. |
| | 68-72 | ①-⑥ | 1-6 | 2 | R | 5 | 5↑, 0 | Alto |
| | 70-74 | ①-⑥ | 1-6 | | 0 | 5 | 0, 5↓ | Xyl. |
| g♮ | 54-56 | ①-④ | 5-8 | 3 | R | 3 | 4↓, 5↑ | Xyl. |
| | 57-59 | ①-④ | 5-8 | | 0 | 3 | 5↑, 2↑ | Alto |
| | 65-68 | ④-⑥ | 4-6 | 4 | 0 | 2 | 6, 4↑ | Xyl. |
| | 65-68 | ④-⑥ | 4-6 | | R | 2 | 4↓, 6 | Alto |
| | 65-68 | ④-⑥ | 4-6 | | 0 | 2 | 2↓, 4↓ | Xyl. |
| | 65-68 | ④-⑥ | 4-6 | | R | 2 | 0, 2↓ | Alto |
| | 68-72 | ①-⑥ | 1-6 | 2 | R | 1 | 0, 1↓ | Xyl. |
| | 70-73 | ①-⑥ | 1-6 | | 0 | 1 | 1↑, 0 | Alto |
| f# | 74-79 | ⑤-⑧ | 1-4 | 3 | R | $\frac{1}{2}$ | 3↓,4↓ 6 | |
| | 75-79 | ⑤-⑧ | 1-4 | | 0 | $\frac{1}{2}$ | 4↓,5↓,5↑ | |
| | 75-79 | ⑤ ⑥ | 5 6 | 6 | 0 | $\frac{1}{2}$ | 1↓,2↓,4↓ | |
| | 92-96 | ⑤-⑧ | 1-4 | 3 | R | 3 | 0, 3↓ | |
| | 92-97 | ⑤-⑧ | 1-4 | | 0 | 3 | 4↓,5↑ | |
| | 92-96 | ⑤ ⑥ | 5 6 | 6 | 0 | 3 | 3↑, 0 | |
| | 93-97 | ⑤ ⑥ | 5 6 | | R | 3 | 5↑, 2↑ | |
| | 97-102 | ⑤-⑧ | 1-4 | 3 | 0 | $\frac{1}{2}$ | 5↓,6,4↑ | |
| | 97-101 | ⑤, ⑥ | 5 6 | 6 | R | $\frac{1}{2}$ | 5↑,4↑,2↑ | |
| | 98-102 | ⑤ ⑥ | 5 6 | | 0 | $\frac{1}{2}$ | 4↑,3↑,1↑ | |
| a♮ | 79-82 | ①-③ | 1-3 | 4 | R | 3 | 0, 3↓ | |
| | 82-85 | ①-③ | 1-3 | | 0 | 3 | 3↑, 0 | |
| | 79-83 | ③ ④ | 3 4 | 6 | 0 | 3 | 5↓, 4↑ | |
| | 81-85 | ③ ④ | 3 4 | | R | 3 | 2↓, 5↓ | |
| | 85-87 | ①-③ | 1-3 | 4 | 0 | 2 | 5↓, 5↑ | |
| | 88-90 | ①-③ | 1-3 | | R | 2 | 3↓, 5↓ | |
| | 90-91 | ①-③ | 1-3 | | 0 | 2 | 4↓, 6 | |
| | 85-89 | ③ ④ | 3 4 | 6 | R | 1 | 5↑,4↑,3↑ | |
| | 89-91 | ③ ④ | 3 4 | | 0 | 1 | 5↓, 6, 5↑ | |

| bars | instruments | durations | dynamics | index of dividing | direction | intervals of multiplication | transpositions |
|---|---|---|---|---|---|---|---|
| 103 | Xyl., Alto | ① | 1  12 | } | + R | 4 | 1↓ 5↓ |
| 103–104 | Xyl. Alto | ② | 2  11 | 12 | + 0 | 4 | 5↓ 3↑ |
| 103–104 | Fl. | ③ | 3  10 | | +OR | 4 | 4↓ 4↑ |
| 105–107 | Alto | ①–⑥ | 7–12 | 2 | 0 | 4 | 3↑ 1↓ |
| 105–108 | Alto | ④–⑥ | 4–6 | 4 | R | 1/3 | 2↓ 3↓ 6 |
| 105–108 | Fl. | ①–⑥ | 7–12 | } | R | 4 | 6 2↑ |
| 107–110 | Fl. | ①–⑥ | 7–12 | 2 | 0 | 1/3 | 2↑ 1↑ 2↓ |
| 107–110 | Xyl. | ①–⑥ | 7–12 | | 0 | 4 | 2↑ 2↓ |
| 108–111 | Alto | ④–⑥ | 4–6, 7–9 | 4 | +OR | 1/3 | 5↑ 4↑ 1↑ |
| 111–114 | Alto | ④–⑥ | 4–6 | | +OR | 4 | 5↑ 1↑ |
| 111–113 | Xyl. | ①–⑥ | 1–6 | 2 | +OR | 1/3 | 3↓ 4↓ 5↑ |
| 111–114 | Fl. | ④–⑥ | 4–6 | 4 | +OR | 4 | 3↓ 5↑ |

| series | bars | durations | index of dividing | dynamics | index of dividing | direction | intervals of multiplication | transpositions |
|---|---|---|---|---|---|---|---|---|
| g# | 2–4 | ① ② | 6 | 56, 78 | 6 | O | 2/2 | 4↓, 6, 4↑ |
| | 5–7 | ①–④ | 3 | 9–12 | 3 | O | 2 | 6, 4↑ |
| | 9–15 | ⑦ | {12 | 7 | {12 | R | 2 | 5↑, 3↑ |
| | 13–16 | ③ | | 10 | | R | 2/2 | 3↓, 5↓, 5↑ |
| | 16–18 | ① ② | 6 | 1–12 | | O | 2/2 | 1↑, 1↓, 3↓ |
| | 19–21 | ③ | 12 | 1–12 | | R | 2 | 2↓, 4↓ |
| | 21–24 | ①–④ | {3 | 1–12 | 1 | R | 2 | 1↑, 1↓ |
| | 25–28 | ①–④ | | 1–12 | | O | 2/2 | 6, 4↑, 2↑ |
| | 29–33 | ③ | 12 | 1–12 | | R | 2/2 | 3↑, 1↑, 1↓ |
| | 34–36 | ① ② | {6 | 1–12 | | R | 2 | 4↓, 6 |
| | 36–40 | ①–④ | | 9–12 | 3 | O | 2/2 | 2↓, 4↓, 6 |
| | 36–44 | ⑦ | 12 | 6 | 12 | O | 2 | 4↑, 2↑ |
| | 40–47 | ⑤–⑧ | 3 | 5–8 | 3 | R | 2/2 | 1↓, 3↓, 5↓ |
| | 46–47 | ① ② | 6 | 12, 11 12 | 6 | R | 2 | 3↑, 1↑ |
| e♭ | 2–4 | ③ | {12 | 10 | {12 | O | 2/1 | 1↓, 3↓, 4↓ |
| | 6–7 | ② | | 3,4,9,10 | | R | 2/1 | 3↓, 5↓, 6 |
| | 9–14 | ⑤–⑧ | 3 | 44, 9–12 | 3 | R | 2/3 | 1↓, 3↓, 4↓, 5↓ |
| | 14–16 | ① ② | 6 | 56, 78 | 6 | O | 2/1 | 5↓, 5↑, 4↑ |
| | 16–21 | ⑤–⑧ | 3 | 5–8 | 3 | O | 2/1 | 5↓, 5↑, 4↑, 3↑ |
| | 22–28 | ⑦ | 12 | 1–12 | 1 | R | 2/1 | 5↑, 3↑, 2↑ |
| | 28–35 | ⑤–⑧ | {3 | 5–8 | {3 | O | 3 | 1↑, 2↓ |
| | 35–42 | ③–⑧ | | 5–8 | | R | 2/1 | 1↑, 1↓, 2↓ |
| | 42–45 | ④ | 12 | 1–12 | 1 | O | 2/1 | 5↑, 3↑, 2↑, 1↑ |
| b♮ | 1–4 | ①–④ | 3 | 1–4 | 3 | R | 3 | 2↑, 1↓ |
| | 5–8 | ④ | 12 | 5, 8 | 12 | O | 2 | 5↑, 3↑ |
| | 9–11 | ① ② | 6 | 12, 11 12 | 6 | O | 1 | 2↑, 1↑ |
| | 11–16 | ⑤–⑧ | 3 | 1–4 9–12 | 3 | R | 2 | 1↑, 1↓ |
| | 16–18 | ① ② | 6 | 1 2 | 6 | R | 2 | 2↓, 4↓ |
| | 16–19 | ③ | {12 | 3, 10 | {12 | R | 1 | 3↓, 4↓ |
| | 19–22 | ④ | | 4 | | O | 2 | 4↓, 6 |
| | 19–27 | ⑤–⑧ | {3 | 5–8 | {3 | R | 3 | 5↓, 4↑ |
| | 23–25 | ①–④ | | 1–4, 9–12 | | R | 1 | 4↑, 3↑ |
| | 26–29 | ③ | 12 | 3, 10 | 12 | R | 2 | 6, 4↑ |
| | 27–29 | ① ② | 6 | 11 12 | 6 | O | 3 | 4↑, 1↑ |
| | 29–33 | ①–④ | 3 | 1–12 | | R | 2 | 4↓, 6 |
| | 34–38 | ④ | 12 | 1–12 | | O | 2 | 1↓, 3↓ |
| | 39–41 | ① ② | 6 | 1–12 | 1 | R | 3 | 3↓, 6 |
| | 41–44 | ③ | 12 | 1–12 | | O | 2 | 3↑, 1↑ |
| | 44–46 | ① ② | 6 | 1–12 | | O | 1 | 1↓, 2↓ |

| series | bars | durations | dynamics | index of dividing | direction | intervals of multiplication | transpositions |
|---|---|---|---|---|---|---|---|
| d♮ | 47–50 | ① ② | 11 12 | | 0 | 3 | 1↑ 2↓ |
| | 47–52 | ③ ④ | 7 8 | 6 | 0 | 3 | 2↓ 5↓ |
| | 47–54 | ⑤ ⑥ | 9 10 | | 0 | 3 | 4↑ 1↑ |
| | 63–72 | ⑧ | 5 | | 0 | 2/3 | 5↓ 5↑ 2↑ |
| | 65–72 | ⑤ | 5 | 12 | 0 | 2/3 | 4↑ 2↑ 1↓ |
| | 67–70 | ② | 2 | | 0 | 2/3 | 1↑ 1↓ 4↓ |
| | 85–90 | ⑤ | 5 | | R | 1 | 4↓ 5↓ |
| | 86–90 | ①–⑥ | 1–6 | 2 | R | 1 | 5↑ 4↑ |
| | 86–90 | ③ ④ | 3 4 | 6 | R | 1 | 1↓ 2↓ |
| | 100–105 | ⑤ ⑥ | 7 8 | | R | 1 | 3↑ 2↑ |
| | 100–105 | ⑤ | 8 | 12 | R | 1 | 6 5↑ |
| | 104–105 | ① ② | 11 12 | 6 | R | 1 | 3↓ 4↓ |
| e♮ | 50–59 | ⑧ | 8 | 12 | R | 3 | 6 3↑ |
| | 52–57 | ⑤ ⑥ | 11 12 | 6 | R | 3 | 5↑ 2↑ |
| | 52–57 | ①–⑥ | 7–12 | 2 | R | 3 | 5↓ 4↑ |
| | 53–56 | ③ ④ | 9 10 | 6 | R | 3 | 2↓ 5↓ |
| | 54–56 | ④ ② | 7 8 | | R | 3 | 2↑ 1↓ |
| | 79–85 | ⑤ | 5 | 12 | R | 3 | 6 3↑ |
| | 80–85 | ①–⑥ | 7–12 | 2 | R | 3 | 1↑ 2↓ |
| | 80–85 | ③ ④ | 9 10 | 6 | R | 3 | 4↑ 1↑ |
| | 82–85 | ② | 11 | 12 | R | 3 | 3↓ 6 |
| | 82–85 | ① ② | 11 12 | 6 | R | 3 | 5↑ 2↑ |
| | 91–93 | ② | 2 | 12 | R | 1/2 | 1↓ 2↓ 4↓ |
| | 91–95 | ③ ④ | 3 4 | 6 | R | 1/2 | 2↑ 1↑ 1↓ |
| | 91–96 | ①–⑥ | 1–6 | 2 | R | 1/2 | 6 5↑ 3↑ |
| | 91–97 | ⑤ ⑥ | 5 6 | 6 | R | 1/2 | 3↓ 4↓ 6 |
| | 91–99 | ⑧ | 5 | 12 | R | 1/2 | 2↓ 3↓ 5↓ |
| b♭ | 54–63 | ⑧ | 8 | 12 | 0 | 2 | 5↓ 5↑ |
| | 56–63 | ⑤ ⑥ | 7 8 | 6 | 0 | 2 | 6 4↑ |
| | 57–63 | ⑤ | 8 | 12 | 0 | 2 | 1↑ 1↓ |
| | 58–63 | ①–⑥ | 7–12 | 2 | 0 | 2 | 1↓ 3↓ |
| | 60–63 | ② | 12 | 12 | 0 | 2 | 3↑ 1↑ |
| | 60–63 | ① ② | 9 10 | 6 | 0 | 2 | 4↑ 2↑ |
| | 73–76 | ② | 11 | 12 | 0 | 1 | 2↑ 1↑ |
| | 73–78 | ③ ④ | 9 10 | 6 | 0 | 1 | 2↓ 3↓ |
| | 73–79 | ①–⑥ | 7–12 | 2 | 0 | 1 | 5↓ 6 |
| | 73–80 | ⑤ | 5 | 12 | 0 | 1 | 6 5↑ |
| | 73–81 | ⑤ ⑥ | 7 8 | 6 | 0 | 1 | 3↓ 4↓ |
| | 73–84 | ⑧ | 5 | | 0 | 1 | 4↑ 3↑ |
| | 94–103 | ⑧ | 5 | 12 | 0 | 3 | 4↓ 5↑ |
| | 95–101 | ⑤ | 5 | | 0 | 3 | 6 3↑ |
| | 96–100 | ①–⑥ | 1–6 | 2 | 0 | 3 | 1↑ 2↓ |
| | 96–100 | ③ ④ | 3 4 | 6 | 0 | 3 | 2↓ 5↓ |
| | 97–99 | ② | 2 | 12 | 0 | 3 | 2↑ 1↓ |
| | 97–99 | ① ② | 1 2 | 6 | 0 | 3 | 1↓ 4↓ |

| series | bars | instruments | direction | duration | dynamics | index of dividing | transpositions 1=halftone |
|---|---|---|---|---|---|---|---|
| f♮ | 1–4 | Xyl. | R | ③ | 3, 5 | 12 | 4↑ |
| g♮ | 1–7 | Xyl. | R | ⑤,⑥ | 5 6 | 6 | 5↓ |
| a♮ | 1–4 | Vibr. | R | ①–⑥ | 1–6 | 2 | 2↓ |
| f# | 1–2 | Vibr. | O | ② | 2 | } 12 | 5↑ |
|  | 3–9 | Vibr. | O | ⑦ | 6 |  | 4↑ |
| c# | 3–10 | Fl. | O | ⑦,⑧ | 7  8 | 6 | 4↑ |
| eb | 4–8 | Vibr. | R | ①–⑥ | 1–6 | } 2 | 1↑ |
|  | 9–12 | Vibr. | O | ①–⑥ | 7–12 |  | 1↓ |
| g# | 7–9 | Xyl. | O | ①–③ | 1–3 | } 4 | 3↑ |
|  | 9–12 | Xyl. | R | ①–③ | 10–12 |  | 5↑ |
| b♮ | 7–12 | Xyl. | O | ④–⑥ | 4-6, 7-9 |  | 5↑ |
| d♮ | 13–15 | Xyl. | O | ①–③ | 10–12 | 4 | 2↑ |
|  | 15–18 | Xyl. | O | ①–④ | 1-4, 9-12 | 3 | 2↓ |
|  | 18–20 | Xyl. | O | ①–③ | 1–3 | 4 | 5↓ |
| e♮ | 14–20 | Vibr. | O | ⑤–⑧ | 5–8 | 3 | 5↓ |
| bb | 12–17 | Vibr. | O | ④–⑥ | 7–9 | 4 | 4↓ |
|  | 18–20 | Vibr. | O | ①–④ | 1–4 | 3 | 5↑ |

| series | bars | dynamics | index of dividing | direction | transpositions | ① = | uniform sequence of attacqs ♩=semiquaver [♩]="diminished"s. [6]="augmented"s. | it is determined by beginning (b) or ending (e) | instruments |
|---|---|---|---|---|---|---|---|---|---|
| f♮ | 47-54 | 1 2 | 6 | O | 2↓ | e♭ | 8 | b | Vibr, Fl. |
| | | | | | | | | | |
| f♮ | 58-61 | 5 6 | 6 | O | 4↓ | f♮ | 4 | b | |
| f# | 61-64 | 7 –12 | 2 | O | 2↓ | e♮ | 2 | b | |
| f# | 64-67 | 7 –12 | | R | 6 | f# | 2 | b | |
| c# | 67-71 | 5 6 | 6 | OR | O | c# | — | — | Fl. |
| c# | 67-71 | 5,6,7,8,9,10,11,12 | | OR | 3↓ | c# | — | — | Xyl. |
| c# | 67-71 | 5 6 | | OR | 3↓ | b♭ | — | — | Vibr. |
| g# | 71-74 | 10 –12 | | R | 3↓ | f♮ | 2 | e | |
| e♭ | 74-76 | 10 –12 | | O | 5↓ | b♭ | 2 | e | |
| e♭ | 75-79 | 10 –12 | 4 | O | 5↑ | g# | 2 | e | |
| b♮ | 78-80 | 7 –9 | | O | 1↓ | b♭ | 2 | e | |
| g# | 81-87 | 7 – 12 | | O | 6 | d♮ | 3 | b | Fl. |
| e♭ | 84-90 | 1 – 6 | | R | 2↑ | f♮ | 4 | b | Vibr. |
| e♭ | 86-88 | 1 – 6 | 2 | R | 3↓ | c♮ | 1 | b | Vibr. |
| b♮ | 86-93 | 7 – 12 | | R | 4↑ | e♭ | 4 | b | Xyl. |
| b♮ | 89-91 | 7 – 12 | | O | O | b♮ | 1 | b | Xyl. |
| g# | 93-95 | 7 – 9 | | O | 4↑ | c♮ | 2 | e | |
| e♭ | 96-98 | 10 – 12 | 4 | O | O | e♭ | 2 | e | |
| b♮ | 98-100 | 10 – 12 | | R | 3↓ | g# | 2 | e | |
| b♮ | 99-103 | 10 –12 | | R | 2↑ | c# | 2 | e | |
| d♭ | 102-105 | 4 – 6 | | O | 3↓ | d♮ | — | — | |
| e♭ | 105-108 | 4 – 6 | 4 | R | 3↑ | e♮ | 2 | b | |
| d♮ | 107-109 | 1 – 3 | | R | 4↓ | d♮ | — | — | |
| e♮ | 109-112 | 5 – 8 | | O | 6 | e♭ | 3 | b | |
| e♮ | 112-114 | 5 – 8 | | O | 4↓ | e♮ | ♪7/3, ♪7/3, ♪/3 | e | |
| d♮ | 114-118 | 5 – 8 | 3 | R | 1↑ | d♮ | — | — | |
| d♮ | 116-120 | 5 – 8 | | O | 1↓ | d♮ | — | | |
| b♭ | 119-124 | 1 – 4 | | R | 1↑ | b♭ | 3 | b | |
| e♮ | 123-126 | 1 – 3 | 4 | R | O | e♮ | ♪7/5=[2] | e | |
| b♭ | 126-128 | 9 – 12 | 3 | O | 3↑ | b♭ | ♪7/5=[1] | b | |
| b♭ | 128-132 | 1 – 3 | 4 | O | 2↓ | b♭ | ♪7/5=[4], 4 | e | |
| b♭ | 132-138 | 1 – 3 | | R | 6 | b♭ | ♪♪7/5=[6]6 | b | |

Diagram IX 147

| | c♮ | c# | d♮ | eb | e♮ | f♮ | f# | g♮ | g# | a♮ | bb | b♮ |
|---|---|---|---|---|---|---|---|---|---|---|---|---|
| ① | ¹ ff sfz ↓ | f sfz ∨ | mf > | mp > | p | pp | ff sfz ∨ | f sfz ∨ | mf > | mp > | p | pp |
| ② | pp | ² ## | f | mf | mp | p | pp | ## | f | mf | mp | p |
| ③ | pp | ## sfz | ³ f sfz ∨ | mf > | mp > | p | pp | ## sfz ∨ | f sfz ∨ | mf > | mp > | p |
| ④ | p | pp | ## | ⁴ f | mf | mp | p | pp | ## | f | mf | mp |
| ⑤ | p | pp | ## sfz | f sfz ∨ | ⁵ mf > | mp > | p | pp | ## sfz ∨ | f sfz ∨ | mf > | mp > |
| ⑥ | mp | p | pp | ## | f | ⁶ mf | mp | p | pp | ## | f | mf |
| ⑦ | mp > | p | pp | ## sfz ↓ | f sfz ∨ | mf > | ⁷ mp > | p | pp | ## sfz ∨ | f sfz ∨ | mf > |
| ⑧ | mf | mp | p | pp | ## | f | mf | ⁸ mp | p | pp | ## | f |
| ⑨ | mf > | mp > | p | pp | ## sfz | f sfz ∨ | mf > | mp > | ⁹ p | pp | ## sfz ∨ | f sfz ∨ |
| ⑩ | f | mf | mp | p | pp | ## | f | mf | mp | ¹⁰ p | pp | ## |
| ⑪ | f sfz ↓ | mf > | mp > | p | pp | ## sfz | f sfz ∨ | mf > | mp > | p | ¹¹ pp | ## sfz ∨ |
| ⑫ | ## | f | mf | mp | p | pp | ## | f | mf | mp | p | ¹² pp |

| durations | c♮ | c# | d♭ | e♭ | e♮ | f♮ | f# | g♮ | g# | a♮ | b♭ | b♮ |
|---|---|---|---|---|---|---|---|---|---|---|---|---|
| ① | | 38<br>49<br>66<br>75<br>81 85 | 77 | 38<br>60 | 33<br>76<br>83 | 34<br>76<br>84 | 34<br>41<br>63<br>82 | 40<br>57<br>63<br>80 | 56 | 38<br>72 | 53<br>89 | 38<br>47<br>53<br>74 |
| ② | 41<br>49<br>74 | | 45<br>45<br>76<br>(79)<br>87 | 45-46<br>45-46<br>75<br>79<br>87 | | (34-35)<br>59<br>83 | 34<br>77 | 36<br>63<br>71<br>76-77<br>81<br>(85) | 39<br>46<br>58<br>74 | 72 | 52 | (54-55)<br>67<br>91 |
| ③ | (55)<br>(91) | 41<br>49<br>66<br>71 | | 77 | 75 | 35<br>41<br>63<br>69<br>82 | (35-36)<br>82 | 83 | 44<br>51 | 58<br>(64) | (38)<br>52<br>74 | 47<br>52 |
| ④ | 47 | (67)<br>86 | 71<br>73 | | (77) | 34<br>75 | 60<br>68 | 34<br>(35)<br>41<br>63<br>(82-83) | 36<br>82 | 40<br>59<br>80 | 38<br>60 | 52<br>53 |
| ⑤ | 73 | 47-48<br>53<br>61<br>66-67<br>69-70<br>74 | 37<br>49<br>(67)<br>75-76<br>81-82<br>85 | 63 | | 47-48<br>88 | 34-35<br>75<br>84 | 63<br>68 | 34-35<br>83 | 35<br>40-41<br>63<br>83 | 36-37<br>50<br>52-53<br>(63)<br>71 85<br>76-77 81 | (55) ?<br>(63-64) |
| ⑥ | 38<br>53<br>73 | 52<br>72 | 42-43<br>49-50<br>64<br>71 | 56<br>85 | 47-48<br>61-62<br>68-69 | | 45<br>(45)<br>(76)<br>79<br>(87) | (75-76) | 37<br>48-49<br>53<br>63<br>76<br>81 85-86 | 35-36<br>82 | (36)<br>(76) | 40-41<br>46<br>59-60<br>80 |
| ⑦ | 40-41<br>46<br>46<br>59-60<br>80 | 38<br>53<br>55<br>72-73<br>(73) | 47<br>61-62<br>67<br>70 | 47<br>54-55 | (67)<br>86 | 62<br>(64-65)<br>(66-67)?<br>69-70<br>(71)<br>73-74 | | (33)<br>76 | 34-35<br>(75-76) | 63<br>68 | 42-43<br>47<br>77<br>79<br>87 | 43-44<br>46<br>78<br>79<br>87 |
| ⑧ | 37<br>50-51<br>52<br>64-65<br>69-70 85-86<br>77-78 81-82 | 54 | 42-43<br>46<br>65<br>70-71 | 47-48 | 46-47<br>54<br>72 | 44-45<br>77-78<br>79-80<br>87 | (63-64) | | 34<br>76<br>84 | 38-39<br>65-66<br>68-69<br>75<br>81-82<br>85-86 | 41-42<br>46-47<br>51<br>58-59<br>80 | 36<br>51<br>63-64<br>70<br>77<br>(81) 85-86 |
| ⑨ | 42-43<br>(47)<br>(77)<br>79<br>(87-88) | (36-37)<br>(76) | 44-45<br>(50)<br>84 | 41-42<br>(49-50)<br>(49-50) | 41-42<br>48-49<br>65-66<br>72-73<br>73-74 | 40-41<br>57-58<br>64-65<br>66-67 | 50<br>89 | 62<br>(69-70) | | 53-54<br>89-90 | (34-35)<br>(75-76) | 38-39<br>60-61 |
| ⑩ | 38-39<br>51<br>61 | 42-44<br>(47)<br>(77)<br>79<br>(87-88) | 44-45 | 54-55 | 36<br>41-42<br>82-83 | 61-62<br>68-69<br>72-73 | 66-67 | 48-49<br>88 | 37-38<br>53-54<br>58-59 | | 55<br>91-92 | 36-37<br>(75-76) |
| ⑪ | 36-37<br>49-50<br>(75-76) | 38-39 | 39-40<br>44-46<br>51-52<br>(80) | 34<br>(76-77)<br>84 | 54-55 | 40-41<br>57-59<br>80 | (55-56)<br>71-72 | 65-66<br>72-73 | 62<br>90-91 | 38-39<br>58-59 | | (33)<br>(76-77) |
| ⑫ | 67-68<br>(77) | (75-77) | 35,41-43<br>51<br>53<br>82-84 | 44-45<br>84 | 43-45<br>(46-47)<br>(78)<br>79-80<br>(87-88) | 67-68<br>84 | 41-43<br>65-66<br>(70-71)<br>72-73 | 39-40<br>57-59 | 54-55 | (48-49)<br>(88) | 37-39<br>53-55<br>(64-66)? | |

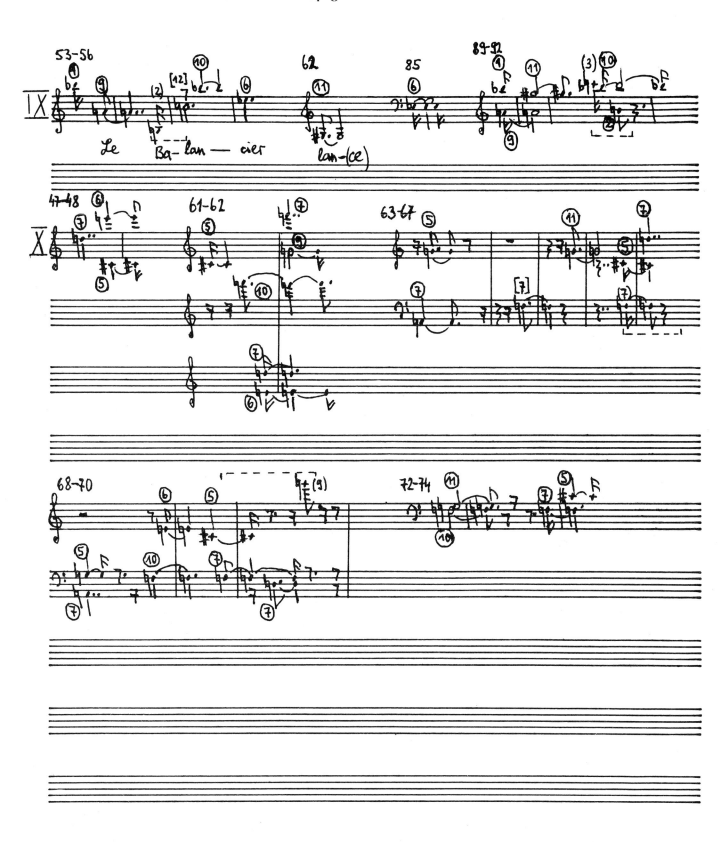

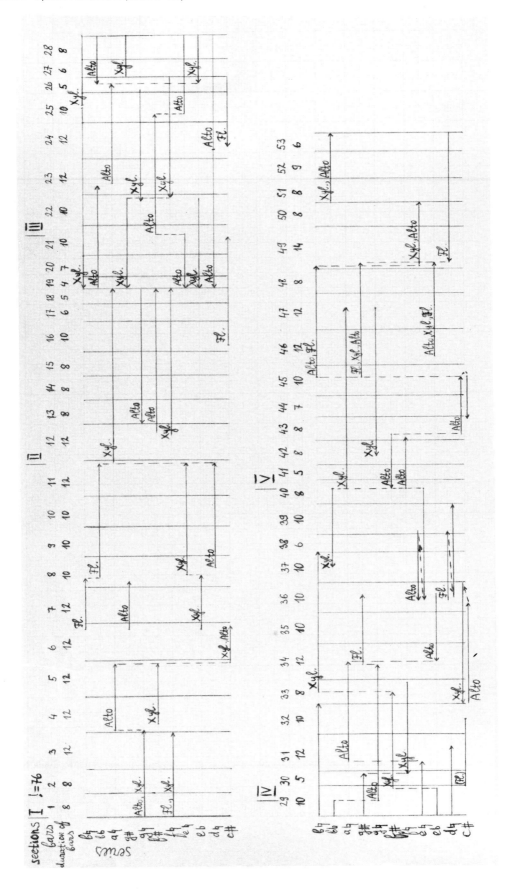

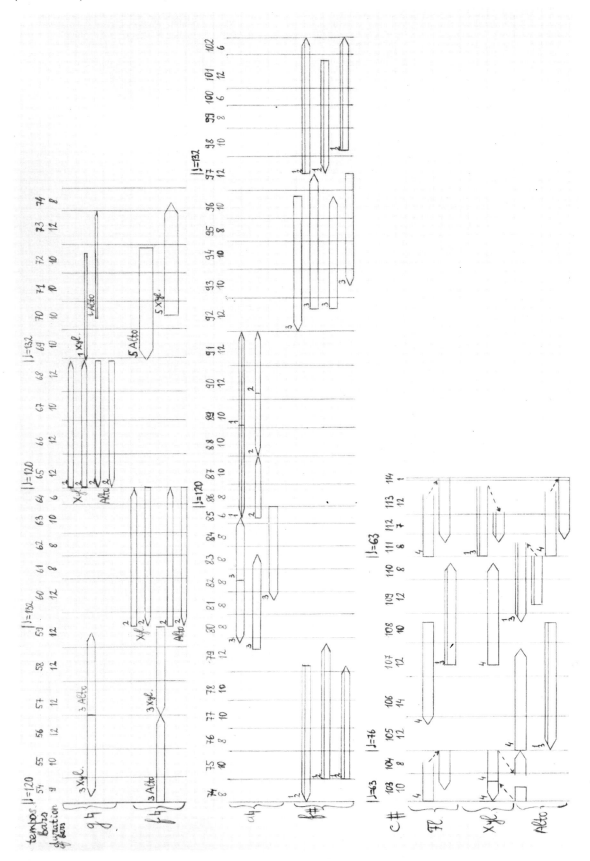

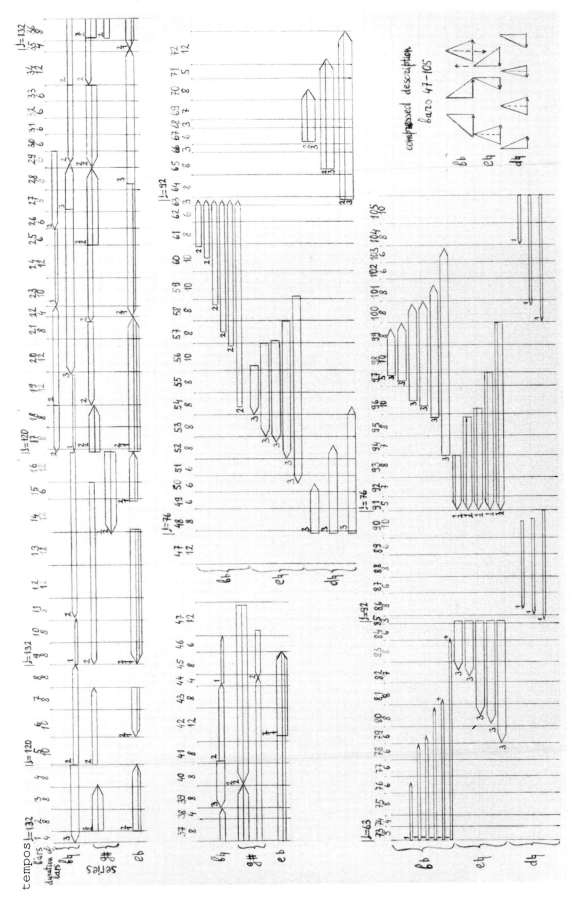

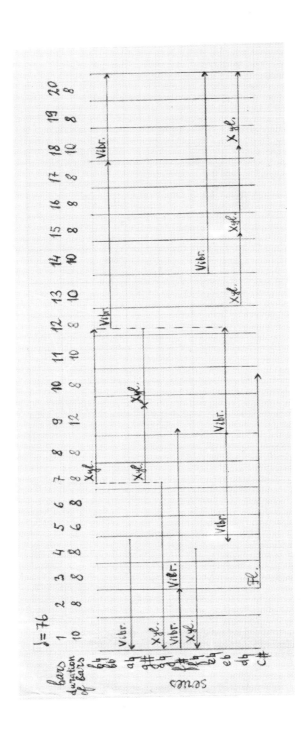

Section I  Bars 1-3 /Fl, Xyl. ①-④ [9-12] f♮ 0

a♮① g#④ ♭b②/c#① c♮④ ⋮ e♮④/f♮③ d♮② ⋮ eb③/f♮① f#② g♮③
pp  p  pp  p

| ④ | ① | ② | ③ | ④ | ① | ② | ③ | ④ | ① | ② | ③ |
|---|---|---|---|---|---|---|---|---|---|---|---|
| c♮ | c# | d♮ | eb | e♮ | f♮ | f# | g♮ | g# | a♮ | bb | b♮ |
| p | pp | pp | p | p | pp | pp | p | p | p | pp | p- |

Bars 1-4 Alto, Xyl. ①-④ [9-12] g♮ 0 .

g♮①/f♮③ ⋮⋮⋮ e♮② f#④/eb① ⋮ d♮④ c♮♭/c#③ bb① g#② a♮③/b♮①
p —

| ② | ③ | ④ | ① | ② | ③ | ④ | ① | ② | ③ | ④ | ① |
|---|---|---|---|---|---|---|---|---|---|---|---|
| c♮ | c# | d♮ | eb | e♮ | f♮ | f# | g♮ | g# | a♮ | bb | b♮ |
| pp | p | p | pp | pp | p | p | p | p | p | p | pp |
| | | | | [p] | | | [pp] | | | | |

Bars 4-5 Xyl. ①-③ 10-12 f# 0

♭b②/g♮② g#③ ⋮ f#① ⋮ e♮(2)/eb① ⋮ f♮③/c#(2) ⋮ e♮①/b♮(3)/a♮①
pp  pp  pp  db③ ⋮⋮

| ① | (2) | (3) | ① | (2) | ③ | ① | ② | ③ | ① | ② | ③ |
|---|---|---|---|---|---|---|---|---|---|---|---|
| c♮ | c# | d♮ | eb | e♮ | f♮ | f# | g♮ | g# | a♮ | bb | b♮ |
| p | pp | pp | p | pp | pp | p | pp | pp | p | pp | pp |

Bars 4-5 Alto ①-③ 10-12 a♮ 0

a♮① ⋮⋮ f♮③ g#(3)/f#① e♮② ⋮ eb① c#(2)/c♮①/b♮(3) d♮③ ⋮ ♭b②/g♮②
p-  p  p

| ① | (2) | ③ | ① | ② | ③ | ① | ② | ② | ① | ② | ③ |
|---|---|---|---|---|---|---|---|---|---|---|---|
| c♮ | c# | d♮ | eb | e♮ | f♮ | f# | g♮ | g# | a♮ | bb | b♮ |
| p | pp | pp | p | pp | pp | p | pp | pp | p | pp | pp |

Bars 5-6 Xyl. Alto ① 12 C# 0

♭b/g♮ g# ⋮ f♮ f#/e♮/eb ⋮ c# ⋮ ♭b ⋮ a♮
pp  d♮/c♮  pp  pp  pp

Bars 6-8 Alto ①② 11 12 g# 0

c#②/b♮②/a♮② ♭b① g#①/f#① ⋮ g♮② ⋮ ⋮ f♮②/d♮①eb②e♮① [c♮①]
pp  pp  pp

| (1) | ② | ① | ② | (1) | ② | ① | ② | ① | ② | ④ | ② |
|---|---|---|---|---|---|---|---|---|---|---|---|
| c♮ | c# | d♮ | eb | e♮ | f♮ | f# | g♮ | g# | a♮ | bb | b♮ |
| pp | pp | pp | pp | pp | pp | pp | pp | pp | pp | pp | pp |
| | | | | | [pp] | | | | | | |

Bars 6-8 , Xyl. ①② 11 12 eb 0

a♮①/g♮①/f#(2) g#② bb② ⋮⋮ eb(1)/c#①(A♮)/c♮(2)/b♮① ⋮⋮⋮⋮ f♮①/d♮② e♮②
pp-  pp  pp

| (2) | ① | ② | (1) | ② | ① | (2) | ① | ② | ① | ② | (1) |
|---|---|---|---|---|---|---|---|---|---|---|---|
| c♮ | c# | d♮ | eb | e♮ | f♮ | f# | g♮ | g# | a♮ | bb | b♮ |
| pp | pp | pp | pp | pp | pp | pp | pp | pp | pp | pp | pp |

Bars 6-8 , Fl. ①② 11 12 b♮ 0

a♮① ⋮ b♮① ⋮ d♮② c#①/c♮(2) ⋮ g♮(1)/f♮① e♮② f#(2)/eb① ⋮ ♭b②/ab②
pp  pp  pp  f♮①  pp

| (2) | ① | ② | ① | ② | ① | ② | ① | ② | ① | ② | ① |
|---|---|---|---|---|---|---|---|---|---|---|---|
| c♮ | c# | d♮ | eb | e♮ | f♮ | f# | g♮ | g# | a♮ | bb | b♮ |
| pp | pp | pp | pp | pp | pp | pp | pp | pp | pp | pp | pp |

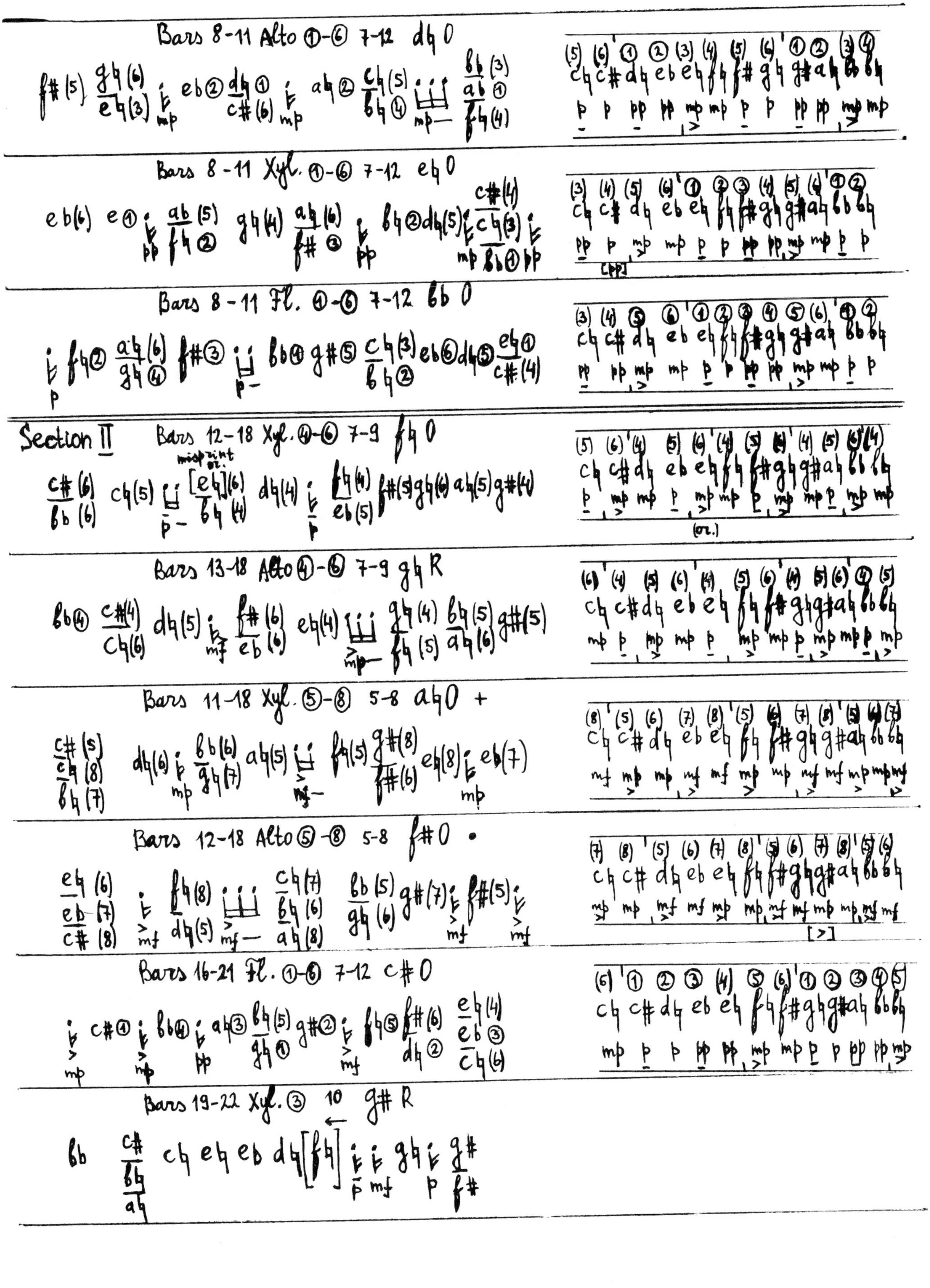

Bars 8–11 Alto ①–⑥ 7–12 d♮ 0

Bars 8–11 Xyl. ①–⑥ 7–12 e♭ 0

Bars 8–11 Fl. ①–⑥ 7–12 b♭ 0

Section II   Bars 12–18 Xyl. ④–⑥ 7–9 f♮ 0

Bars 13–18 Alto ④–⑥ 7–9 g♮ R

Bars 11–18 Xyl. ⑤–⑧ 5–8 a♮ 0 +

Bars 12–18 Alto ⑤–⑧ 5–8 f♯ 0 ·

Bars 16–21 Fl. ①–⑥ 7–12 c♯ 0

Bars 19–22 Xyl. ③ 10 g♯ R

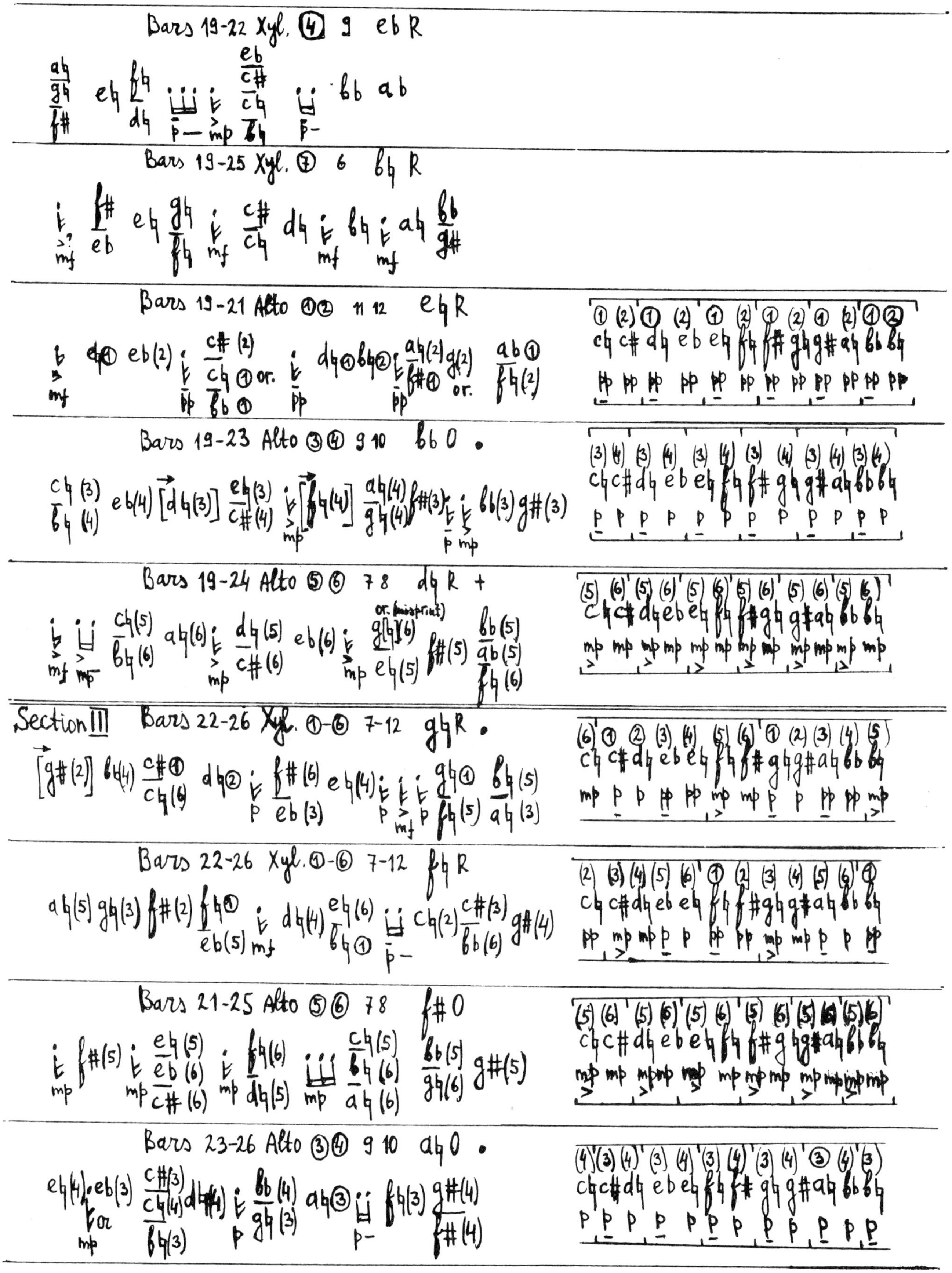

Bars 19-22 Xyl. ④ 9 eb R

Bars 19-25 Xyl. ⑦ 6 b♮ R

Bars 19-21 Alto ①② 11 12 e♮ R

Bars 19-23 Alto ③④ 9 10 bb 0 .

Bars 19-24 Alto ⑤⑥ 7 8 d♮ R +

Section III    Bars 22-26 Xyl. ①-⑥ 7-12 g♮ R .

Bars 22-26 Xyl. ①-⑥ 7-12 f♮ R

Bars 21-25 Alto ⑤⑥ 7 8 f# 0

Bars 23-26 Alto ③④ 9 10 a♮ 0 .

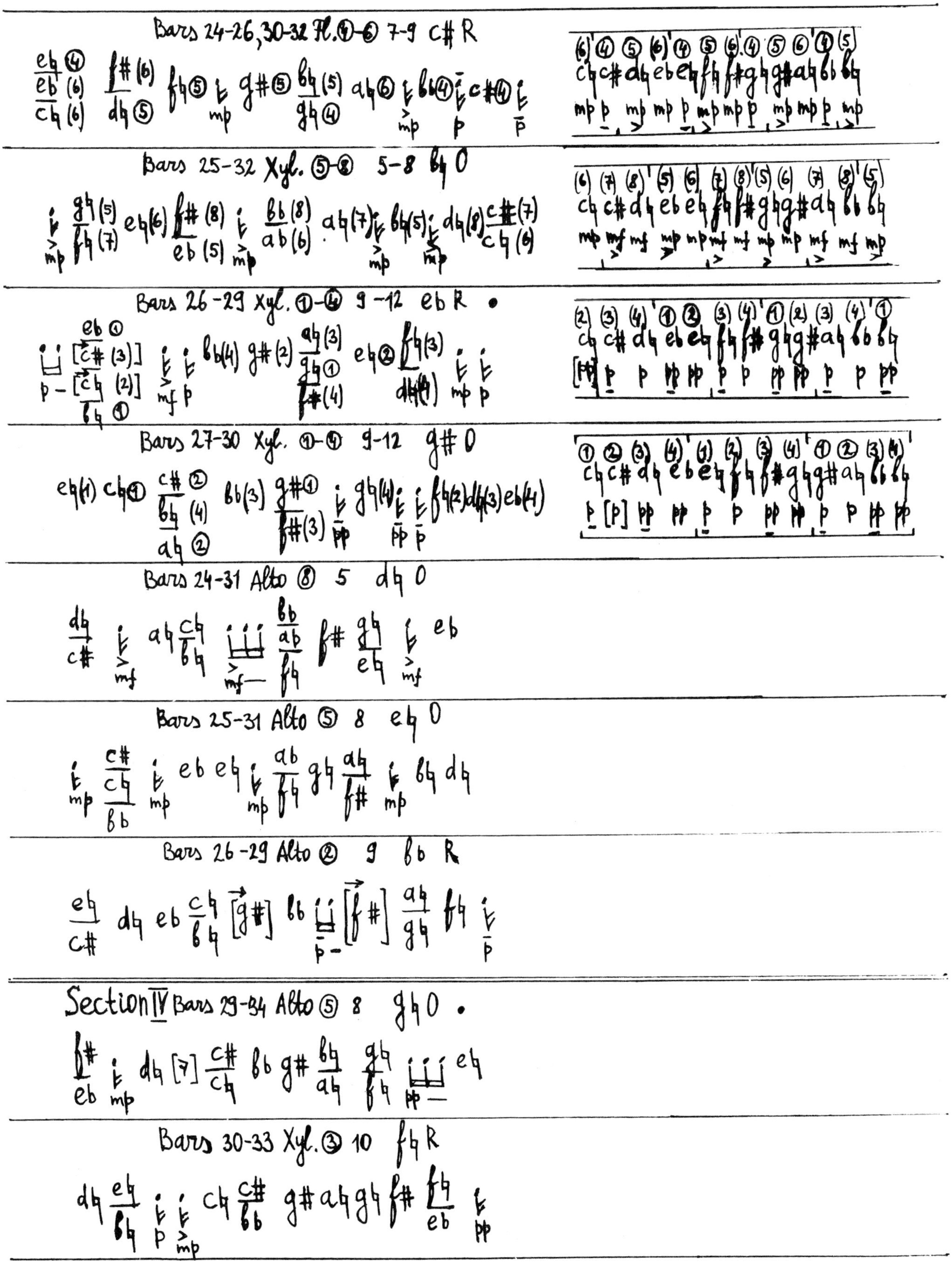

Bars 24-26, 30-32 Fl. ①-⑥ 7-9 c# R

Bars 25-32 Xyl. ⑤-⑧ 5-8 b♮ O

Bars 26-29 Xyl. ①-④ 9-12 e♭ R ·

Bars 27-30 Xyl. ①-④ 9-12 g# O

Bars 24-31 Alto ⑧ 5 d♮ O

Bars 25-31 Alto ⑤ 8 e♮ O

Bars 26-29 Alto ② 9 ♭b R

Section Ⅳ Bars 29-34 Alto ⑤ 8 g♮O ·

Bars 30-33 Xyl. ③ 10 f♮ R

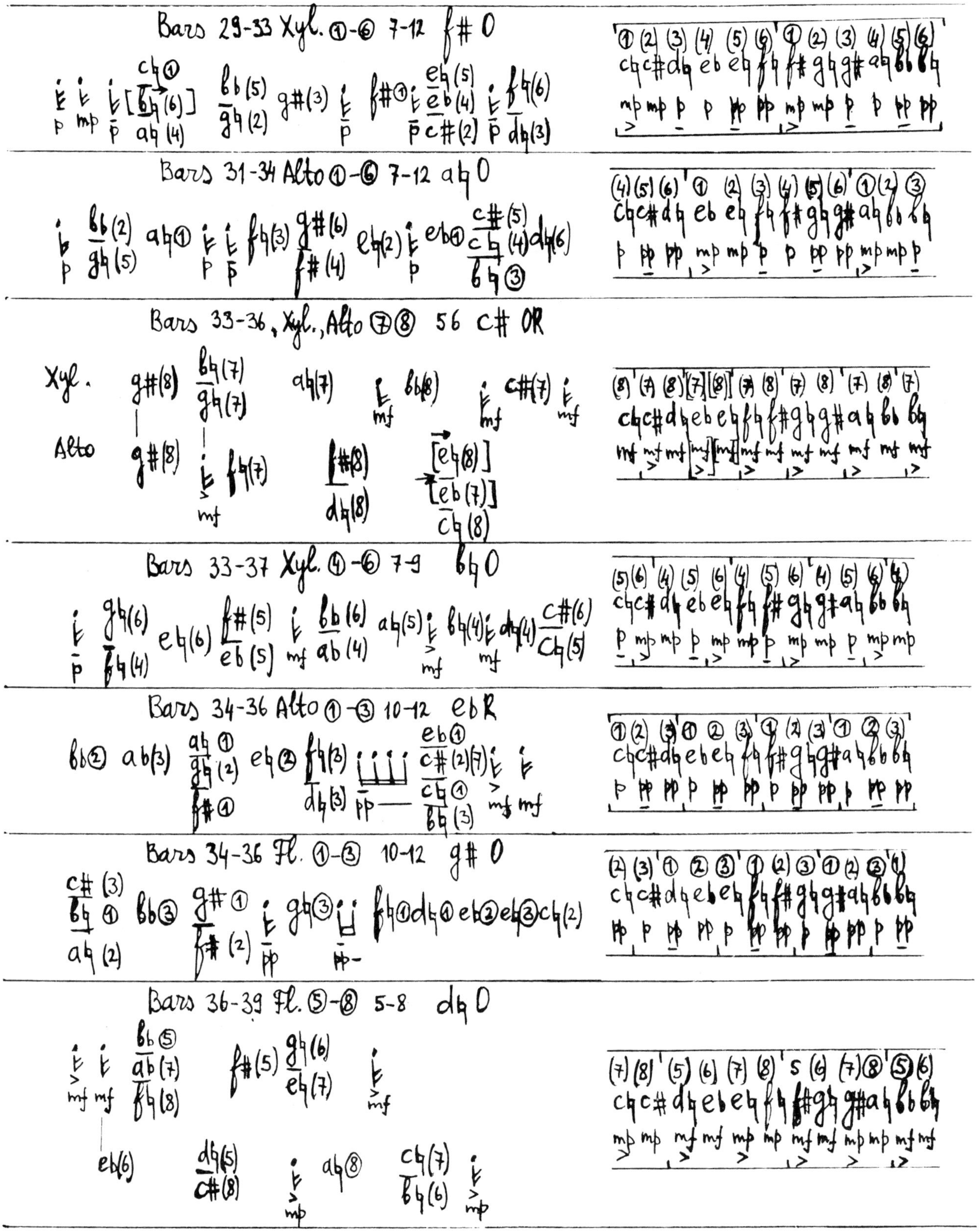

Bars 29–33 Xyl. ①–⑥ 7-12 f# 0

Bars 31–34 Alto ①–⑥ 7-12 a♮ 0

Bars 33–36, Xyl., Alto ⑦⑧ 56 C# OR

Bars 33–37 Xyl. ④–⑥ 7-9 b♮ 0

Bars 34–36 Alto ①–③ 10-12 eb R

Bars 34–36 Fl. ①–③ 10-12 g# 0

Bars 36–39 Fl. ⑤–⑧ 5-8 d♮ 0

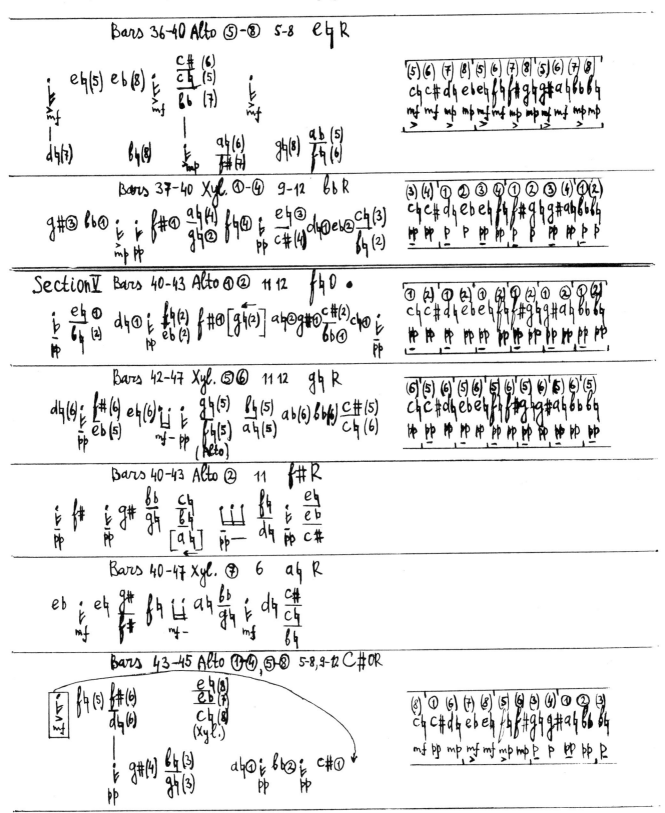

Bars 45-49 Alto, Fl. ①-⑥ 7-12 b♮ 0 +

Bars 45-49 Fl., Xyl., Alto ①-⑥ 7-12 g♯ 0 ·

Bars 46-49 Alto, Xyl., Fl. ①-⑥ 7-12 e♭ 0

Bars 49-50 Xyl., Alto ①-③ 10-12 c♮ 0

Bars 49-53 Fl. ④-⑥ 7-9 d♮ R

Bars 51-53 Xyl., Alto ①-③ 10-12 b♭ 0

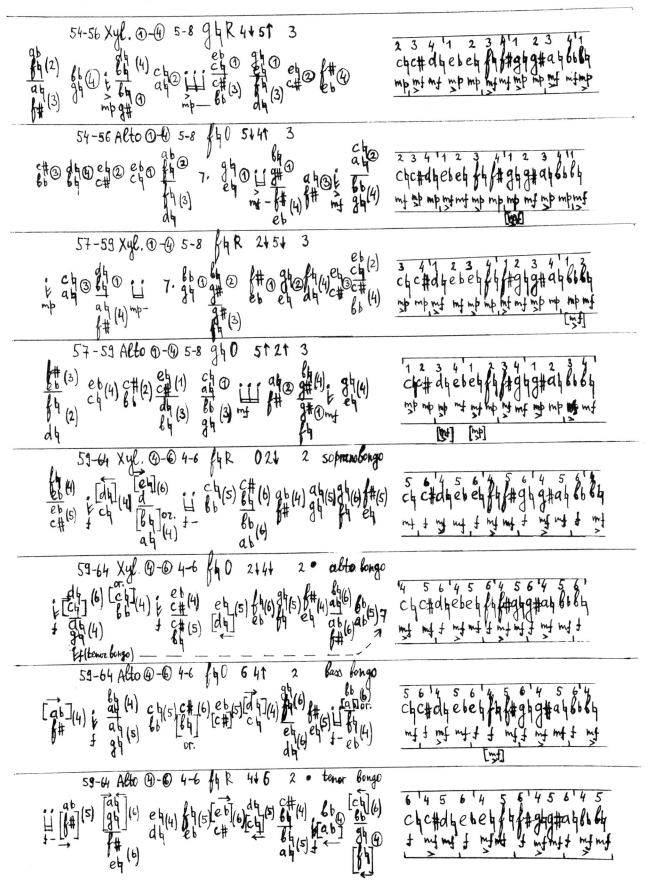

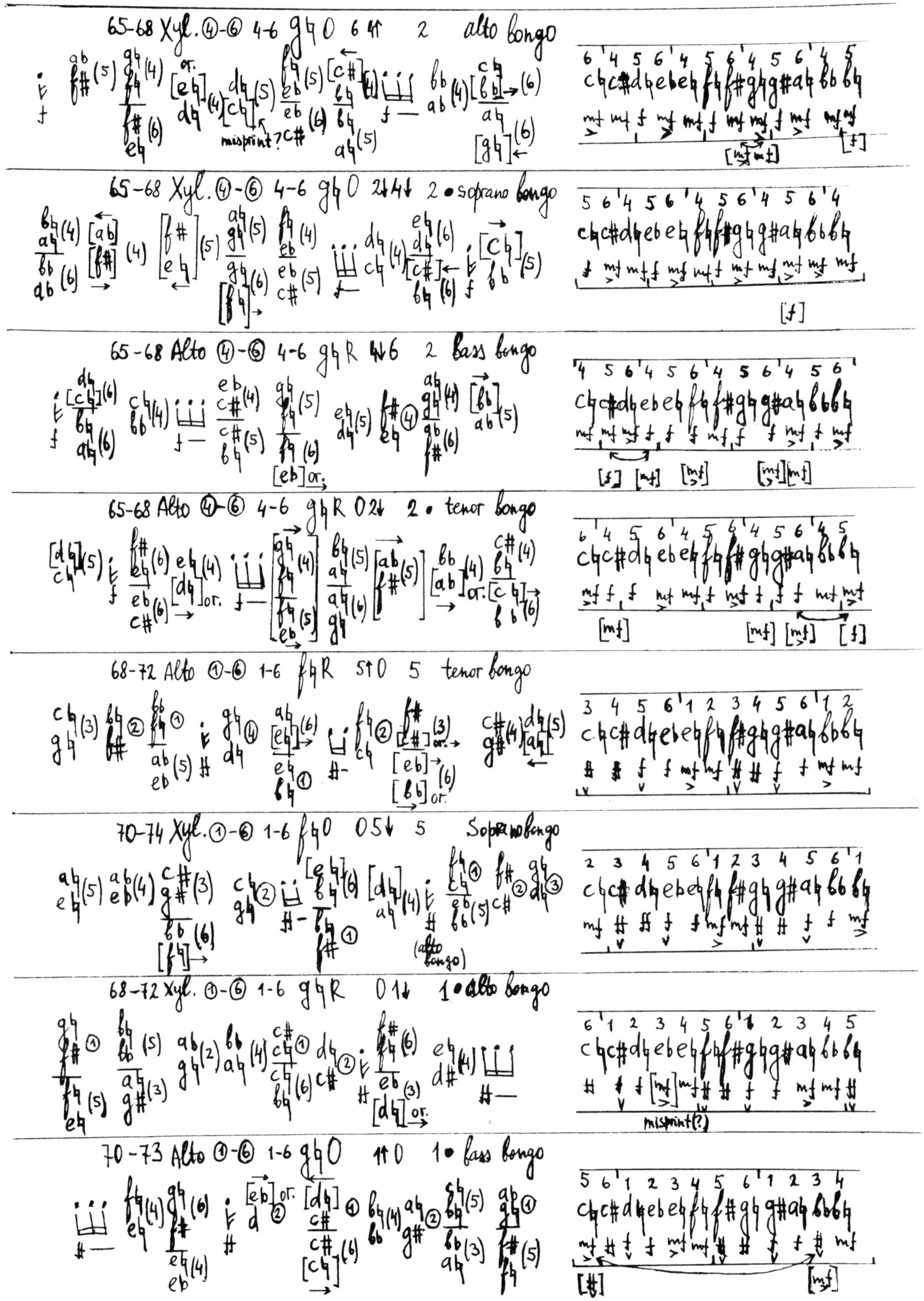
65-68 Xyl. ④-⑥ 4-6 g♮ O 6↑↑ 2 alto bongo
65-68 Xyl. ④-⑥ 4-6 g♮ O 2↑4↓ 2• soprano bongo
65-68 Alto ④-⑥ 4-6 g♮ R 4↓6 2 bass bongo
65-68 Alto ④-⑥ 4-6 g♮ R 02↓ 2• tenor bongo
68-72 Alto ①-⑥ 1-6 f♮ R 5↑0 5 tenor bongo
70-74 Xyl. ①-⑥ 1-6 f♮ O 05↓ 5 Soprano bongo
68-72 Xyl. ①-⑥ 1-6 g♮ R 01↓ 1• alto bongo
70-73 Alto ①-⑥ 1-6 g♮ O 1↑0 1• bass bongo

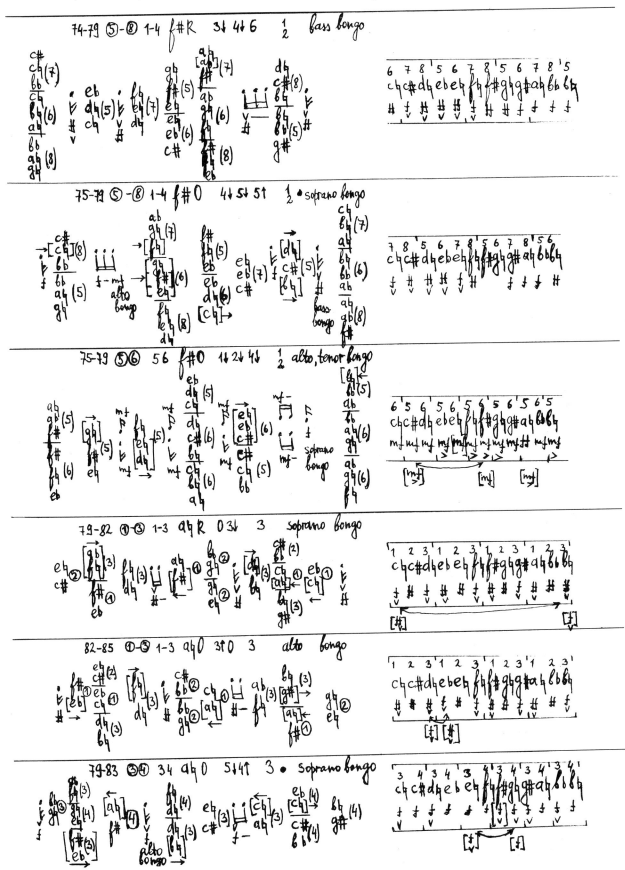

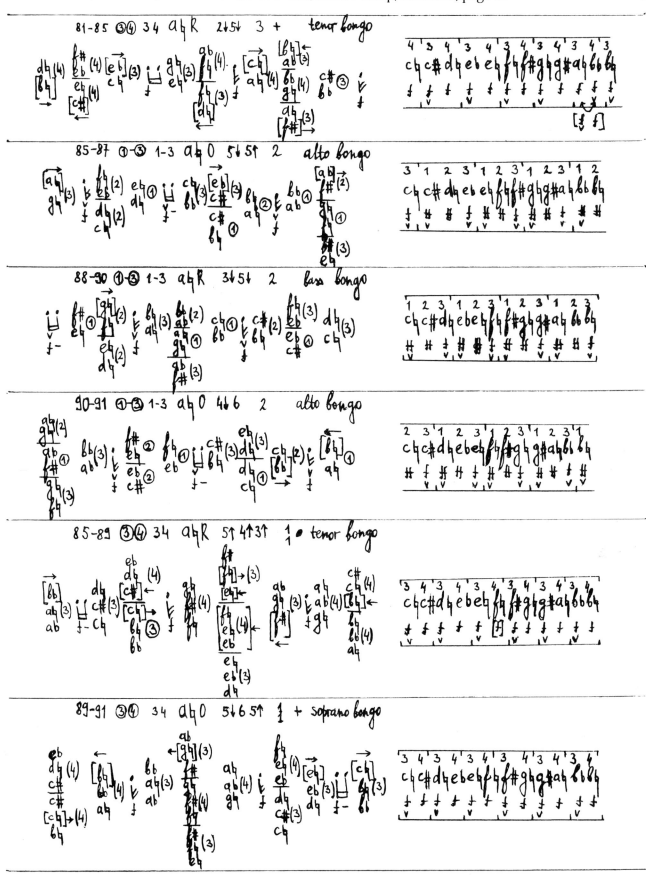

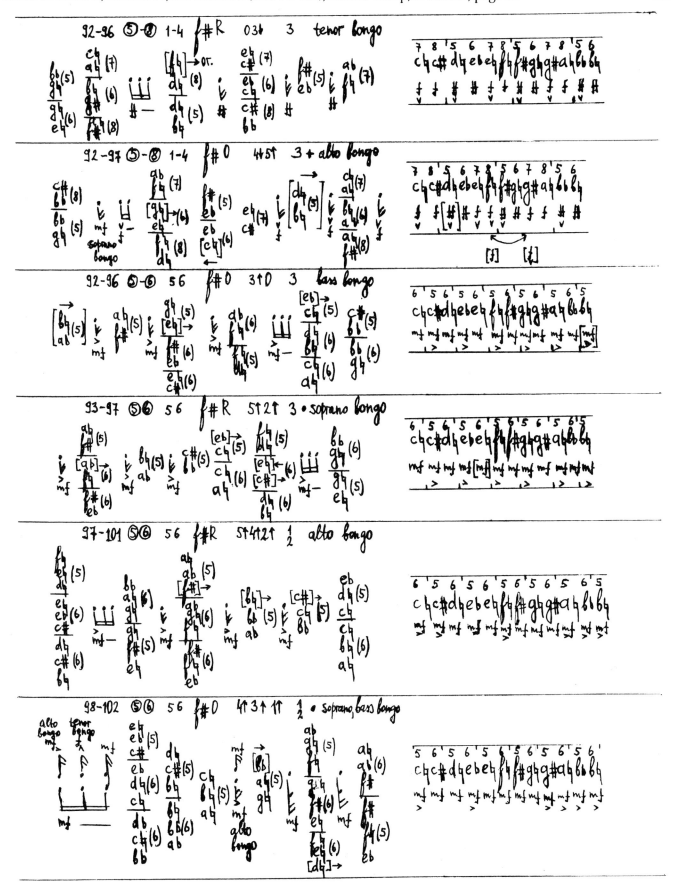

Tables of Series II, Section VI, Movement 2 (bars 74–102), series F sharp, A natural, (bars 103–114), Series C sharp, page 13

170

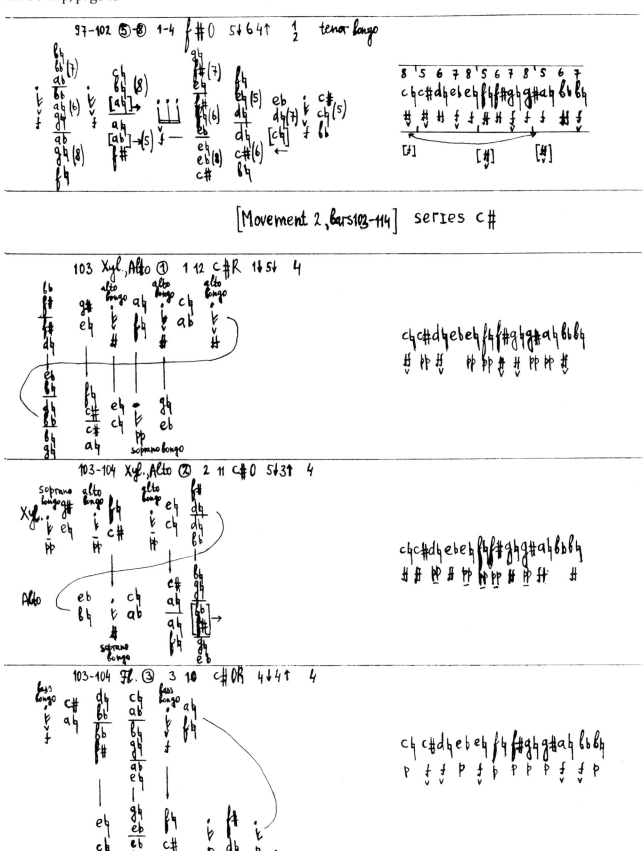

[Movement 2, bars103-114]  series c♯

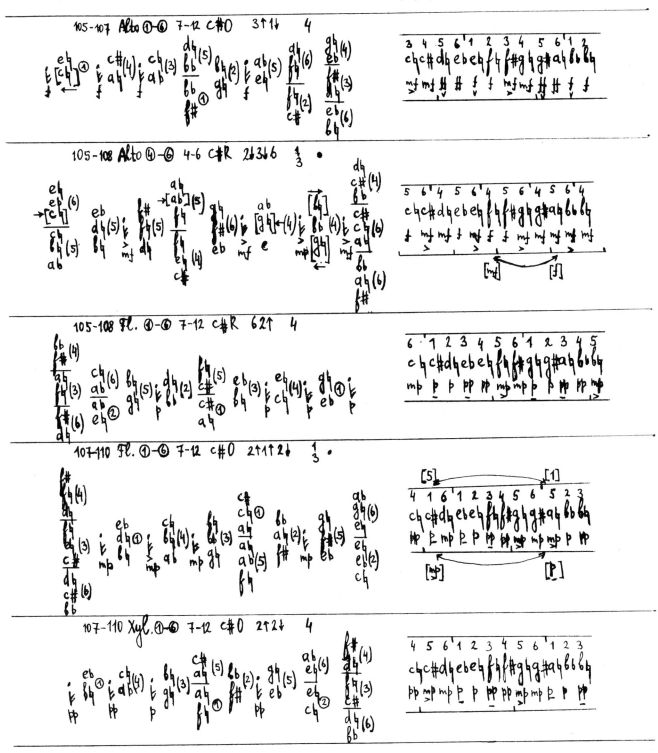

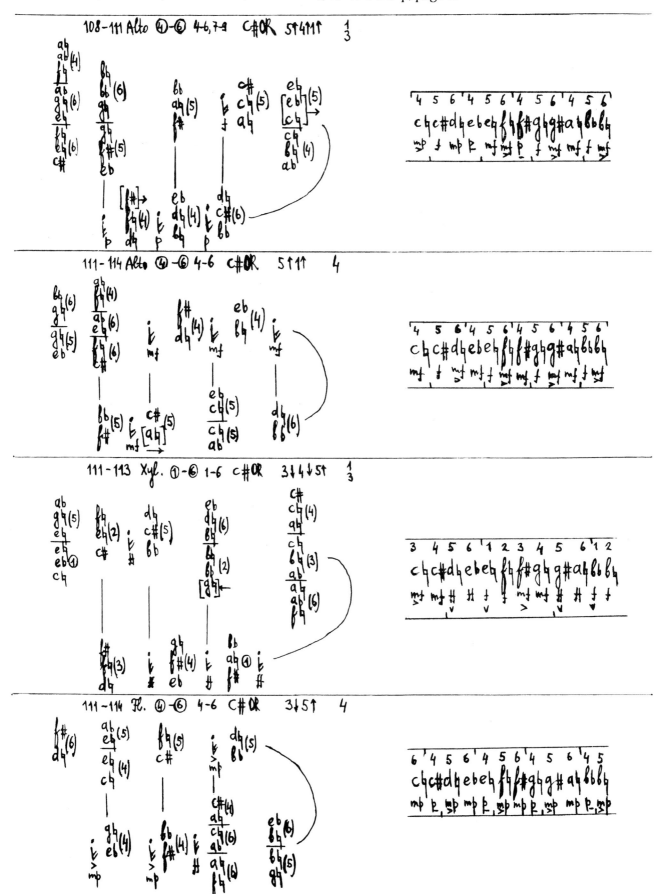

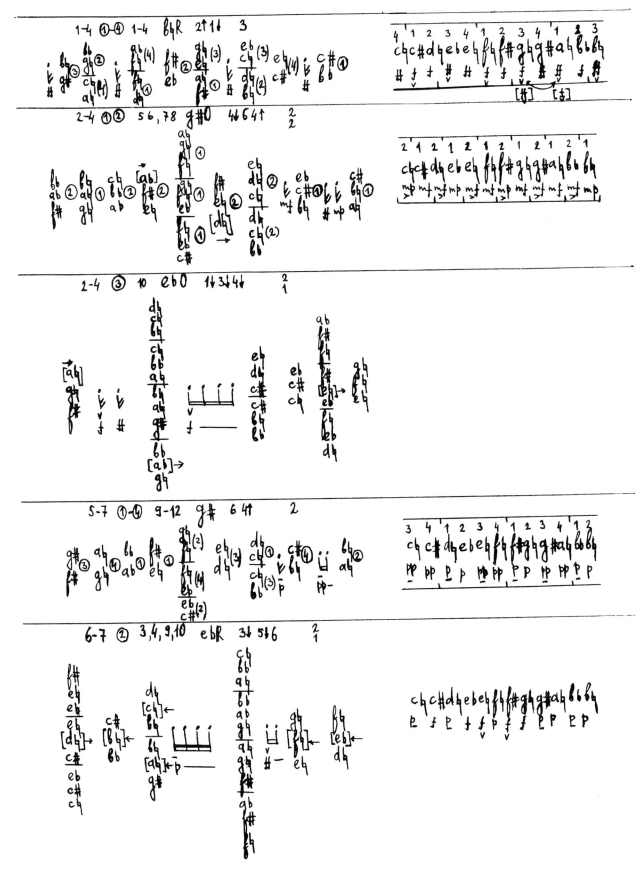

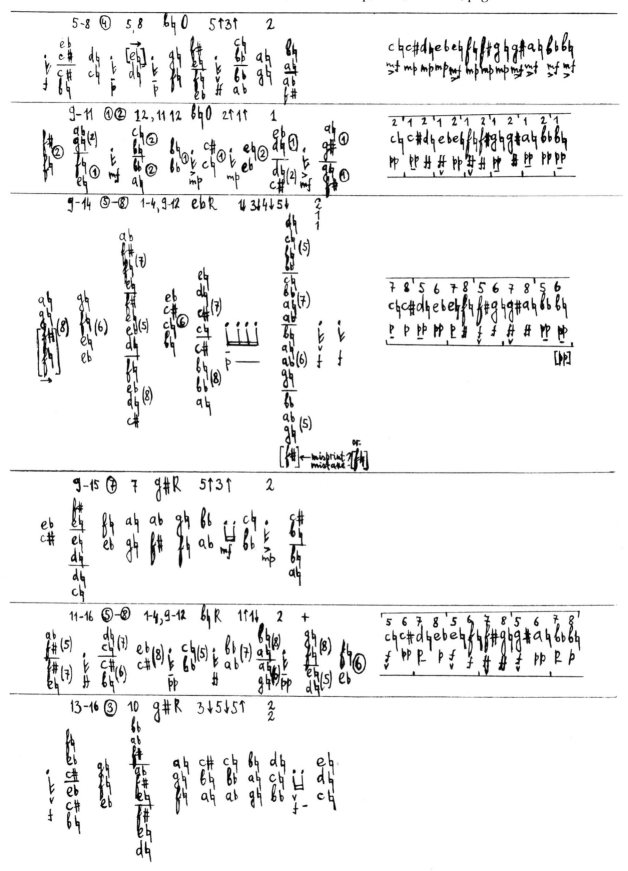

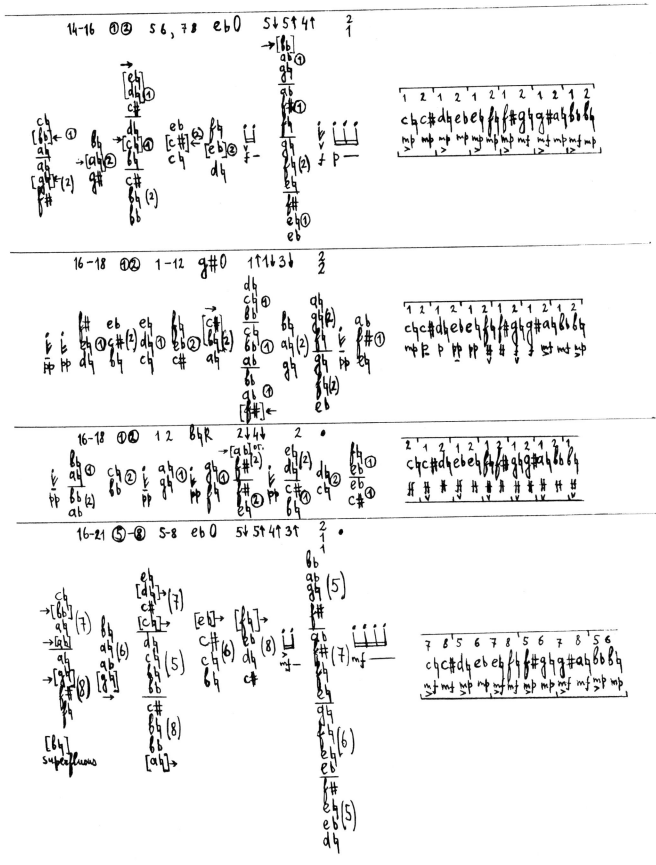

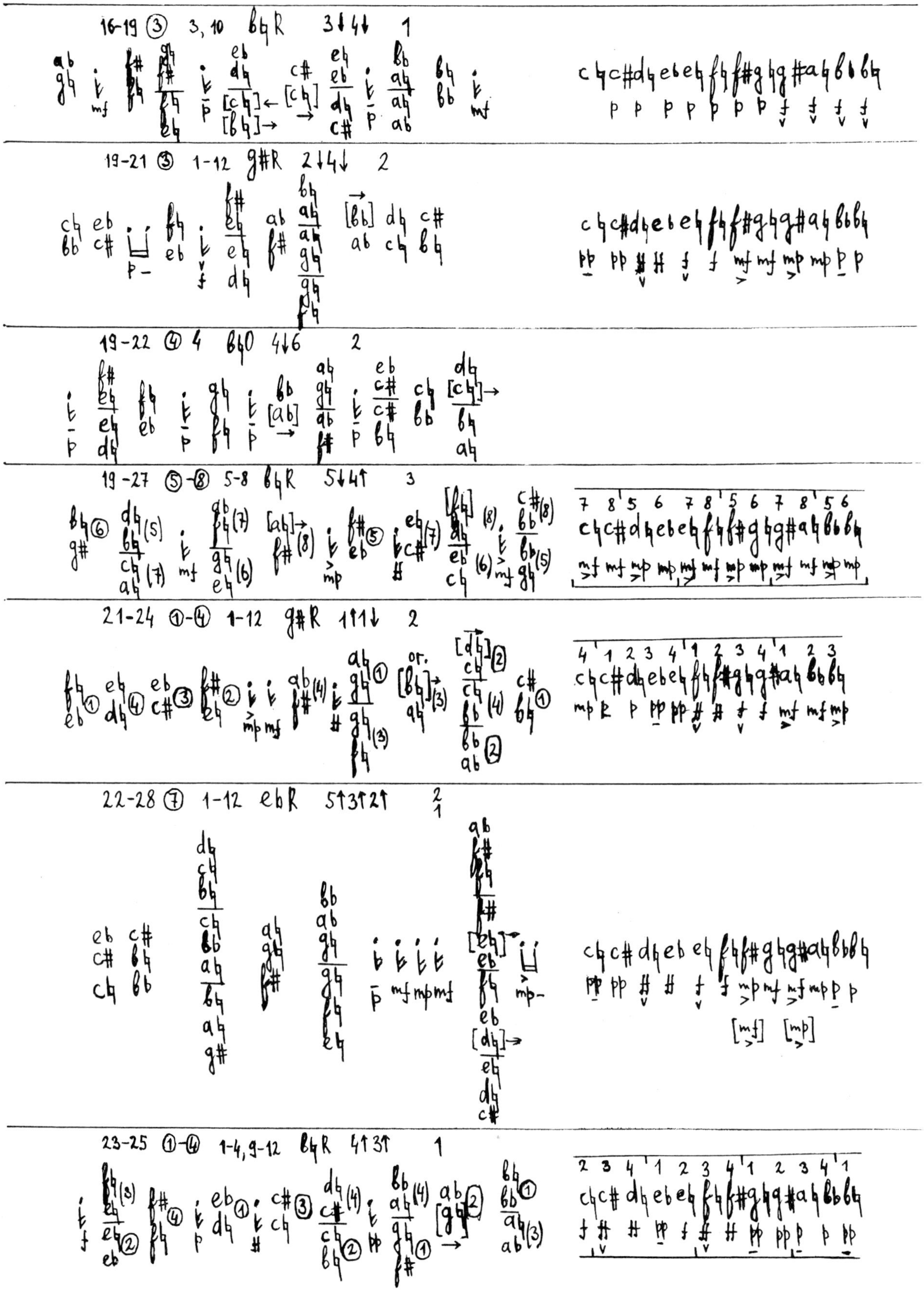
16-19 ③ 3, 10 b♮R 3↓4↓ 1
19-21 ③ 1-12 g#R 2↓4↓ 2
19-22 ④ 4 b♮O 4↓6 2
19-27 ⑤-⑧ 5-8 b♮R 5↓4↑ 3
21-24 ①-④ 1-12 g#R 1↑1↓ 2
22-28 ⑦ 1-12 ebR 5↑3↑2↑
23-25 ①-④ 1-4, 9-12 b♮R 4↑3↑ 1

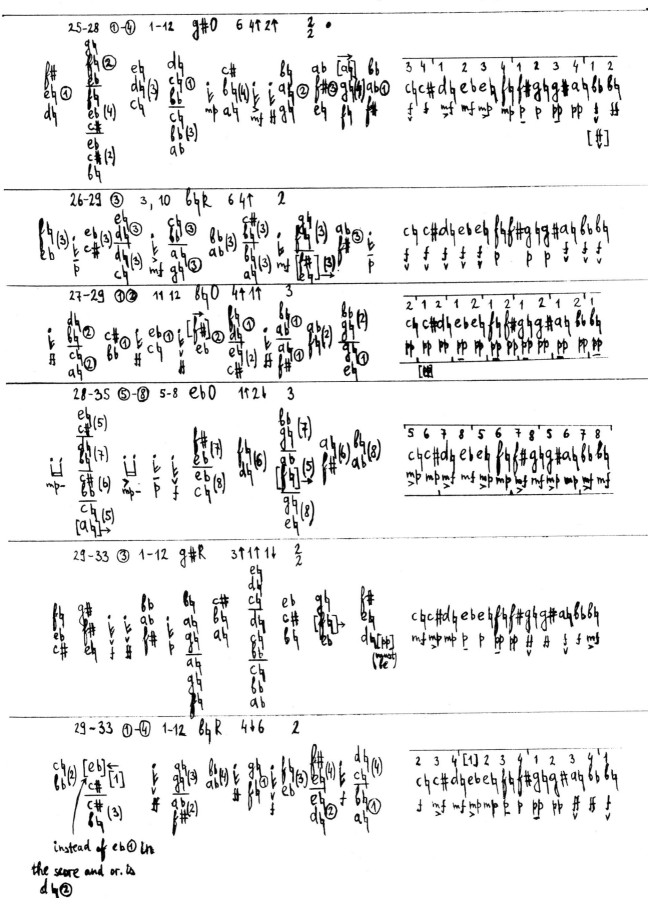

34–36 ①② 1–12 g#R 4↓6 2 　　*deviation of duration system*

35–42 ⑤–⑧ 5–8 ebR 1↑1↓2↓ 2/1

36–40 ④–④ 9–12 g#0 2↓4↓6 2/2

36–44 ⑦ 6 g#0 4↑2↑ 2

39–41 ①② 1–12 b♮R 3↓6 3

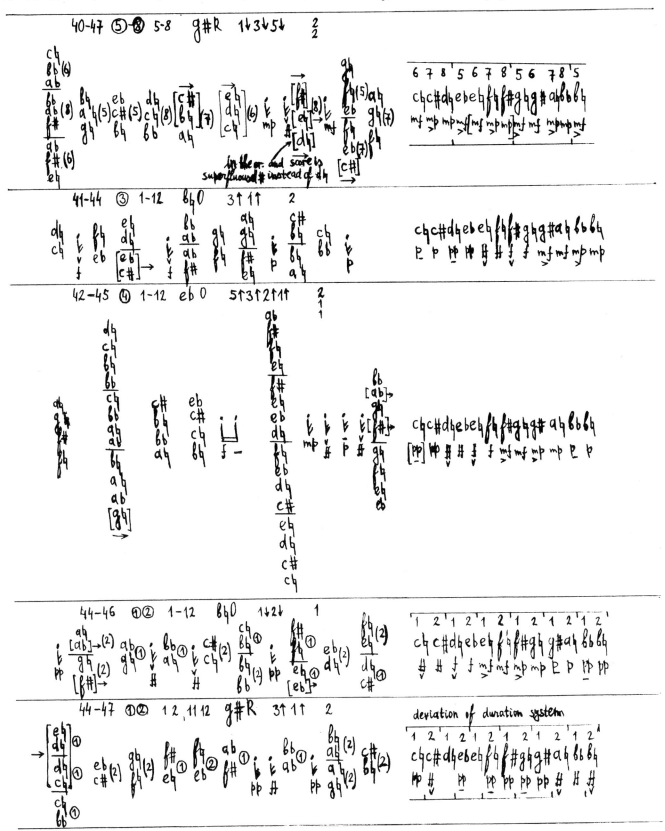

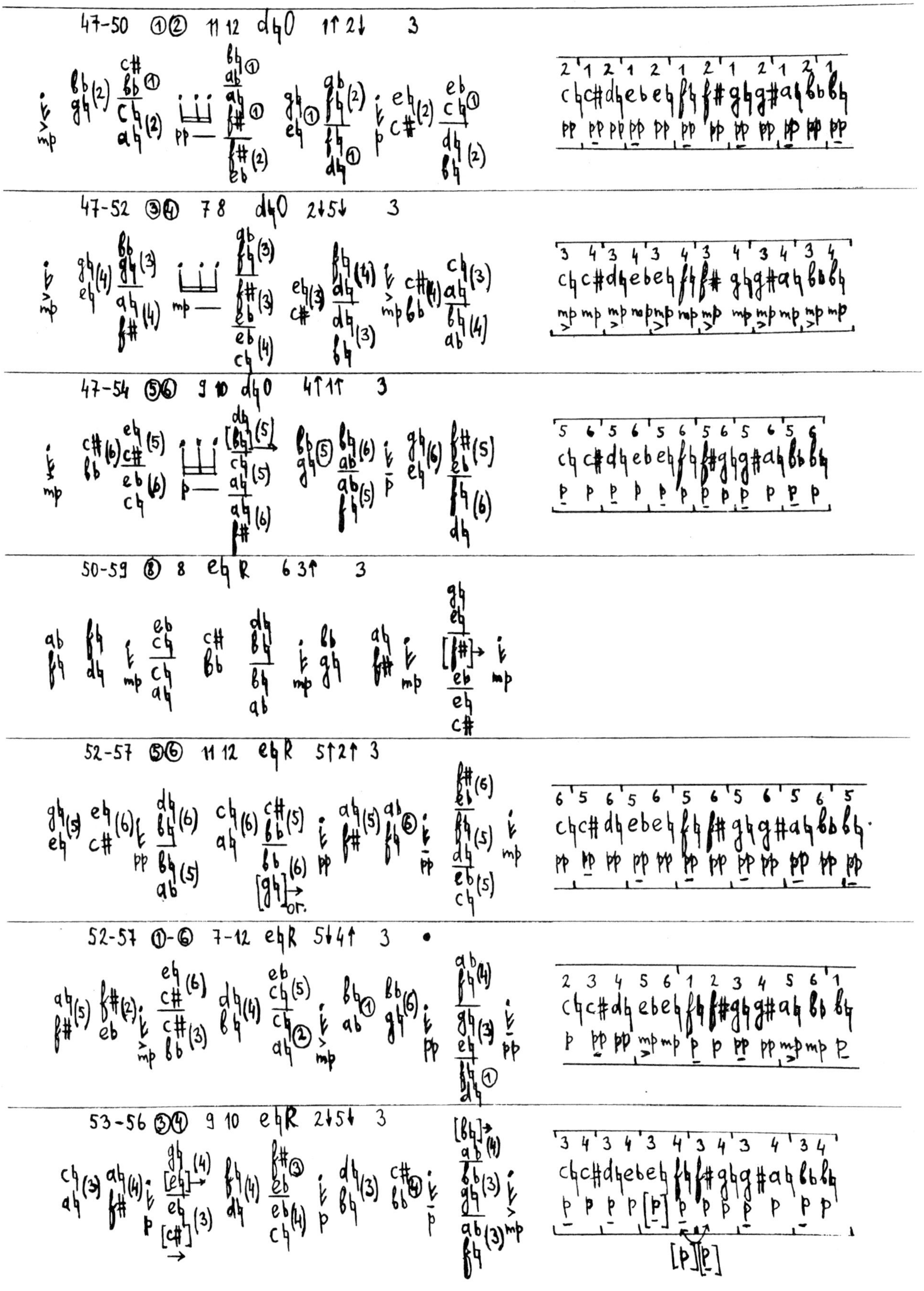
47-50
47-52
47-54
50-59
52-57
52-57
53-56

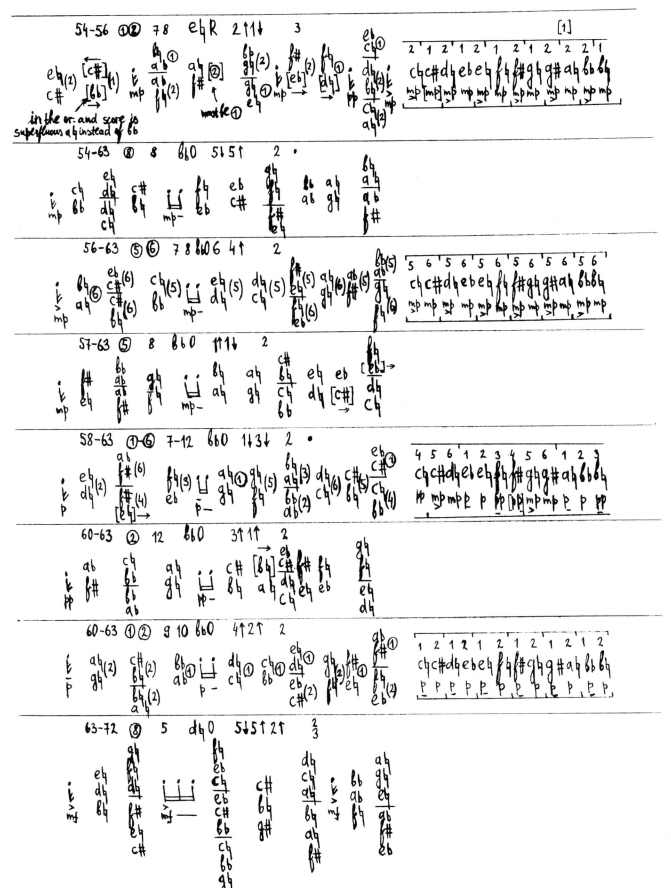

two semiquavers overlap with the next attack

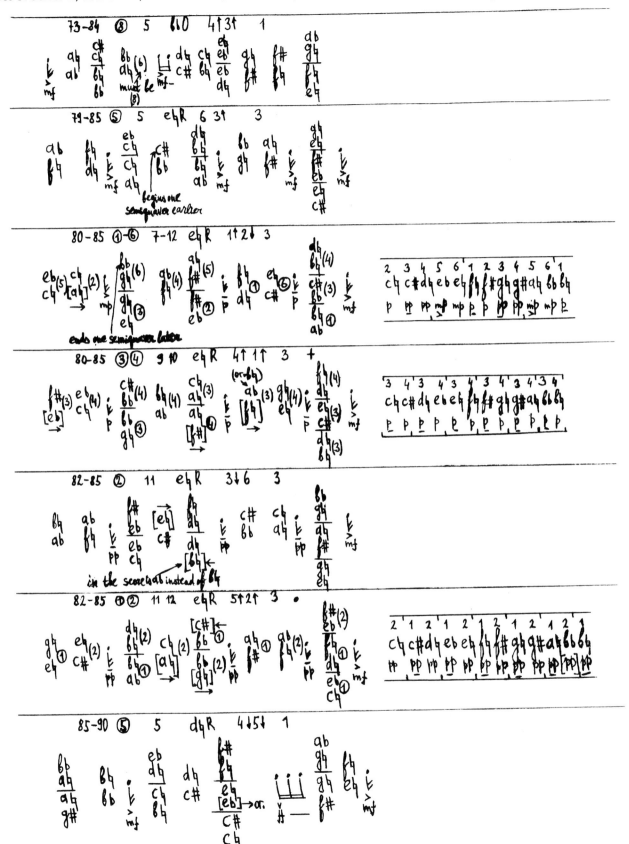

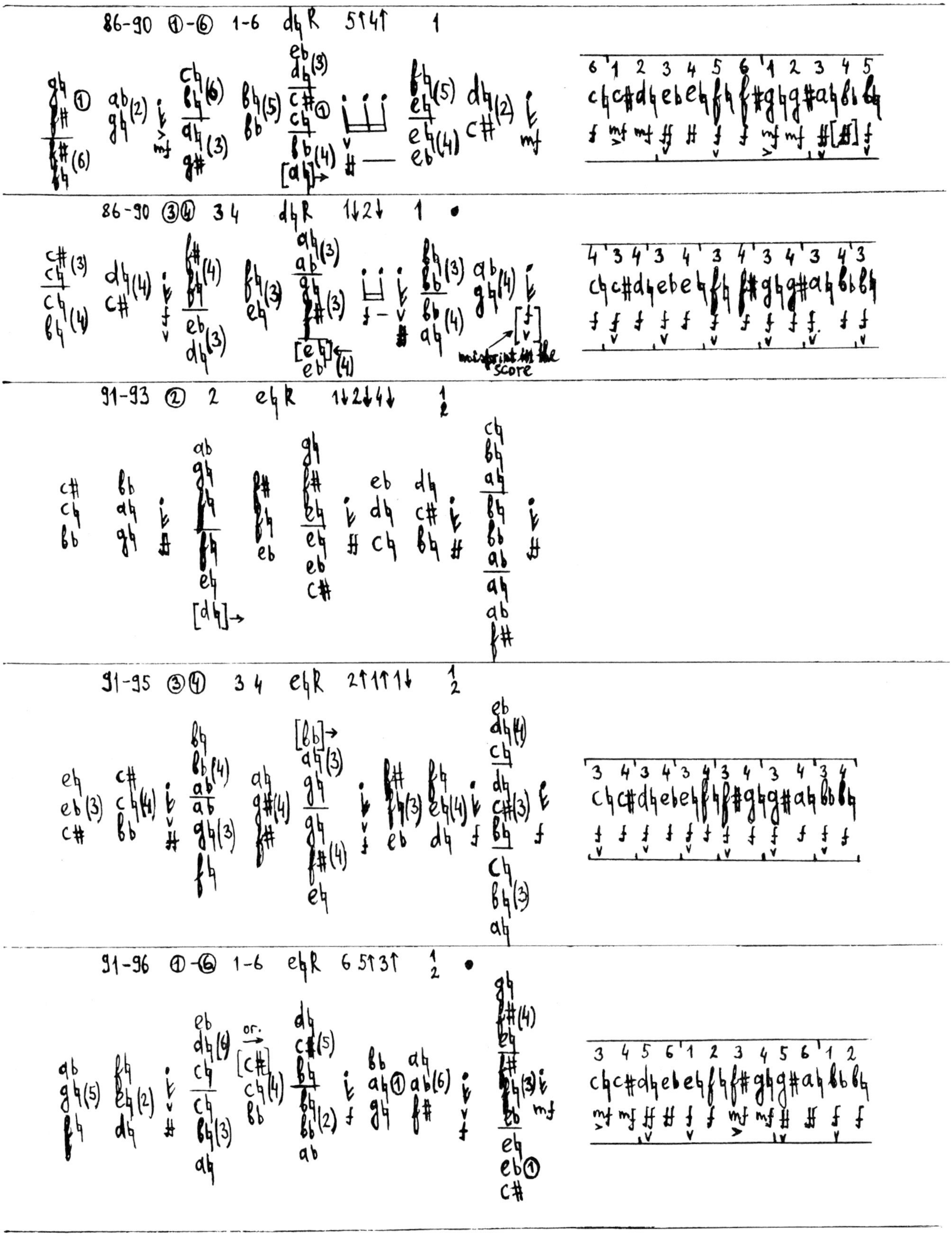
86-90
86-90
misprint in the score
91-93
91-95
91-96
or.

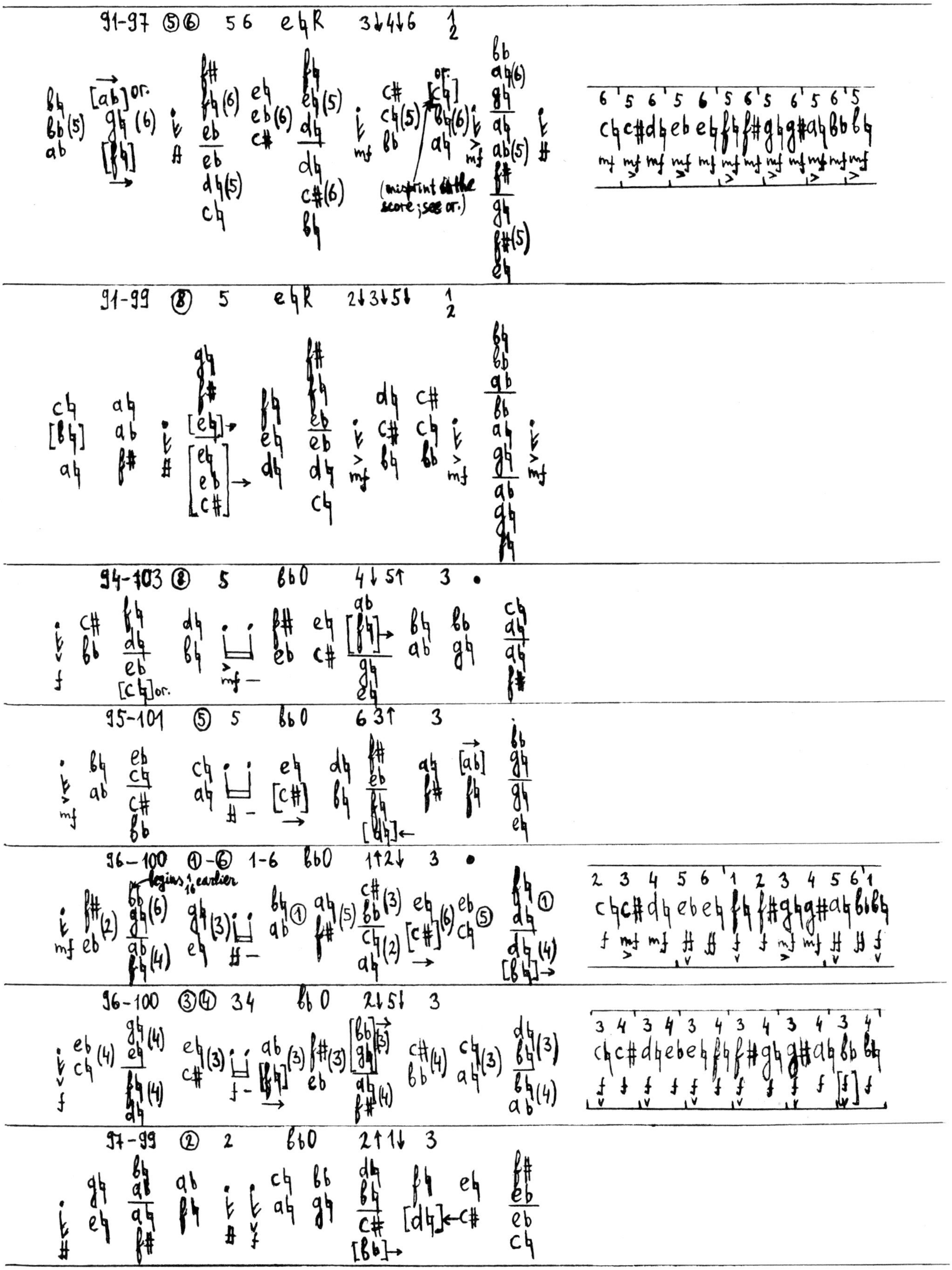
91-97 ⑤⑥ 5 6 e♮R 3↓4↓6 1/2
(misprint in the score; see or.)
91-99 ⑧ 5 e♮R 2↓3↓5↓ 1/2
94-103 ⑧ 5 b♭0 4↓5↑ 3
95-101 ⑤ 5 b♭0 6 3↑ 3
96-100 ①-⑥ 1-6 b♭0 1↑2↓ 3
begins 1/16 earlier
96-100 ③④ 34 b♭0 2↓5↓ 3
97-99 ② 2 b♭0 2↑1↓ 3

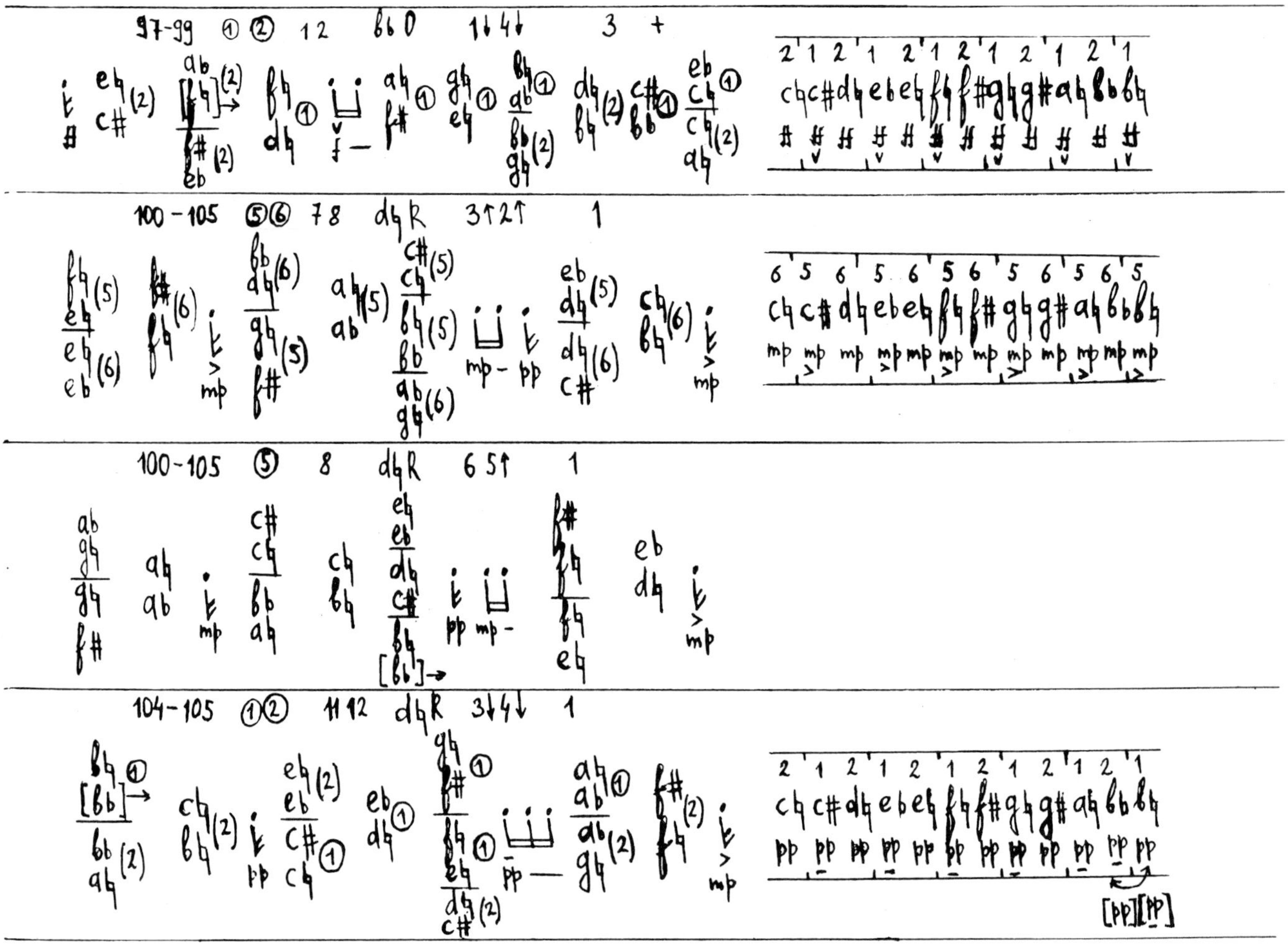

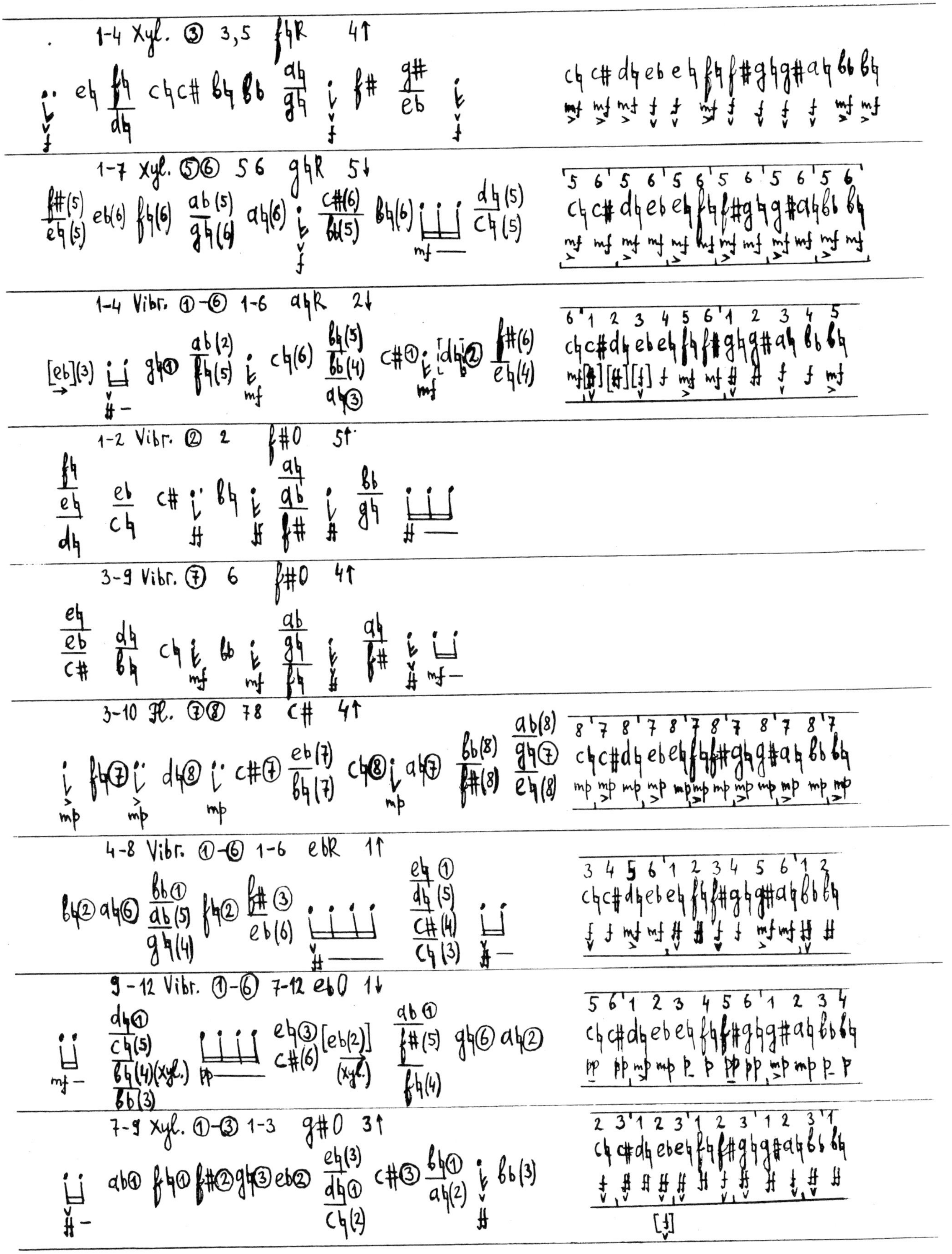
1-4 Xyl. ③ 3,5 f♮R 4↑
1-7 Xyl. ⑤⑥ 5 6 g♮R 5↓
1-4 Vibr. ①-⑥ 1-6 a♮R 2↓
1-2 Vibr. ② 2 f#0 5↑
3-9 Vibr. ⑦ 6 f#0 4↑
3-10 Fl. ⑦⑧ 7 8 c# 4↑
4-8 Vibr. ①-⑥ 1-6 ebR 1↑
9-12 Vibr. ①-⑥ 7-12 eb0 1↓
7-9 Xyl. ①-③ 1-3 g#0 3↑

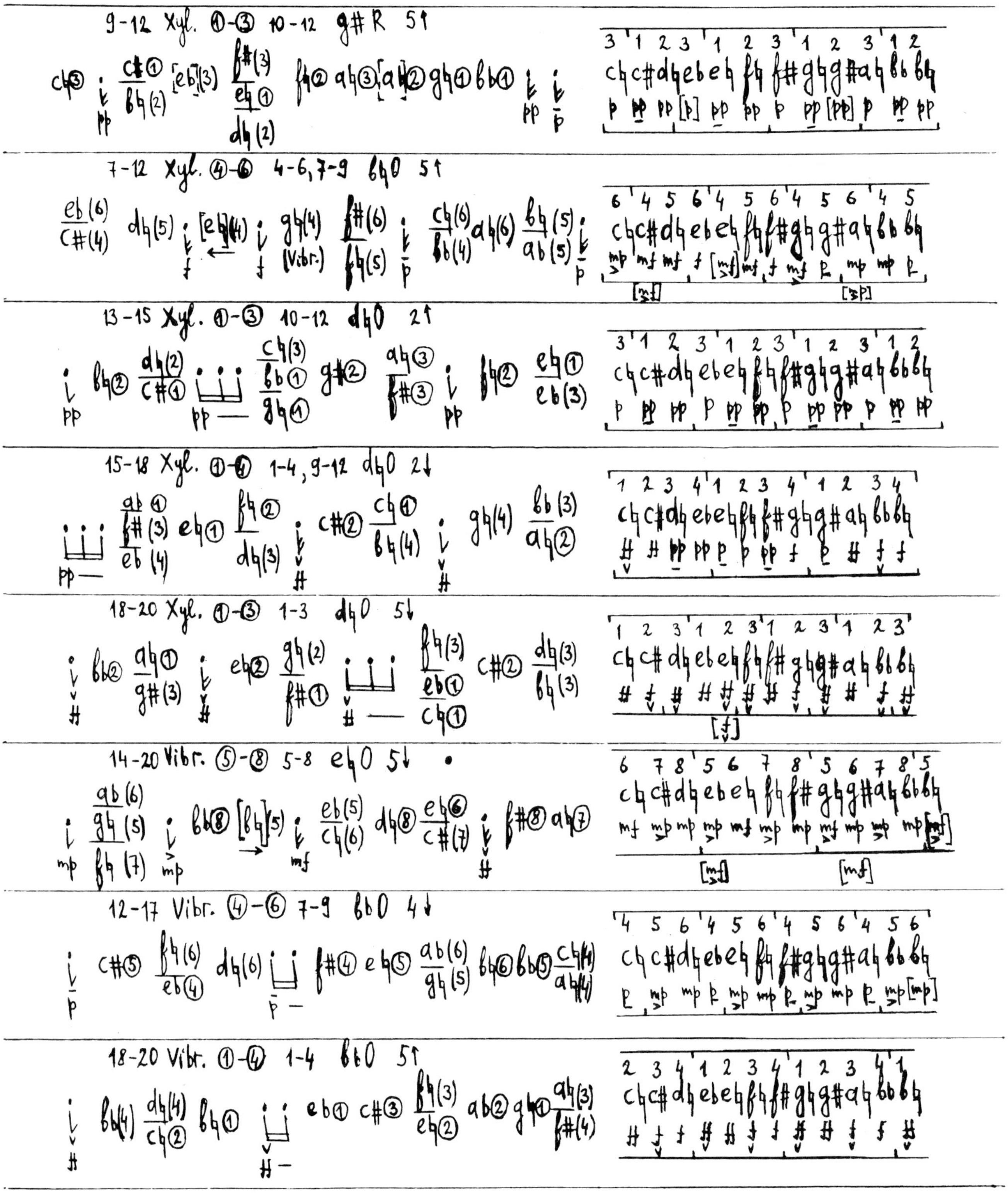

9-12 Xyl. ①-③ 10-12 g# R 5↑

7-12 Xyl. ④-⑥ 4-6,7-9 b♮0 5↑

13-15 Xyl. ①-③ 10-12 d♮0 2↑

15-18 Xyl. ①-④ 1-4,9-12 d♮0 2↓

18-20 Xyl. ①-③ 1-3 d♮0 5↓

14-20 Vibr. ⑤-⑧ 5-8 e♮0 5↓ •

12-17 Vibr. ④-⑥ 7-9 b♭0 4↓

18-20 Vibr. ①-④ 1-4 b♭0 5↑

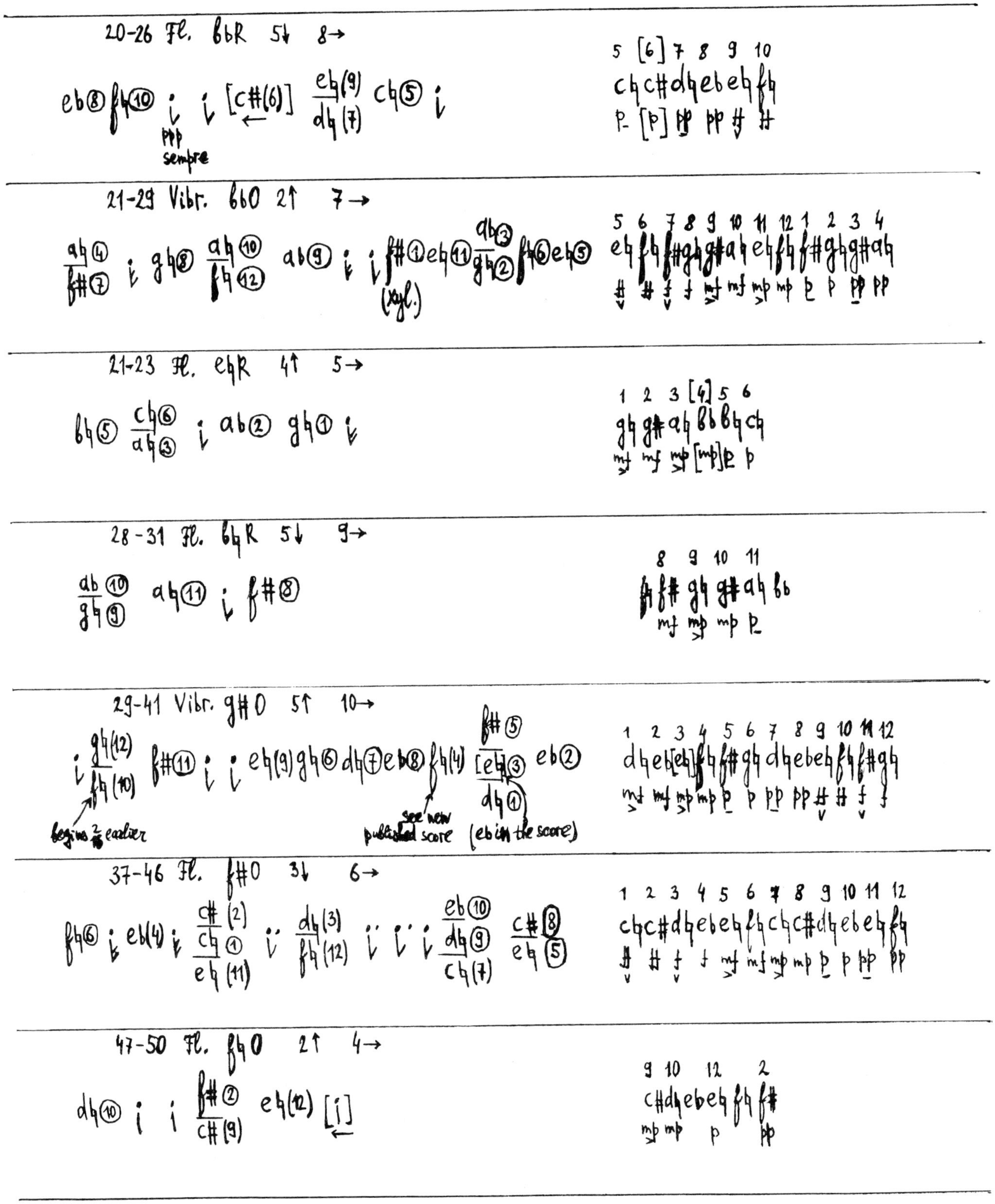

20–26 Fl. b♭R 5↓ 8→

e♭⑧ f♮⑩ i i [c#(6)] $\frac{e♭(9)}{d♮(7)}$ c♮⑤ i
   ppp
   sempre

5 [6] 7 8 9 10
c♮ c# d♮ e♭ e♮ f♮
p- [p] pp ppp ♯ ♯

---

21–29 Vibr. b♭O 2↑ 7→

$\frac{a♮④}{f#⑦}$ i g♮⑧ $\frac{a♮⑩}{f♮⑫}$ a♭⑨ i i f#①e♮⑪$\frac{d♭⑫}{g♮②}$ f♮⑥e♮⑤
(xyl.)

5 6 7 8 9 10 11 12 1 2 3 4
e♭ f♮ f# g♮ g# a♮ e♮ f♮ f# g♮ g# a♮
♯ ♯ ♯ ♯ mf mf mp mp p p pp pp

---

21–23 Fl. e♮R 4↑ 5→

b♮⑤ $\frac{c♮⑥}{a♭③}$ i a♭② g♮① i

1 2 3 [4] 5 6
g♮ g# a♮ b♭ b♮ c♮
mf mf mp [mp] p p

---

28–31 Fl. b♮R 5↓ 9→

$\frac{d♭⑩}{g♮⑨}$ a♮⑪ i f#⑧

8 9 10 11
f♮ f# g♮ g# a♮ b♭
mf mp mp p

---

29–41 Vibr. g#O 5↑ 10→

i $\frac{g♮(12)}{f♮(10)}$ f#⑪ i i e♮(9)g♮⑥ d♮⑦e♮⑧ f♮(4) [e♮③ e♭② $\frac{}{d♮①}$]
f#⑤

begins ⅔ earlier      see new published score (e♭ in the score)

1 2 3 4 5 6 7 8 9 10 11 12
d♮ e♭ e♮ f♮ f# g♮ d♮ e♭ e♮ f♮ f# g♮
mf mf mp p p pp pp ♯ ♯ ♯ ♯

---

37–46 Fl. f#O 3↓ 6→

f♮⑥ i e♭④ i $\frac{c#(2)}{c♮④}$ $\frac{}{e♮(11)}$ i i $\frac{d♮(3)}{f♮(12)}$ i i i $\frac{e♭⑩}{d♮⑨}$ $\frac{c#⑧}{e♮⑤}$
c♮⑦

1 2 3 4 5 6 7 8 9 10 11 12
c♮ c# d♮ e♭ e♮ f♮ c♮ c# d♮ e♭ e♮ f♮
♯ ♯ ♯ ♯ mf mf mp mp p p pp pp

---

47–50 Fl. f♮O 2↑ 4→

d♮⑩ i i $\frac{f#②}{c#(9)}$ e♮(12) [i]

9 10 12 2
c# d♮ e♭ e♮ f♮ f#
mp mp p pp

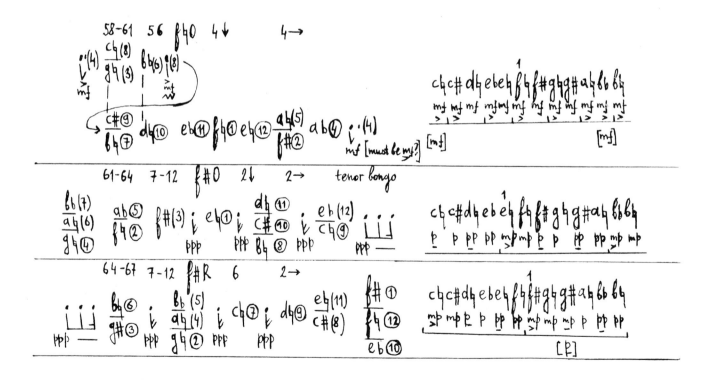

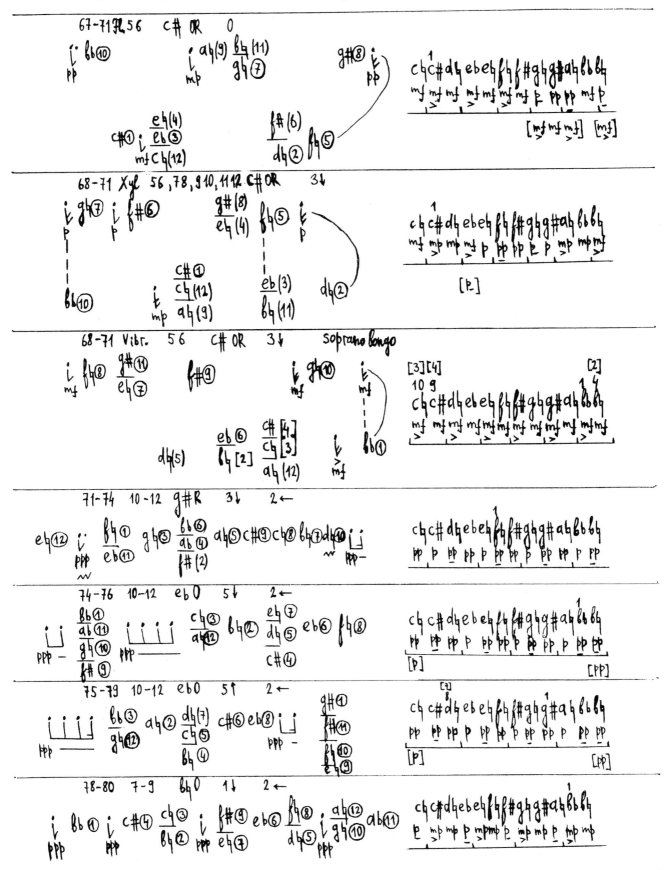

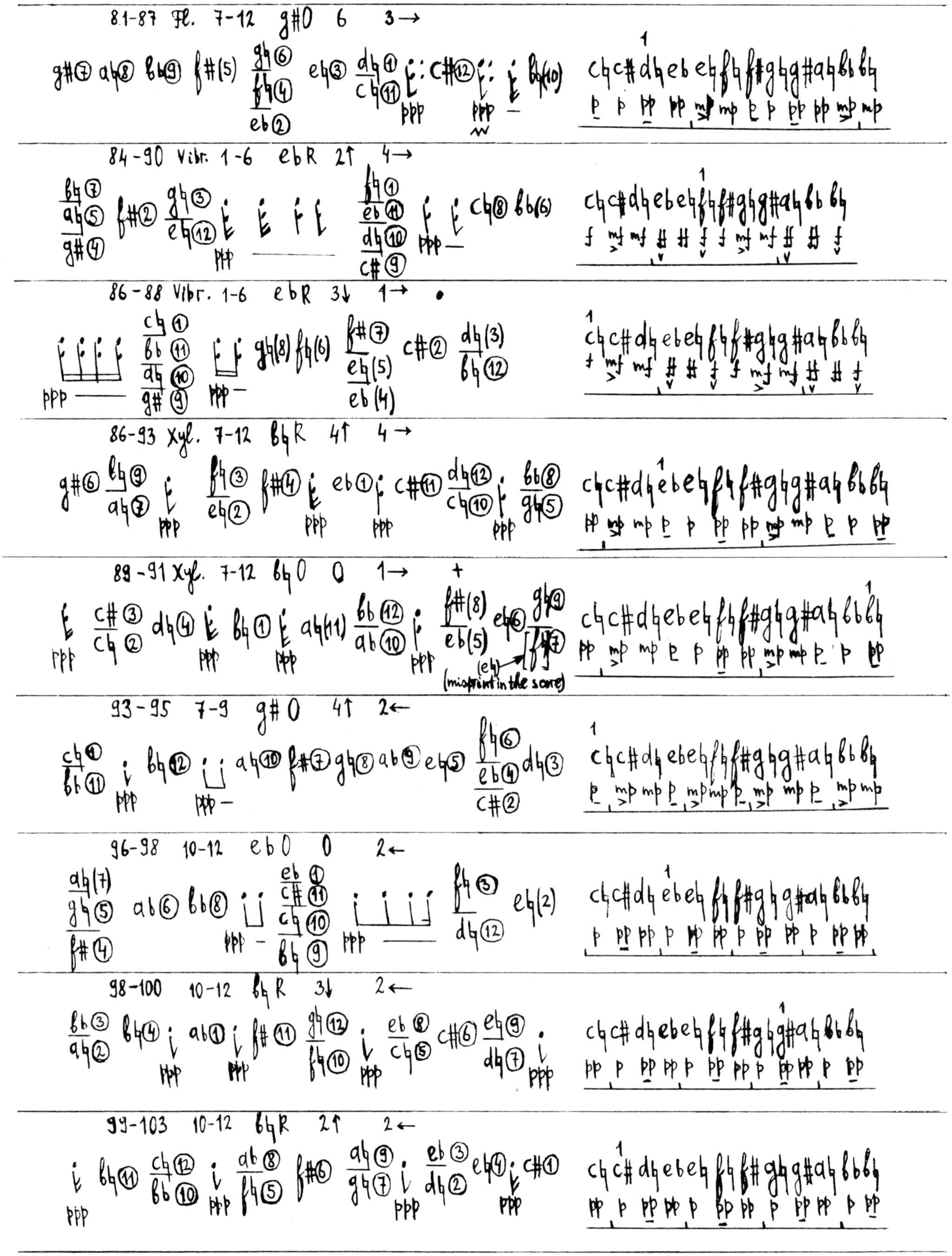
81-87 Fl. 7-12 g#0 6 3→
84-90 Vibr. 1-6 ebR 2↑ 4→
86-88 Vibr. 1-6 ebR 3↓ 1→
86-93 Xyl. 7-12 b♮R 4↑ 4→
89-91 Xyl. 7-12 b♮0 0 1→
(misprint in the score)
93-95 7-9 g#0 4↑ 2←
96-98 10-12 eb0 0 2←
98-100 10-12 b♮R 3↓ 2←
99-103 10-12 b♮R 2↑ 2←

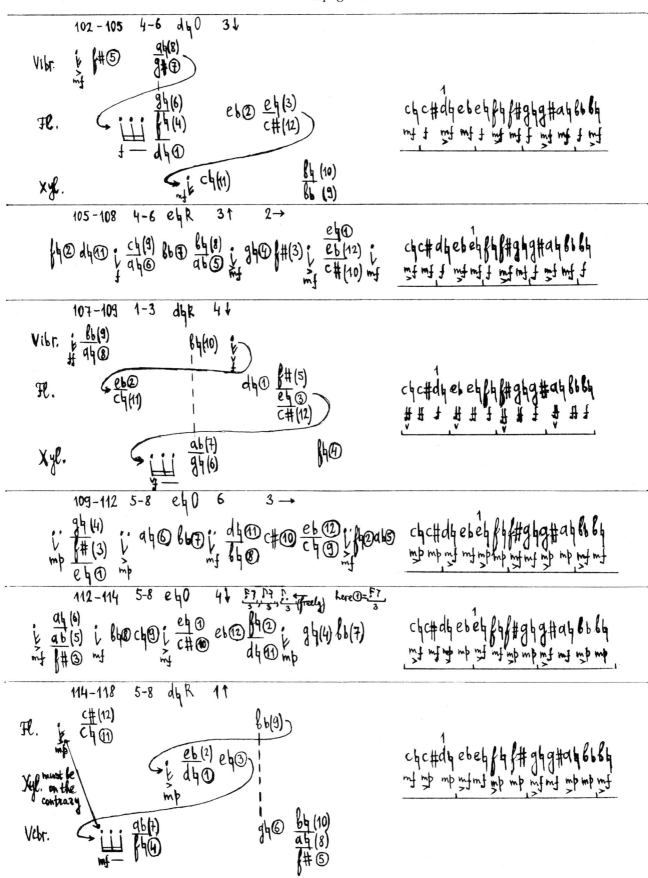

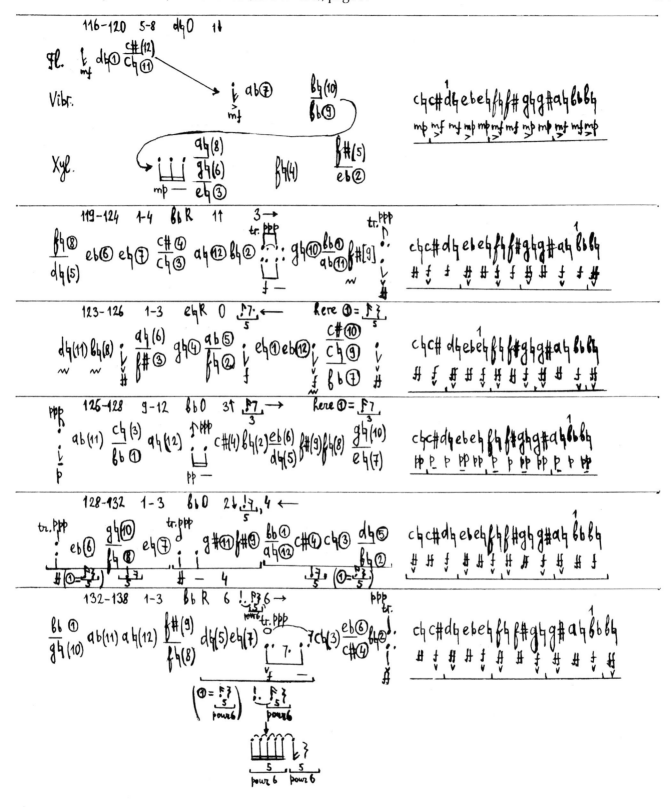

# Le marteau sans maître

Fragments of the Score with Analysis

le marteau sans maître

pierre boulez

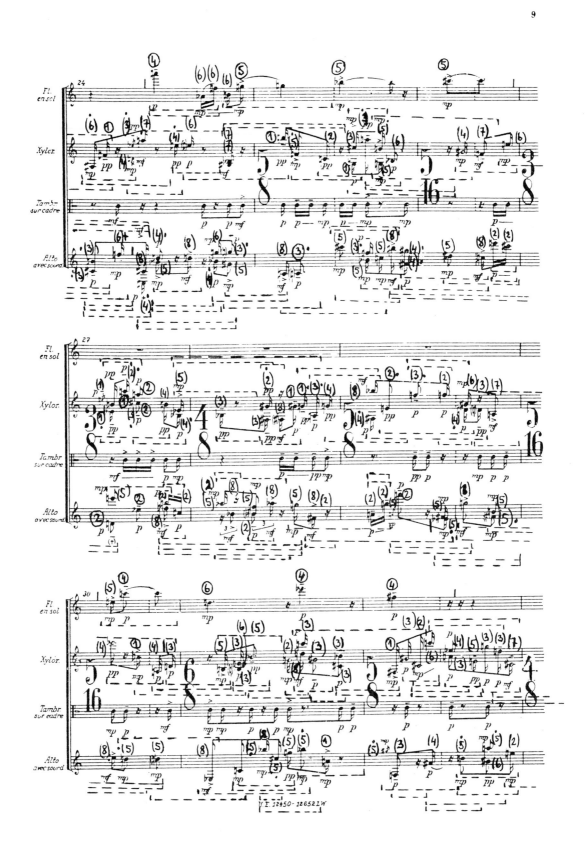

14

# III.
## ‹l'artisanat furieux›

# IV.
## commentaire II de ‹bourreaux de solitude›

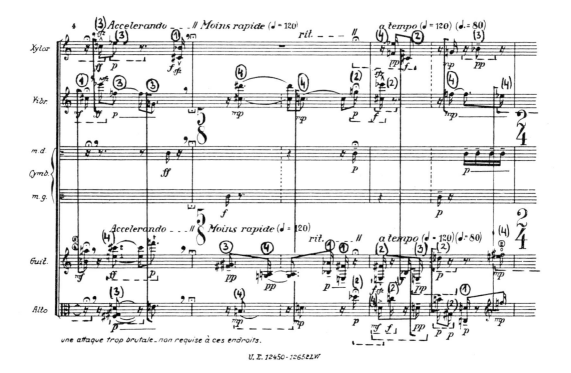

U. E. 12450 - 12652 LW

213

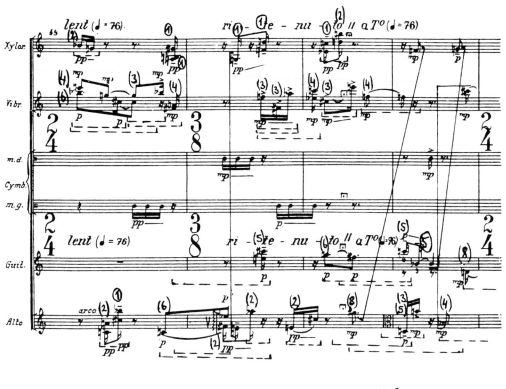

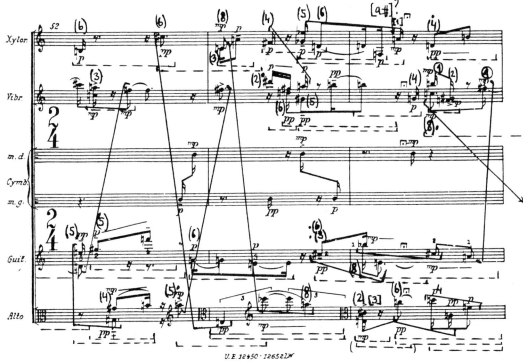

U.E. 12450 · 12652 JW

217

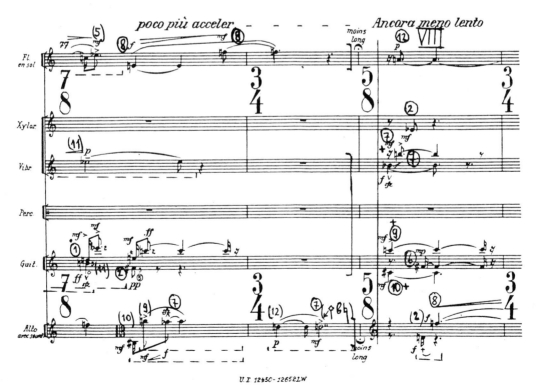

U.E. 12450-12652LW

U.E. 12450-12632LW

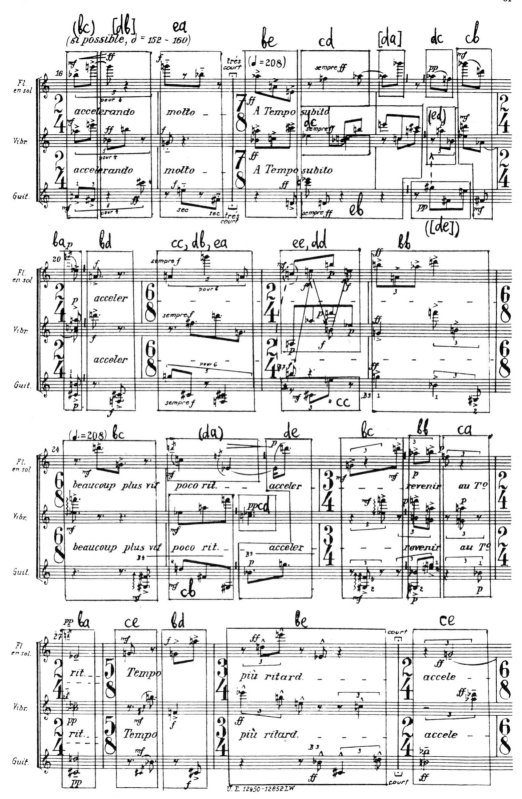

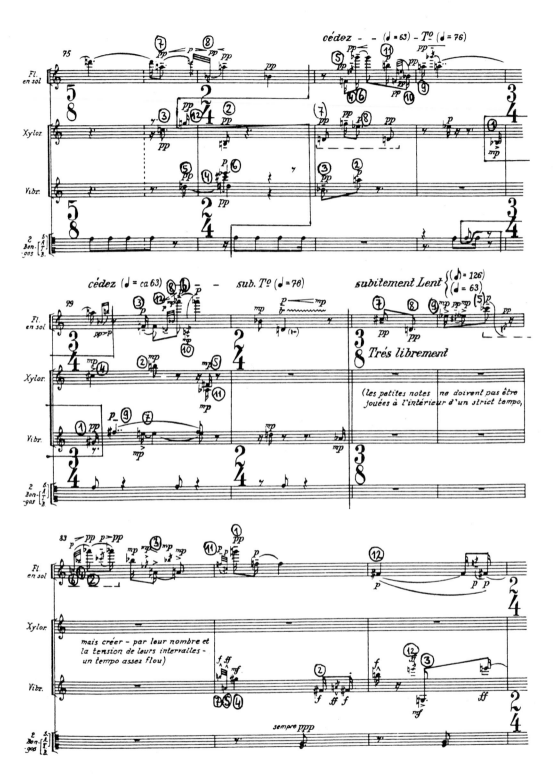

80

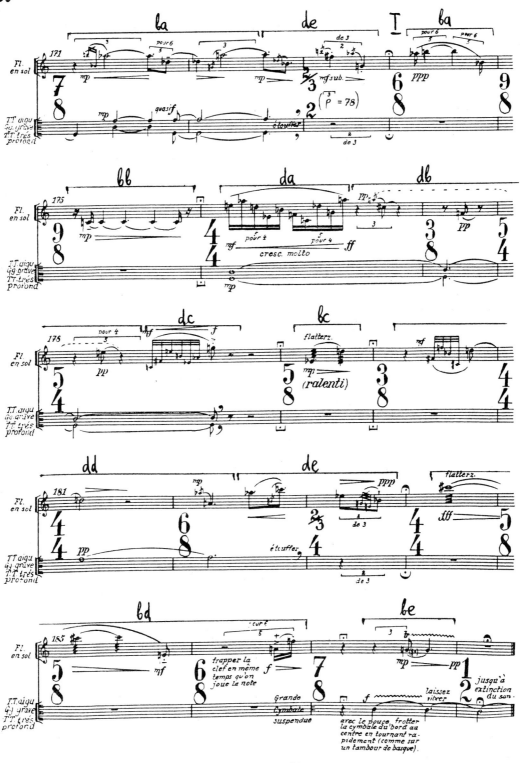

U. E. 12450·12652LW

Waldheim-Eberle, Wien VII.

# INDEX